AF815145

Fresh Feathered Eggs

By John F. Burgess
and
George D. Burgess

Copyright © 2005 by John F. Burgess &
George D. Burgess

All rights reserved. No part of this book shall be reproduced or transmitted in any form or by any means, electronic, mechanical, magnetic, photographic including photocopying, recording or by any information storage and retrieval system, without prior written permission of the publisher. No patent liability is assumed with respect to the use of the information contained herein. Although every precaution has been taken in the preparation of this book, the publisher and author assume no responsibility for errors or omissions. Neither is any liability assumed for damages resulting from the use of the information contained herein.

This work is about actual people, places, and events from the authors' pasts. However, from the authors' imaginations come some fictional situations and people (the Brockmans and others), used to protect real friends and family from embarrassing, hard-to-believe-people-would-do-such-things scenes. Much accuracy is combined with fiction.

ISBN 0-7414-2682-X

Published by:

INFINITY
PUBLISHING.COM

1094 New DeHaven Street, Suite 100
West Conshohocken, PA 19428-2713
Info@buybooksontheweb.com
www.buybooksontheweb.com
Toll-free (877) BUY BOOK
Local Phone (610) 941-9999
Fax (610) 941-9959

Printed in the United States of America

Printed on Recycled Paper

Published August 2005

PREFACE

Fresh Feathered Eggs has two major thrusts: *humor*...to make you laugh and ask for more...and *love*...of family, friends, neighbors and God.

It's a story of the 1940s and '50s, of how two brothers experienced the world, all from rural America, bumping from activity to activity—sometimes with amusement, sometimes with philosophical results. The story tells how they, and their family, dealt with various challenges...relying on trust, faith, and perseverance.

Fresh Feathered Eggs is fresh! And, it's all true...*or could be*. The brothers, Freddy and George, live through fresh feathered eggs, 'accidental' car rides, bathroom episodes, one-pig diners, Aunt Maggie's blue jays, milking school, being a hop too slow, the wrong color calf, a lily-livered puff, painting like P. Kosso, the seating of pew number three, cow-tail skiing, church-camp undercover undressing, and more. And, they meet the challenges by falling back on family values developed from their Christian walk.

And what about neighbors? This is also the real-life story of real-life friends and family. Sometimes, that story is disclosed by the fictitious Brockman family... those people that don't quite get it right (every neighborhood has them) and who end up on the short end of many practical jokes and self-inflicted humorous events.

Why include a pretend family in a life-story book? Answer: The funny things that happened to real people can now be told without embarrassment. Shorty Brockman can make the dumb mistakes, and with each one, a real person in the story can duck being put on the spot. So important is the Brockman bunch, that a 'looks real' genealogy table is included on the next page.

The book also tells of colorful ancestors and relatives, whose sometimes quirky behavior is fun and entertaining. There are plenty of laughs and practical philosophies, as the boys tell their story.

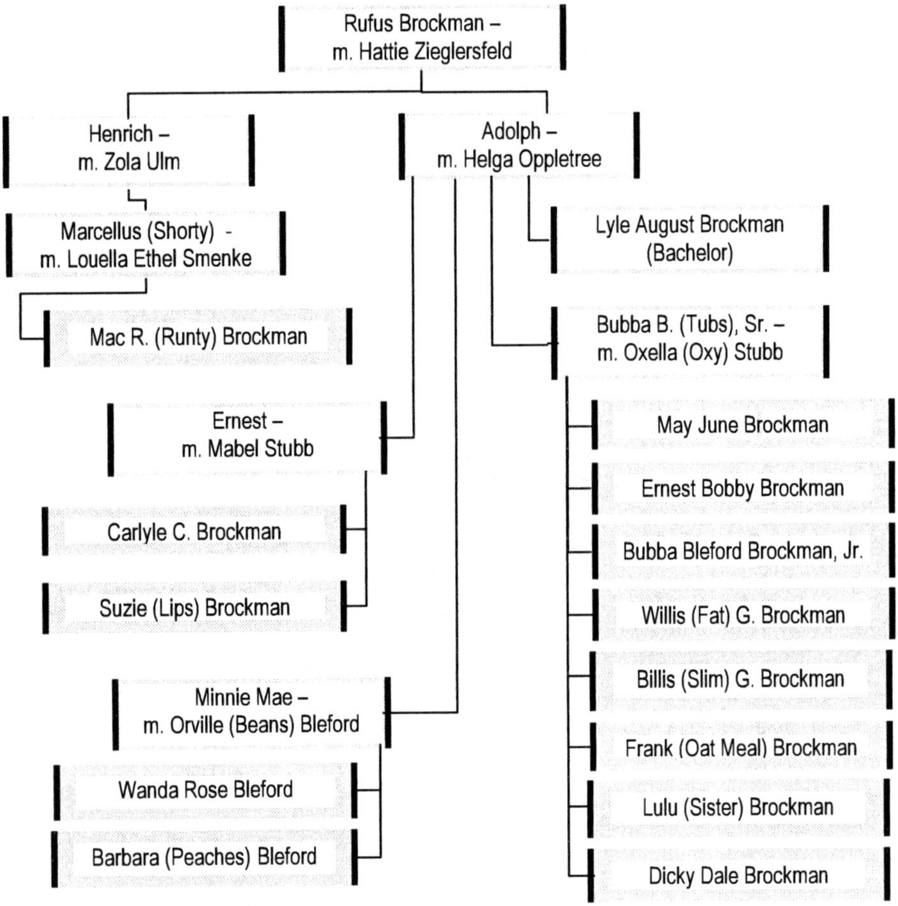

BROCKMAN GENEOLOGY
Pottawatomie County Kansas ~ Circa 1948
(A fictitious family found in this book and in the sequel called The Creep of Her Outfit *to be published in 2006.)*

AUTHORS' NOTE

Our story involves real people, real locations, and real situations…*most of the time*. Family members, friends, and neighbors may find some of their own history recorded in these pages…and we hope…that when they do, they'll feel good about their roles in our story. We wouldn't have one without them.

That said, please recognize we do not in any way want to dishonor, put down, mistreat, or libel any one. This is our best recollection of what was done and what was said…with a few cases of poetic license to make the story flow and give it full meaning. We invite anyone mentioned in this story to contact us about what they find…after they buy a copy of the book. ☺

God's blessings on all of those, living and dead, who helped make *Fresh Feathered Eggs* a joy to write. We dedicate this book to you.

John and George

SPECIAL THANKS

Many—too many to mention all—contributed to this compelling story. However, two people deserve special thanks. For one thing, they patiently nurtured and encouraged the writers as only loving, long-suffering wives can.

Carol Burgess read, questioned, and offered suggestions for many of the scenes, which in some cases added strength to the episodes. She spent many hours editing and proofing the work, and offered encouragement throughout its writing.

Susan Burgess contributed in a myriad of ways, including reading, re-reading, proof-reading, and testing the humor, plus drawing our maps and the concept of our cover. Thank you.

Cousin Bob Burgess, one of two second-generation survivors shared his recollections and his humor, especially about Grandpa David. His information added to the story.

Cowboy poet, Dwight Burgess, gets special mention for sharing his knowledge and lore of the family—especially about his grandfather, Tom. Dwight's poem in the next section sums up much of what we lived in the *Fresh Feathered Eggs* tale.

Some family members deserve thanks for providing information and background. Others deserve thanks for their moral support and encouragement. The list below names everyone we remember who helped in some way, including our sisters Joyce Elcock and her husband, Doug, Judy Leonetti and husband, Steve; the raft of cousins, in addition to Bob and Dwight; Kathleen Ramonda, Becky Gordon Lindbloom, Gary Gordon, Jim Gordon,

Dr. Barbara Burgess, Denny Burgess, Beverly Burgess Loukota, Ruth Elaine Burgess Archimede, Karen Burgess Meek, Ben Meek, Dean and Sally Burgess, Dan Burgess, Dwayne Burgess, Brad Burgess, State Rep. Michael Burgess, and David and Susan Burgess—plus the others we failed to mention (if we missed someone, we apologize in advance).

Our thanks goes to the good people of Wamego, Louisville, Westmoreland, Flush, St. George, Laclede, and Hartford who added so much life to the story. Thanks, too, to the citizens of Pottawatomie County and Kansas for being you!

Finally, we give thanks to the Almighty for life, love, and family. He surely must smile at some of our antics.

A TALE OF TWO BROTHERS

We close our eyes and in our mind visualize,
A story that begs to be told.
About growing up poor, yet with blessings galore,
And memories more precious than gold.

A story with charm of life on the farm,
Of pastures and clear sparkling streams.
A family with love and the blessings thereof,
Of two brothers and their plans and dreams.

Who learned early on that fine paragon,
That states your bond is your word.
And learned paramount that family does count,
With a love for the flag and the Lord.

Of Freddy, the one, that lived life on the run,
Whose curiosity reached to the sky.
Of George, the one who, reasoned things through,
Being reticent, quiet, and shy.

As different all right as day is from night,
Embarking on different careers.
Yet loyal each brother, and true to each other,
With a bond that has held through the years.

So, just close your eyes and with us visualize,
This story that begs to be told.
Of boys' plans and schemes and childhood dreams,
And memories more precious than gold.

by Cowboy Poet and Rancher,
Cousin Dwight Burgess
of Wamego, Kansas – 2004

TABLE OF CONTENTS

ONE

SAVING THE CAR, WHAT'S IN A NAME, AND TALKING TO THIN AIR

[*Westmoreland Recorder* - September 11, 1933] **THREE LOUISVILLE STORES ROBBED** - Some time Monday night at the store of C.W. McNay, butter and meats and other articles were taken. The Shaw store lost a gun and several other articles. The post office was entered but information has not been obtained as to the loss there. The J.C. Kornemann store was not entered. It is probably lucky that an attempt was not made to rob this store as Mr. Kornemann sleeps in the store with a loaded shotgun beside him. It is believed that the robberies are by local talent.

TAKING THE CAR FOR A RIDE

"Yikes, we're moving! Oh, my…goshhh! What do I do?" Freddy shouted, clinging to the steering wheel of the '28 Chevrolet. In contrast, the old car showed no alarm. At first, it made almost polite, gravel crunching sounds and inched over the bank, with the noise increasing when it picked up speed on the downslope. Weeds, buckbrush, and small hackberry trees were like markers of an obstacle course. The car's wooden-spoked wheels, bumpers, fenders, and running boards whacked at the plant life, while the windows and doors chattered and the tired metal body rocked and groaned.

The bug-eyed, five-year old squeezed the steering wheel and stared ahead. He gritted his teeth while his heart pounded like a hammer. This was his first white-knuckle ride. What if he wrecked the car? What would Mom say? We were just playing….

His eyes darted to the pedals far down on the floorboards. If only he could stop the car, like Dad. Yikes, here comes a tree! With a jerk, he steered left, missing a small hackberry...almost. Branches screeched along the right side, scratching the black paint from fender to fender.

With a jolt and more chafing, the car rocked and

tipped side to side across some two-foot high buckbrush. With a drawn-out scrunch, it slowed for a bit, and then headed for a big red and gray boulder. That rock, pushed there by a melting glacier eons ago, seemed bigger than a wheat shock and dwarfed the weeds and brush. Hitting it meant curtains.

Straining, Freddy muscled the car around the granite mound. Missed it, he thought, with a deep breath. A half-hearted smile of cockiness crossed his face, though it soon faded when the car picked up speed again. Now, near the bottom of the slope, a big oak tree loomed and he veered right, only to find the car heading for the huge tin granary with the summer's precious wheat inside. At the last instant, the bouncing car—as if by itself—moved away from the tin tower. Freddy gasped. Where was his smile now?

Though the slope had flattened out, the speeding car rolled on and on. Would the thing ever stop? In desperation, Freddy steered toward a five-foot high wild plum thicket off to the right. Crunchhhh…thunk, thunk, thunk! The Chevy slowed and came to rest atop the mashed-down trees. It rocked back and forth, then up and down, at last settling motionless, with the thumping shower of ripened wild plums the only sound.

Freddy, still standing on the seat, stared ahead and then sighed. That was some ride, he thought. Man oh man, that was something. Then his smile returned. "Mom will be so glad. Mom will be so glad I saved the car!"

MOM, I SAVED THE CAR

During the breathtaking ride, three-year-old George had watched from the top of the slope with his mouth wide open. What happened? Why did the car go away? We were just playing, he thought. He remembered what his brother had told him.

"I'll get in the car and steer and you watch me move the front tires." George had shaken his head thinking, I don't know. We're not supposed to play with the car.

"Ah, don't worry scaredy-cat. I'm just going to see if I can move the tires like Dad does," Freddy had said.

As commanded, George moved to the front of the car, and stared at the tires. "Did it move?"

"No."

"How about now?"

"A little, I think."

Smiling, Freddy moved the steering wheel a few more inches. "Well, how about now?"

George moved closer to the left front wheel. "Yeah, it moved some. Try moving it the other way."

Freddy had yanked the steering wheel hard. Off balance, his knee had jammed the gearshift. Whoops! The car had started to roll, and George had jumped out of the way just in time, for it eased forward and headed down the slope.

"Come back, come back. Stop. Wait." He had taken a couple of steps downhill and then stopped and had started to blubber—surely both Freddy and the car would soon be dead. His brother couldn't drive! "Don't die!" he yowled. "Don't die!"

The bawling had triggered his mom's intuition. What was going on outside? The trip to Mr. Kornemann's general store in Louisville would have to wait. She ran to the door and stared at emptiness and a crying three-year-old in the space where she'd parked the car. "What's going on?"

With flashing hazel eyes, she looked at George. He pointed at the plum thicket far below. "...they're dead!" he stammered. "Dang that old car. Dang that old car." Sobbing, he tottered down the slope.

His mom pulled up her hem, and with red hair flying, dashed past him. When she reached the car, she gasped for breath. "What have you done to the car? I told you two not to play with it! Just what have you done?"

She stood, hands on hips, and surveyed the car perched up on the flattened plum trees. It showed a few scratches, but no real damage. She sighed at her redheaded five-year-old inside standing on the seat. Was he safe? After a short pause, in a quavering voice, she asked, "Oh, Freddy, are you all right? Are you hurt? Oh, why did you roll the car down here?"

Freddy, still gripping the steering wheel, smiled and puffed out his chest. "Mom, aren't you proud of me? I saved the car! It's a good thing I missed the granary, isn't it? Aren't you proud of me, Mom?"

Proud? Yes, even though she was upset, she felt proud. He *had* saved the car and missed the granary and he was safe. Tears welled in her eyes when she thought of what might have been. At that instant, she felt thankful—for both her sons.

With Freddy in tow, she trudged up the slope to meet George and hugged both boys. She then bowed her head in thanksgiving, and hugged the boys again.

§

The hugs erased our tensions. We felt so close to our loving Mom. That day, we knew she was the most wonderful person in the world!

And, what a day we had begun! In just a few minutes, we experienced heart-pounding excitement, avoided disaster, received love and forgiveness, and ended up okay. We learned, too. We wouldn't play with the car again—at least until we were teenagers—but that, of course, would be another story.

Mom's forgiveness came through her tears, hugs, and prayer. We were her sons, her pride and joy, and until our sisters, Judy and Joyce, came along more than a decade later, we were her focus.

As for the car, when Dad got in from the field, he started it right up, backed off the plum trees, and drove up to the house, without saying a word. The damage—scratched fenders and side—became the topic of many conversations.

"Oh, it got a good scratching alright. Must

have sideswiped a sapling. But, the boy came through it without harm. Isn't that something? I guess the car isn't really that important in the long run, 'cause you can always replace it. That boy is worth a lot more than any car," we heard Dad say many times.

We knew the folks cherished us. We were flesh of their flesh, their offspring. Even before we were born, they had dreams for us. And, they gave us worthy names that perhaps hinted in some way of our future.

§

NAMES, NICKNAMES, AND SUCH

"What's in a name?" The Bard of Avon posed this question centuries ago. Did he assume names did or did not matter? Just what's in a name?

"Veda, do you think a baby's name will have an effect on what he'll be?" John asked his pregnant wife as they sat side by side in the hayloft that Sunday afternoon. A dusting of snow sparkled through the arched doors and several white and gray pigeons roosted high on the rafters. Outside, a chilly January breeze gusted, yet the barn seemed warm.

Veda snuggled next to her husband. "Well, I don't know," she said. "Why?"

"I heard somewhere that people try to live up to their names."

She raised her eyebrows and stared at him. "That's pretty farfetched, isn't it?"

"I don't know, but what if men with bold sounding names like Hercules are bold, and women with names like Faith and Grace have those qualities?" he asked.

"Well, maybe. I do know Faith Broderick is a faithful, God-fearing woman."

He smiled and said, "Yes, that's true. Maybe, when our baby is born, we should call her Faith."

"Maybe Faith would be okay. But, what if it's a boy? You don't want to name him Hercules...for goodness sake. Anyway, if it's a boy, we have to call him John...after his father. Oh, I'm so excited. I wish he'd hurry up and get here."

A few weeks later, during the start of a mighty snowstorm, Veda's time arrived. They hurried the seven frozen miles to tiny Genn Hospital in Wamego. There, the wait began, while outside the storm grew worse. Within a couple of hours, two or three inches of heavy snow had fallen. Drifts began building across the roads.

"Oh, John," Veda said, "You just have to go home now and tend to the stock before the roads get too bad. The doctor is here, and the nurse. I'll be alright. Your offspring may not get here for hours," she said, grimacing with another contraction.

"Maybe I should go. I just don't want to get snowed in here."

"Go on, John. I'll be alright."

"Okay," he said. "I'll call the hospital in the morning, unless the storm knocks out the phone." Coming back to her side, he gave her a kiss. "I love you, you know."

"Yes, and I love you, too. Now, go on. The baby won't be here for a few hours and you can come see him in the morning. Babies always come in the middle of the night, don't they?"

So, in the early hours of February 24, 1934—while the snowstorm still raged outside—Veda's child arrived. Later, after the tiring labor and painful birth, she lay filled with joy, holding the most wonderful baby ever born. Soon she dozed.

Just before 6:00 a.m., the nurse shook her. "Your husband just called. He wanted to know how you are and if the baby is here. I told him he has a wonderful son, and that everyone is fine. He says he's snowed in at the farm and can't come to town until the storm breaks and the roads get cleared. He wants you to call him if the doctor lets you out of bed in the next day or two."

"He also wants to know what you named the baby,"

the nurse said over her shoulder as she left the room.

Veda, left alone with her son, moved the baby to her left breast and stroked his fine, reddish hair. "We need to call you John, like your papa, don't we?" she asked him. "You'd like that, wouldn't you, John?"

That afternoon, she was allowed to walk down the hall—as was the custom, new mothers usually stayed in bed several days—to call the farm. After telling the details of the birth, she asked, "Would John Frederick Burgess be a good name? It has a nice ring to it."

"Hey, that's a great name. Sounds pretty official," the new father said. "So, who is this John you named him for? And Frederick?"

"He's named John after you, silly. And the Frederick is from my dad, Fred," she said. "Are you sure you like both names?"

"You bet. Darn, I can't wait to see John Frederick, honey. If this dang storm ever lets up, I'll be there."

Unfortunately, the wait was seven days, until the weather turned fair and the drifts got cleared out. At last, with Grandpa and Grandma Burgess along, John the elder met his son, John the younger.

"Why, Veda, baby John is just wonderful. And look at him, see how active he is."

"He's so special...at least I think so. Isn't John the best baby in the world, John?" Veda asked. As she finished speaking, a puzzled look crossed her face. "Why you're both John. You know, that might cause me a lot of confusion. How will I know which one I'm talking to? I love the names, but...."

For Veda, and for others, the same-name game did bring about confusion. After a time, when young John moved to the toddler stage, Veda made a decision. "Let's give him a nickname. Let's call him, Freddy."

From then on, she told the family, "It's a whole lot better now that we call him Freddy. No more confusion with his dad. It was just getting to be too much."

So, John the younger became Freddy. His active approach to life kept his mother happy, though very busy. And, two years later on a cold day in March, the family's liveliness increased even more when a second child came along. And again, John and Veda went through the naming business and, this time, settled for George David. There would be no confusion with that name, but for Freddy, while his mom was unconfused, he faced an identity crisis time after time.

FREDDY THE TEDDY

Freddy, in his church tie and overalls, had lots of nicknames.

Was he Freddy or John or John Frederick? Later, official school records used John F. Burgess, but his teachers wrote Freddy on his report cards.

Besides, what kind of a name was Freddy? Everyone had an opinion. "Where'd you get that goofy name, Freddy?" older cousin Ben Gordon asked a few years later while they looked over an old barn. He nodded to his brother Rollie and laughed.

"Yeah," said Rollie. "It sounds like Reddy or Deady or Teddy."

"Hey, that's great. He's Freddy the Teddy," said Ben, stepping up to examine a hole in the barn wall. "Yeah, let's call him Teddy."

Freddy frowned, and shook his red head. Guys aren't teddy bear cuddly. I don't want to curl up on anybody's lap!

"No, better yet, you're Froggy," said Ben. "Like the kid that wears glasses in the *Little Rascals* movies. From now on, you can be Froggy."

"No, I'm Freddy. That's my name." Then he fired a comeback that stopped the teasing for a while. "Don't you forget that, Benny the penny and Rollie Polly!"

George picked that moment—he had excellent timing—to step on a dry, discarded bullsnake skin in the far end of the barn. "Yikes!" he yelled, and Ben and Rollie ran to examine his find.

Meanwhile, Freddy kicked at some owl droppings and started thinking. Maybe Froggy would be okay. He had learned how to make a growly voice like that movie kid. He smiled and started to practice. Bet the kids at Sunday school will laugh.

The next morning, his Sunday school teacher told her helper, "Listen to that boy talk in that scratchy voice. He sounds like that Froggy from the movies. He's always doing something. Look at him now," she said, while Freddy made an airplane out of modeling clay-like material.

"Freddy," she said politely, "Jesus didn't ride into Jerusalem on an airplane. It was a donkey. Why don't you make one of those?" So the airplane crashed and the kids laughed. While all eyes were on him, he crafted a talent-less burro with elephant ears. More laughter.

This making kids laugh was fun, and he soon developed many ways of doing it. Besides his weird artwork, he'd sing strange songs, make up poems about classmates, and tell what he thought were funny stories. He did some physical stunts too, like making funny faces and buggy eyes, and head lolling with a flapping tongue…or imitating animals.

Once, during second-grade recess, he horse-galloped toward a group of girls. "Here comes Freddy," Betty Haid said as he nuzzled up to a gathering of girls near the blackboard. There, he motioned with his head for Betty to get on his back.

"No, I don't want to ride," pretty Betty said. "Go away."

Since she wouldn't ride, Freddy changed gears. "Won't you feed the horsey? Pleeeeeze," he said, blinking his eyes at her. The other girls laughed.

"Oh, alright, here's some oats," she said, holding out her hand…which Freddy pretended to lick. "Oh, quit it. You're awful." The girls laughed again.

And, so his image developed. And, his antics

normally worked well, unless he over did it, or played to an ungrateful audience. Of course, his need for attention, his name, his red-haired appearance, and from the fourth grade on, his round, wire-rimmed glasses made him easy tease bait.

"Hey, carrot top, why don't you quit flirting with the girls?" fifth grader Bobby Wagoner asked. "Hey Jim, look at ole four-eyes pester those poor girls." It hurt to have an older boy tease him, and since his open expressions betrayed his feelings, that led to more teasing. Frustrated when picked on, he'd move to the point of tears and that increased the teasing.

However, after a few years, two things happened. He became the oldest boy in the one-room school, and he also told his new teacher to call him John. It worked. The teasing ended.

TALKING TO THIN AIR

However, he was still Freddy to relatives and neighbors, and at home. However, when the conversation was official or when his behavior needed correcting, he was John Frederick.

"John Frederick Burgess, you make me so mad. Why don't you sit still and pay attention?" his mom said many times during his early years. "Think before you do something, for goodness sake! Oh, I might as well be talking to thin air. You've just got to straighten up, young man!"

His fiery-tempered, redheaded mom—because she loved him and wanted him to be the best—found plenty of reasons to correct him, for Freddy fidgeted more than a hunting dog with a colony of fleas. And, like the dog, he had his own agenda, even in public.

"Remember, you're wearing good clothes, so don't do anything to get them dirty," his mom said, as the two boys—still preschool—accompanied her to a monthly Home Demonstration Unit meeting.

Freddy, for reasons unknown, ran through the door

and somersaulted past the gathered ladies the length of the room. When he popped to his feet, he looked around the circle of chairs to see how he had done. The polite farm ladies, mostly aunts and cousins, tittered and then laughed.

"Veda, you poor dear. How in the world do you keep that boy clean?" Ben and Rollie's mom, Aunt Helen asked. "You could end up scrubbing clothes all day long. On the other hand, you could do what I do with Rollie. I don't wash his hand-me-downs until they get too heavy for him to lift."

Aunt Helen looked at Freddy and gave a nodding smile. He, in turn, grinned and bowed. More laughter followed, and even his mom giggled while she said, "That boy," under her breath.

So, the question remained. Did the name Freddy inspire the fast-forward farm boy from Kansas to be the center of things? Did that sharpen his wit and hone his verbal skills? Did saving the car—and other outrageous feats—nurture a certain boldness?

Did the name lead to his ability to read an audience and become a good communicator and teacher? Later, as Professor John Frederick Burgess, his practiced humor endeared him to students, and perhaps his youthful tease-bait encounters gave him empathy for those who struggled.

In any event, Dr. Burgess did 'learn' students, with many of his classes overflowing. In addition, more than 300 different colleges used his three co-authored McGraw-Hill published textbooks. In the final analysis, Freddy did indeed learn to communicate. Was it because of his name?

And, what about George? What did his name bring him?

TWO

MR. BLUE RING BOWL, WHISPERING HOPE, AND GEORGIE PORGIE

[*St. George News* – April 1, 1938] **POTTAWATOMIE COUNTY FARM BUREAU NEWS NOTES** by R. F. McNitt, County Agent – Bindweed meetings were held in Wamego, Fostoria, Emmett, Flush, Swamp Angel School House, Olsburg, and Belvue last week. It is hoped, however, that the county will soon be well organized to cooperate in controlling bindweed successfully. [Finest Easter Suits $14.50 to $22.50 at Larson's, Wamego.]

BEHAVIOR MODIFICATION

"Now look what you did! I told you to straighten up, or you'd spill something!" his mother said.

George stared at his upside down cereal bowl that lounged in a pool of thick, heavy cream. Near it floated oatmeal islands, and a gentle, milky waterfall trickled from the table to pool on the worn kitchen linoleum. "Just look what you did! Oh, how can you be so careless?"

The white-topped four-year-old stared without expression at the sand-colored bowl with the soft blue ring, a newly acquired feed store bonus. You dumb ole bowl, he thought. You're no friend of mine. Now see what you've done. You got me in trouble with Mom. Why did you have to flip over?

For a moment, Mr. Blue Ring Bowl said nothing, acting innocent, like bowls can do. Then, as if it could talk, George heard, "Hey, I'm no toy and I'm not a play thing. Anyway, it was your fault." George started to debate the point, but before he could speak, his dad's frown penetrated like an arrowhead. The youngster looked down and away.

As she jerked the mop from the rack, his mom had more to say. "Why are you such a careless boy? If you don't be careful, George David Burgess, God is going to put a black mark by your name in His Big Book In

Heaven. And you know what that means!"

George inched lower in his chair. Oh no, not more black marks. Soon, just his scalp showed above the table and his entire face sunk far inside his milk glass. Darn that ole bowl.

"I don't know, John, it just never fails. Every time we eat, one of the boys is acting up. What are we going to do with them?"

George's stomach turned. Why am I always getting into trouble with God and the folks?

§

It seemed one of us—or maybe both—acted up or had an accident at most meals. Our parents, saddened by the long list of offenses, searched for ways to overcome our problems. In general, animated scolding worked the best, though gentle chiding and civil discussions had some effect. In truth, reaching our parents goals and aims—to turn us into tiny bodies of perfection—required the corrective measures of behavior modification; long before that concept made the textbooks.

To us, this training and re-training sometimes seemed harsh. Our giant parents—owners of stern looks and gruff voices—intimidated us with ease. The rule, as we understood it was: "You act up, and you'll be punished."

Intimidated or not, we did learn to catalog Mom's long list of corrective measures. Her favorites included, 'If I Yell Loud Enough Maybe I'll Get Through,' 'Put the Fear of God in the Kid,' 'No Dessert This Time,' and 'Don't Forget Who You Are.'

As with many mid-century parents, the technique of last resort—probably the most effective—was, 'Go Getta Switch!'

§

"John Frederick, you go outside right now and bring me a switch! We're not going to put up with any more of your shenanigans," his father said, after his eldest dropped the bread he'd tried spinning on one finger. Strawberry jam stained his school shirt, his chair, and the floor.

"Look at you! Just how am I going to clean that shirt now?" his mother asked. "You just go get that switch like your father said. And, take the shirt off so I can wash it. You'll have to wear your work shirt to school." With that, Freddy left the table, peeled off his shirt, and hurried from the tension of the room, slamming the screen door in protest...which brought another stern look from his dad.

At the Schlegel Place, Mom holding George, Freddy at the '28 Chevrolet, and the F-12 Farmall in the background.

While he was gone, time seemed to crawl by and in the hush, George again pulled down inside his glass. He sensed his brother was stalling...and that would probably cause another outburst from his mom. Will he ever get back? If Dad would only forget about it.

That did not happen, for after several minutes, the boys' dad went to the door to look for his son...only to find him dawdling on the porch. "Get in here right now, young man. You've just got to learn to think before you do things. Come on, let's get this over with."

Freddy handed over a rather dry box elder branch and grabbed his ankles. "Awwww...oh...ouch! Ayieeeee...oh. That hurts. Oh, that's enough!" This brittle switch spanking, through thick bib overalls and underwear, produced minimal pain. And, although his dad tried to seem stern, his heart wasn't in it so that he delivered semi-harsh swats. The result was that Freddy—more uneasy with himself than harmed—did feel sorry about messing up.

Did Dad's being upset with him also upset God? Or, did a spanking rub out God's black marks? Did *He* see me drop the bread or George upset Mr. Blue Ring Bowl? Can God see inside of George's milk glass? Does God judge us every time we do something bad? These questions remained unanswered in Freddy's head until that evening at supper he asked, "How can God see us? We can't see him."

His folks exchanged glances; each hoping the other would field the question. At last, his dad said, "Well, God's not like us. He had the power to create the whole world in seven days, so I guess he knows what we do all the time. He sees our failings, and he also must see how we pray to him and try to help others as Jesus taught. Someday you can ask him that question in person."

§

AVOIDING BLACK MARKS

Regardless of who God was, where he lived, or what he saw, we realized our parents took him seriously. And, we sensed we had better do the same. We also learned that avoiding black marks was a good way of avoiding penalties—the earthly kind for sure. In truth, our folks' corrective actions didn't seem to last. What about God's?

The big picture of God—we guessed that was him—hanging from a nail in the wall at Laclede Baptist Church, looked kind of stern, as if we annoyed him. Was he going to take a switch to us? Were we going to get another black mark and how many could a person get before being in serious trouble? Would he forgive us in the end—like Mom?

We could count on her mercy, even though she felt God tallied up a person's wrongs, and if there were too many marks, that person would miss out on heaven. Mom had developed definite rules of life from what she understood of the Missouri Synod Lutheran church's teachings, what she learned from her devout Norwegian immigrant mother, and from her somewhat severe father. To her, right was right and wrong was wrong, and that there were no gray areas.

In contrast, Dad's view of religion was less black and white. Although he had strong views of right and wrong instilled by his mother and the Episcopal Church, forgiveness—if a person was really sorry and said so—seemed the key to his understanding. He said he believed that God loved us and wanted us to love him back, and we could do that by serving others and worshiping regularly.

In those days, getting to worship every Sunday could be difficult. Rain, snow, and barely passable roads made even short trips a challenge. However, while living on the Schlegel place on Indian Creek—where Freddy saved the car—we could make it the three miles to the tiny, bright Laclede Baptist Church quite often.

That church had a God-fearing congregation—about half were relatives—that filled the pews and worshiped him with prayers, hymns, and heavy preaching. And, one August Sunday, we heard our folks add to the worship with a special song, that stirred our hearts.

We could not believe our ears. Our parents stood on the raised platform making the most beautiful music. A bit shaky at first, they soon found the rhythm, and with the aid of the old upright piano, created harmony sweeter than a flock of meadowlarks. Dad's soft Irish tenor held the melody, and Mom followed with the echo in a clear, though timid, alto.

'Whispering...whispering...hope,
Oh, how wel...come...thy voice,
Making my heart...
In its sorrow rejoice."

Neither of us fidgeted, or made a sound. In the other pews, no one moved, except for movement of ladies' arms, fanning away the summer's heat. Everyone seemed awed by the music, and when it ended, polite applause sounded from every seat. And look, wasn't that big picture of God smiling a bit? No, it was just the sunlight...or...no...it was a smile!

§

The next day while the boys played on the floor, George asked his brother, "Do you think Mom and Dad could get a job on the radio? Maybe they could sing along with Edmund Denny at WIBW." Denny, accompanied by Miss Maudie at the piano, had just finished singing *The Old Rugged Cross* in a rich, warm voice over the powerful Topeka station. "Wouldn't that be swell?"

Freddy nodded yes, and then moved next to the borrowed, battery-powered RCA radio when another WIBW performer, Little Jimmie Dickens, started singing his favorite song. It was about a '*bird of paradise*' flying up someone's nose and an elephant caressing with its toes. The nonsense song rhymed, so Freddy, strumming a pretend guitar sang along…trying to harmonize.

Little Jimmie was his hero, and Freddy knew from posters at the Columbian Theater, how he held his mouth just so when he sang. Maybe, he thought, I can get a job at WIBW and sing like that. I bet George would like it if I was a star.

GEORGIE PORGIE

George, who never had thoughts of stardom, approached music—and life in general—in a more relaxed way. He stayed quiet most of the time and seemed to like daydreaming. If he sang by himself, he did it softly, not wanting to have people look at him. He seemed slow to act, and mulled the choices for each decision over and over. Playing checkers with him took forever.

"If you don't make you move soon, I'm going to put the checkers away," his dad said. "You're slower than molasses in wintertime."

"Do you suppose George is slow because he embarrasses so easily?" his mother asked, as if her son wasn't in the room. "He hates to make mistakes."

"He does get red in the face at the drop of a hat. Yeah, that may be why he's so shy. But you know, he has a way with people. He seems pretty likable."

"Yes, I think you're right, John. He is pretty cuddly."

First grader George has a smile and lots of ears as he poses for his picture.

A few weeks later, the family and other relatives gathered for Thanksgiving dinner. While the ladies prepared the meal, George became the topic of conversation. "Have you ever seen a skinnier kid?" Aunt Helen said. "I'm surprised the wind doesn't just blow him away. We'd better make sure he gets a lot of those mashed potatoes today. Maybe he should use a trough instead of a plate...and a great big fork...or maybe a scoop shovel!"

"You know," Aunt Dorothy said, "he could have a tapeworm or something. Did you ever think of that, Veda?"

"Well, he did have worms a year ago. John gave him enemas with Rinso dish soap for three straight days. I'm pretty sure we got them all. It was a pretty ugly sight."

"Well, I should hope so. Goodness that sounds awful."

"Yeah, George is skinny, but he's a good boy. It does seem to take him forever to join a conversation. He just stands there with a blank expression," his mom said. "And, when people look at his blue eyes and that helpless appearance, they want to give him a hug or a squeeze."

As if on cue, George came into the house for a drink of water, and right away his Aunt Dorothy tried to put her arms around him. Oh, no, he thought, sliding behind his mother and hiding in the folds of her dress. Not more hugging...and no kissing with those big lips.

"Oh, Georgie, just look at you, you're such a poor urchin, let me give you a hug," Aunt Dorothy said.

I've got to get out of here, he thought. But how? With caution, he stuck out his moppet head, only to have his aunt rub it as if he were a tabby cat.

Like a terrified turtle, he pulled his long neck behind his mom. Ugh, he thought, and un-rubbed his hair. Then, holding his breath, he ran for the door.

NAME LIABILITY

Later, when he entered the combined school—both grade and high—at Hartford, he discovered Georgie gave him plenty of name liability. A new menace surfaced...*teasing*.

"Why do the girls have to call me Georgie?" he asked his brother. "I just get red all over and they tease more."

"Hey, don't let it bother you. You could tease them back, you know. Give them a dose of their own medicine."

That wasn't so easy, the six-year-old thought. The girls in my class say that poem every time I see them. I hate it. Why don't they pick on somebody else? I'm not the only boy in school. Oh, no, here they come again.

Georgie Porgie, puddin' and pie;
Kissed the girls and made them cry.
When the girls came out to play,
Georgie Porgie ran away.

In a panic, he headed for the boys' bathroom. Kissed the girls and made them cry? Not me…not ever.

When he went back to the classroom, a couple of girls spotted him. "So, Georgie Porgie, where have you been? To the toitie? Don't spend too much time there, you might fall in." He took his seat and acted as if he hadn't heard them. They knew better—his face turned beet red.

Later, during morning recess, he headed to the restroom again, just as the bell rang. Now, maybe I can go without them seeing me, he thought. A minute later—without eye contact—he scurried to his seat, as the room started to become quiet. Then he heard it…

From across the aisle, in a loud whisper, Stella Colglazer said, "Georgie, your barn door is open." Everyone seemed to look at him and snicker. Without moving his head, his eyes looked down. She was right. For a time, he sat in reddened silence, but slowly realized he had to do something. So—at a snail's pace—he slid his reader downward, and with his hands hidden, started fastening the three buttons.

Again, Stella helped. "One, two, and three," she hissed. Oh man, will girls ever leave me alone…or will they tease me forever?

An answer to his question would come a year or so later when, midway through the second grade, the family left Hartford, and the girls had to find another poor soul to tease. At his new school—it had only one room—there would be only seven or eight girls total and just two of them would be in his grade.

And happily, in 1946 and 1948, sisters Judy and Joyce would join the family. That helped him appreciate girls, for his sisters were very special, and of course, so was his mom...but she really didn't count. She was just Mom.

For now, however, George was months away from relief and still had to face the daily dose of teasing. And, there were other challenges—of major proportions—for the bashful youngster.

"Okay class, you are dismissed for today. You can wait in the classroom for your bus or you can go outside to the playground," his first-grade teacher, Mrs. Secrest, said. George collected his take-home papers, lunch pail, jacket, and cap and headed outside.

Only a couple of other kids came out, so he climbed on a swing and watched a couple of dogs chase each other across the street. Overhead, he heard the high-pitched whistle of a red tail hawk, and wondered what the bird was saying. Would it understand me if I whistled back? Then, grinning to himself, he remembered he didn't know how to whistle yet.

Next, a flying beetle joined him on the swing, and he shooed it away with his cap. For a few moments he sat there, enjoying the low sun and the things nature served up that afternoon.

NUMBER TWO

Then it hit him—a feeling of panic and other things. "Ah...." I need a bathroom, and in a hurry, he thought. *Number Two!* He jumped from the swing and quick-stepped to the school door and started down the stairs toward the restrooms, locker rooms, and gymnasium.

Halfway down, he heard voices. They came from the boys' locker room. The football team is suiting up for practice, he thought. And I have to go by them to get to the toilet. He tiptoed down a few more steps. But, what if they see me and make fun of me?

At the door, he held his breath and slowly pulled it part way open. Screeeeech! He froze, for through the opening, he saw the team, half-naked, putting on their shoulder pads. Giants!

By now, the urge to get into a stall was very strong, but he just couldn't enter. In panic, he turned and started back up the stairs.

Nature now took over. He wheeled and once more moved down the stairs. Toward the voices. He wanted to go in—he had to go in. Loud laughter erupted, and George bolted back up the stairs.

Just as he reached the landing, the full force of his intestines took over. He felt what he dreaded, but was unable to stop. There he stood—paralyzed—and filled his pants, right on the spot—a full-blown bowl movement!

I've got to get to the open air. Outside, outside....

The school janitor, coming up the front steps, noticed the youngster shuffling along bow-legged, trying to hide his strained, deep red face.

"Are you alright, son?" asked the kind janitor.

"Uh-huh," George said, to which the janitor shook his head and continued into the school.

What do I do now, George thought. My pants feel awful, and the smell is awful. How can I sit on the bus in this mess? What will the others say? What will the folks say?

His initial solution was to be the first on the bus so he could sit in the back. He waddled to the rear window seat and draped his jacket across his lap. Next, he put his papers and lunch pail alongside his hip so no one could sit next to him. Maybe this will work, he thought. Then he realized he had to face another obstacle. He had to walk past lots of kids to get off the bus! Oh, man.

A DEAD MOUSE IN THE HEATER

"What's that smell?" Freddy asked, when he walked down the aisle to sit beside cousin Kathleen Wilson. "Somebody must have died in here."

The bus driver nodded that he smelled something, too. By now, all the kids chimed in with a chorus of whews and ughs. Everyone, except George. "There must be a dead mouse in the heater," the driver said. "We can't do anything about it now, but I'll look for it at the end of my run."

George sucked in his breath, feeling sick to his stomach. This is going to be a bad trip, he thought. Can't this bus go any faster? Man, oh, man.

By the time George, Freddy, and Kathleen reached their drop-off spot, the bumpy bus had traveled five miles over some rough roads and chugged through several stops and starts. When George inched down the steps, the driver sniffed a bit and then smiled, but said nothing. He had been a first-grader once himself.

The humiliated George walked downwind from his brother and Kathleen, hoping his aroma would be confused with normal barnyard smells. His luck held, for the other two ran on down the lane leaving him to labor on alone.

Would anyone besides the bus driver—and, of course, his mom—discover George's little secret? For the next few weeks, he expected someone to tease him about the day he had number-twoed in his pants, but no one did. This made him more confident and the teasing slowed. Then, when he was almost eight, the family moved and the label of 'Georgie Porgie' was left behind. R.I.P.

About the time of the move, George discovered that he liked the world of make believe and its fantasy heroes. In particular, he felt inspired by the feats of the legendary St. George of dragon-slaying fame. So, once at the new farm, George, also known as St. George, dedicated himself to protecting the family from all kinds of fire-breathing menaces.

A MIGHTY DRAGON SLAYER

So, as the March days grew longer, George began honing his fighting skills. With a dogwood-switch sword—a la Douglas Fairbanks—he whacked, sliced, and stabbed dozens of imaginary monsters. The constant battling improved his swashbuckling, but it also slowed his assigned chores to a crawl.

The one-minute walk from the house to the granary now consumed ten minutes. The simple task of watering the chickens used up half an hour—though it did leave the deceased bodies of several make-believe dragons strewn about. He moved at a snail's pace, shuffling through the brisk sun-drenched morning, dressed in a heavy winter coat and a red-checked flop-eared cap. His ducking and circling left erratic footprints in the snow.

Again and again, his mom had watched him waste time from the kitchen window. She shook her head and thought, just look at that kid poke along. He can be such a picture of slow. There, he's stopped again to fight somebody.

When her patience gave out, she commanded from the kitchen door, "George David, you go take care of those chickens this minute. Stop poking along and do your work." Her stern voice got his attention…and also scared away a redbird in the box elder tree and startled the blackbirds at the cattle pen.

George didn't see the birds, but did attempt—with little success—to heed his instructions. The mighty dragon slayer retraced his battle route, and wasted ten minutes going and another ten coming back. Again, the simple process of feeding two pounds of cracked corn to a couple of dozen Leghorn hens was still a 30-minute activity.

Looking back, one could see that perhaps the names—Georgie, Georgie Porgie, and St. George—all had a bearing on what he would one day become. The cuddling of Georgie by relatives and the teasing of Georgie Porgie seemed to cultivate caution and deliberateness. And, it is possible the St. George role taught him boldness and determination?

Many years later, he successfully commanded Air Force units as Colonel George D. Burgess and flew huge jet aircraft around the world. He found thoughtfulness and caution to be valuable traits. Thorough and calculated planning, attention to detail, and meticulous execution led to safe and efficient trips to exotic places like Vietnam, Europe, Africa, South America, the Middle East, and Australia.

§

When the two of us were young, we hadn't heard of most of those far-off places. Our world was confined to a small section of Eastern Kansas, except for a couple of trips to Michigan to visit Mom's family. During one of these trips—we were five and three—we saw check-row corn in Iowa, the mighty Missouri and Mississippi Rivers, and the barges moving iron ore up the waterways from mine to foundry.

What we saw impressed us. However, the highlight of the trip was not the scenery, but a man. That man was our Great Uncle Tom, a true family character. We could go on all day about him....

THREE

UNCLE TOM'S FORD, THOSE HARD TIMES, AND KITTENS IN THE OVEN

[*St. George News* – April 1, 1938] **THE ROUTE ONE REPORT** – March 28. Cool and rainy and it was badly needed. The Mt. Zion Ladies Aid will meet with Mrs. Nannie Oppy Thursday afternoon, March 31. ~ Guests of Mr. and Mrs. Ed Guilfoil and family were his mother and a brother and family of Kansas City. ~ Doris Mae Seematter was in St. Marys Friday evening. She was in the St. George high school play put on there. ~ Antone Voelker sawed wood for Will Oppy Friday. ~ Sylvester Umscheid has a new car.

UNCLE TOM'S FORD

"We'll keep the water jar up front. The food can go in here," Uncle Tom—really the boys' great uncle—said, loading a flour sack containing homemade bread, a quart of canned beef, and two Mason jars of peaches into the trunk.

He nodded to the boys and said, "Okay, you cowboys, it's time to load the stage. Freddy you sit in the back with Aunt Mabel and your mom. Georgie Porgie, you sit with your dad while he drives, and I'll ride shotgun."

As the early morning spring sun beamed down, everybody moved toward the black '35 Ford. Except three-year-old George. He stood dead in his tracks staring at the car.

"Come on George," his mom said. "My mama's sick, and we need to get going." Nothing. He stayed put. His eyes began to water. "What's the matter with you?" she asked, watching George point toward the back seat.

"Oh, alright," she said. "You can ride in back and Freddy will ride up front."

George slid across the backseat and clung to his mom. For most of the trip, he left her side only for the occasional roadside picnic, for a good bush to heed the call of nature, or when everyone got out while the men fixed a tire.

And many punctures occurred, rain or shine, during the long, straight-through trip over the challenging pre-freeway roads.

Highway 24 was paved to Kansas City, but when the travelers angled across Missouri, Iowa, and Wisconsin, they hit mostly sand and gravel roads. Except for the few stretches of pavement near some cities, twenty-five to thirty-five miles an hour was their best speed, for most rural roads were rutted and dusty unless it rained.

"Dang, there goes another tire," John said, herding the car to the side of the road somewhere in Missouri. "Hear the whap, whap? The right front tire is flat this time."

"Alright, out you go everybody," he said. "You can wait out of the drizzle under that big elm over there. We'll have this fixed in a jiffy."

While the boys pestered a line of ants climbing the tree, Uncle Tom jacked up the car's front end, and the boys' dad loosened the wheel lugs. Soon, the tube's puncture was scraped and a circle of patching material glued on. After drying a few minutes, they remounted the tire, pumped it up, and the Ford continued the 980-mile trip to Michigan's Upper Peninsula.

Any other stops were for the cheapest gas or at small-town grocery stores—after the food in the trunk gave out—to buy canned peaches, sardines, bricks of cheese, and loaves of bread or crackers that served as dinner plates. With limited eating utensils, Uncle Tom's trusty pocketknife opened tin cans, speared the peaches, or sliced the cheese.

As the car pulled away from a small Iowa store, Aunt Mabel said, "Tom, you're not going to cut cheese with that old knife. It is not even clean. Just look at it. Someone is going to get sick."

Silently, and with great drama, Uncle Tom unfolded the longest knife blade, gripped the orange brick of longhorn, and carved downward in one motion. Smiling, he stabbed the thick slab, reached into the backseat, and offered it to George.

"There ya go, Georgie...did you ever see a nicer slice?" George hesitated. Uncle Tom pressed the knifepoint closer, and dropped the cheese in George's lap. "You can tell my knife is clean, can't you, Georgie? I've been polishing it in my pocket for nearly ten years. And besides...I just skinned a skunk with it last week. That would clean it if anything would."

The two women shook their heads. Uncle Tom was at it again. George on the other hand, took the cheese and held it at arm's length. He stared at it for a long while, and turned to his mother and tossed it onto her lap.

To the family, Uncle Tom was a treasure—most of the time. Grandpa Burgess' younger brother was both witty and funny. And, though he ended up with much of the farm his Irish-immigrant parents had assembled, people often said he would rather jaw and josh than farm.

"Isn't this some car? Isn't this Ford sleek? This style is a whole lot better then the old models. And, don't you just love the V-8 engine? Listen to that purr," Uncle Tom said. "Why I wouldn't have any other kind of car. Especially since ole Henry Ford took up my suggestion."

To himself, Freddy marveled that someone famous like Henry Ford had received help from his relative. Uncle Tom must really be a smart man, he thought, though I wish he'd stop sliding into me on the corners.

"Course, I didn't talk to Mr. Ford directly, but I did tell the dealer in Manhattan I'd buy a new Ford if they'd make one that had a better look to it. I'm sure glad I did that. Humm."

At that moment, he looked out the window toward a farmer cultivating corn with a pair of mules. "You know," he said to Freddy, "those surely look like side-hill mules, don't they? Yep, no doubt about it. They were bred for side-hill work, don't you think?"

Freddy stared as the team walked around a low hill. How could he tell what the mules were? They looked black to him...and that was all. Uncle Tom provided the answer. "You see how those mules have level backs, even though they're on a hill?"

Freddy looked.

"...that's because the uphill legs are shorter. On flat ground, they can't walk level, but they are great for hills...if you only go one direction."

"Humm," he said. "I wonder if mules in places like Colorado have even shorter legs on the steep up-slope side? What do you think? Humm."

Just before twilight, somewhere near the Iowa border, Uncle Tom provided his fellow passengers with another observation. "Don't you just feel sorry for some folks? Some people just plain don't have it easy."

"For example, take that Louella Ethel Brockman. I surely do feel sorry for her. Saw her a few days ago hoeing corn like a hired man, while Shorty sat watching the cows to keep them from getting in the field. You might not agree with me, but that Shorty sure knows how to get out of work."

"Poor Louella Ethel," he said, "She drove her hogs to a bad market when she married that guy. Yep, she surely did."

This kind of remark, plus stories and jokes he made up, entertained the travelers during the long, long trip. Uncle Tom also was full of poems and limericks.

§

We sat in awe in the bumpy car when he recited the entire Robert Service poem, *The Cremation of Sam Magee.* Somewhere further north, he spouted what seemed like a hundred verses of *The Strawberry Roan.*

Years later, our Uncle Tom used his interesting and convincing rhetoric, to get himself elected to the Kansas State House of Representatives, and he served two full terms. To his credit, he sponsored the bill making *Home on the Range*—composed a few miles from where we lived—the Kansas State Song.

On our trip, we sang that song...and others...traveling north, crammed in the Ford. The hurried trip—straight through—left us exhausted, but we arrived in time. Grandma Scott had turned for the better by the time we got there, and in a few weeks had recovered.

As for us, we made the trip home with more stories and a less hurried pace. We even ate at a diner and stayed the night in a Traveler's Court cabin near the edge of Hannibal, Missouri.

§

"Tom," Aunt Mabel said, "Veda and I are getting tired of sitting back here. Let's stop somewhere for supper. George is going to waste away if we don't."

"Oh, that would be nice," Veda said, with hope in her voice. She looked at her husband in the rearview mirror and asked, "Do you think we can afford it, John?"

"Now don't you ladies worry about money. We can stop and eat," Uncle Tom said. "When we get home, I'll sell a hog to pay for it. But, don't over eat; I don't want to sell two. Just keep your eyes open for a one-hog diner."

Soon, alongside the Mississippi River, the travelers sat at the single table behind the only five stools in the place. The meals were blue-plate specials, well-done roast beef and gravy on thick slices of bread with corn on the side. The women shared with the boys, and the adults had coffee in thick, brown pottery cups squeezed at the middle like their belts were too tight.

"You know, boys," Uncle Tom said after a good belch, "it was right near here that ole Tom Sawyer came up with a way to make a lot of money. He had this scab, and he'd let his friends look at it for cash. Isn't that a dandy idea?" he asked.

"Yep, Georgie, we could scrape you up some, put a big piece of flour sack around it, and you'd be in business. And, you could attract a lot of lookers if you moaned just right. Maybe we ought to do some moaning practice in the car tomorrow. You need to try to sound like a fresh weaned calf. Humm."

From his diner's seat, Tom demonstrated with a long, loud moan. The noise startled the cook, who dropped a pan, and caused the two customers on stools to spin around like they had something to hide.

As the sound died away, Aunt Mabel just shook her head and started for the door, heading toward the little cabin court across the gravel drive. It had been a long day...and she wanted no more of Tom's nonsense.

So that night, for the first time on the trip, the travelers didn't sleep in the moving car, but rather stayed in the roadside lodging—not often available in those days—all in the single cabin to save money.

A day later, the trip in Uncle Tom's Ford was over and Grandma Scott was well again, thank God. However, the folks had spent money they couldn't afford, for they had little cash. Those were difficult times.

HARD TIMES

Hard times came with the Great Depression of the 1930s. People lost jobs—about 25% of all men were unemployed—and if farmers raised anything, prices for it were at rock bottom.

The productivity of the United States fell more than one-third, making cash money hard to come by. Previous economic downturns hurt, but this was the most devastating financial time in history.

In Kansas, John and Veda married on May 27, 1933, and immediately faced problems. They had little money, suffered through the crop killing Dust Bowl, and other disasters. Into the hardships and the poverty Freddy and George were born.

"We'd have never made it," the boys' dad said to the family gathered at the kitchen table, "but for the Grace of God and lots of hard work. It was a hard time to start farming. The country was a mess, and Freddy was born the year the Dust Bowl winds blew topsoil as far as the Atlantic Ocean," he said, nodding toward his oldest.

"We lived upstairs at Grandpa and Grandma Burgess' that first year. The next year, we rented the Fortune place on shares." The boys were silent.

"We had almost no rain and the winds just blew and blew. Sometimes dirt drifted as high as fence posts in Western Kansas and Oklahoma. Dust covered everything, even in the house. Some people said half of Kansas landed in Missouri and the other half in Iowa."

"The next year was dry again and had more dust," the boys' mom said, "but your dad got some corn started and I had a pretty nice garden. Then the grasshoppers came. They ate anything green and even clothes on the clothesline."

"We just didn't have any money. Finally, your dad got a job helping build roads for Union Township. He only made one dollar a day."

§

The story amazed us. On the road building job, Dad worked long days for a dollar. And he furnished his own team. The horses pulled a little tumblebug scraper that moved dirt from high spots to fill in the dips. He worked most of the fall until road building stopped for the winter.

The money was a blessing, but during that winter of 1935, with no income at all, they ate chickens and chicken eggs, and not much else. On one occasion, Dad traded a case of 30 dozen eggs for a case of canned green beans, almost the only vegetables they had all winter.

In our early years, we were dressed in hand-me-down clothes, and Christmas and birthdays brought few presents. But, our family struggled on until the late '30s when drought and insect plagues ended and crops survived to provide a harvest.

During the struggles and with the successes, Mom and Dad taught us to do our share. We started helping out early in life, for even at age 6 or so, we had chores each day. Our responsibilities grew as we did, for pretty small boys could gather eggs, feed the chickens, or even milk a cow.

We learned about animals, the earth, and making do. We learned to work together...and that God was on our 'team' and always with us. We had a home, maybe not much by some standards, but real to us.

The home was friendly space, held familiar belongings, and had the feel of family. Like the people of history who lived in caves, tents, or huts, we found peace with what we had. Our homes were tiny, as few as three rooms, but love and security prevailed…even in the face of the hardship of depression, drought, and poverty.

People taught us lessons, too. Some adults you could 'read like a book,' while others hid their real feelings. Some were just characters like Uncle Tom. Others faced hardship with calm resolve. Each had a story, including our parents.

YOU DON'T GET TO PICK YOUR PARENTS

We didn't get to pick our parents. But when we looked around at the neighbor kids, and later in school, we decided we liked what we had…at least compared to some. Our folks weren't mean, or drinkers, or like those who skipped out on their families in the hard times.

Mom and Dad used strong values raising us. They were focused. Work came before play. They strived to do right, and we were to do the same. They pushed us to be the best, especially Mom.

We learned to compete, to be good citizens, and without putting it into words, to be what God created us to be. We tried to excel at school, sports, and in our work…most of the time. The words citizenship, trustworthiness, honesty, and deportment—sometimes we forgot that one—had meaning.

John Michael & Veda Helen Burgess on their wedding day, May 27, 1933. They took their vows seriously.

We felt supported and guided, sometimes with tough love and a spare-the-rod and spoil-the-child approach, by John Michael Burgess and Veda Helen Scott Burgess. They were great parents.

§

"Dad, who were you named after?" Freddy, now six-years-old, asked. The family had just finished supper, a platter of chicken fried steak and fresh green beans. They sat outside on the stoop while insects of the night began to sing in the early summer dusk. The family had time to talk, for it was a time before television.

"How did you get your name?"

"Well, the John came from my grandfather, John Irving Burgess. He came from Ireland in 1868 and homesteaded in Union Township. He was a great farmer and a good man to be named for, though he could be pretty stern."

"I guess my second name, Michael, came because I was an angel to my mother. She named me after the Archangel Michael, at least that's what she said. Maybe I am an angel...don't you think so, Veda?" he said, and then laughed.

"I can't imagine where you got that idea," the boys' mom said, humor lighting her large eyes and brightening her face. "You don't look much like an angel wearing those dirty clothes you farmed in all day. Still...."

"Maybe...sometimes." She smiled again.

Freddy missed the adult humor because he was thinking up another question. George missed the humor because he was tying a string to a big, brown June bug.

"What about you, Mom?" Freddy asked. "Who were you named for and where did they come from?"

"You know my father's parents came from Scotland. My dad is Fred Scott, the Postmaster of Bergland, where I grew up in Michigan. Your grandma, Sigrid Olson Scott, came from Norway when she was 19."

"But, who were you named after?" Freddy asked again.

"When she first came to the states, your grandmother worked for a family in Iowa. She liked their little girl named Veda, so that's what she named me. I think Veda was the name of some lady from Greek mythology."

"Coming from Norway, your grandmother knew a lot about mythology for they had all kinds of strange people like Odin and Thor...and even trolls. They didn't have anything to do with my second name, though. The name Helen came from Helen of Troy. My mom must have liked that name, too."

As they sat on the stoop, their dad continued the story. "Your ancestors came from Ireland, Scotland, and Norway. Some say the Burgesses moved from England to Ireland during the time of Cromwell, but no one knows for sure...and maybe never will."

While George watched his knot unravel and the June bug fly to safety, he asked, "So, are we English or Irish?"

"We don't know; we just don't know."

The English-Irish issue persisted for years, and

finally at a Sunday family gathering, George asked Uncle Tom about it. "So, Uncle Tom," he said, "if the Burgesses were first in England, and then went to Ireland, does that make us English or Irish?"

Looking down his long nose with a bit of disdain, Uncle Tom said, "Well, let me ask you a question, Georgie. Tell me this. If the cat had kittens in the oven, would you call them biscuits? Well, would you?"

§

We never knew for sure what the question meant. Or the answer to it. We laughed, and certainly felt convinced...of something! We also decided his Irish immigrant parents, John I. and Margaret Burgess, must have kissed the blarney stone, and that Uncle Tom had the stone's power, too.

English or Irish, his older brother was our grandfather, David, and our grandmother was Mary Anna Shea Burgess. Both came from Irish immigrant families so we assumed that settled the question.

Those ancestors helped give us our many physical and mental characteristics. Dad, for example, was good at logic and math, and had played basketball and baseball. He stood five foot ten, and one feature about him, although having nothing to do with ancestry, was unique.

§

"Dad, what happened to your hand?" Freddy asked. "How come you only have part of a finger?"

"Well, I did a stupid thing when I was about 10-years old and lost a third of it," he said, poking Freddy in the chest with the stubby index finger of his right hand. "Aunt Dorothy and I went to the well by the cow shed to get some water."

"We wanted to couple the windmill shaft to the

pump, but couldn't find the bolt. Finally, I stuck in my finger in place of it. That was a horrible mistake. The spinning windmill pulled the shaft, pump, and me, up and down 'til my finger broke off," he whispered. "It was a stupid thing to do. Don't you do something like that!"

§

We heard this story, over and over, for Dad preached safety. He was cautious, and people respected his judgment. He was honest and a good farmer. Our dad thought people should reap what they sowed, and he worked hard to make things happen.

Our mom was tall, a little over five eight, according to her. She had deep auburn hair and freckles. She liked to laugh and sing, and was full of ideas. Her fiery emotions made her hazel eyes flash...especially when we messed up.

Mom also cried at the drop of a pin...from sadness, gladness, or in frustration. Dad would tease, saying she could cry when the stoplight changed color. Fortunately, she laughed more than she cried, and found humor in the most everyday things.

"Look at that, he's going to fall off the porch," Mom said, laughing at our dog, Pep. His name was a misnomer, for he lay like a pile of old rags that panted and sometimes scratched. His head and drooling pink tongue hung over the edge of the porch's cool concrete. "Just look at him lie there. Doesn't that look uncomfortable? I wish I could be that relaxed."

Mom, in contrast to Dad, did have trouble being calm in pressure situations. She got flustered and frustrated easy, and that led to some spark-producing conversations.

"I guess I'm the nervous type," she said. "I just worry about everything."

Our mom did worry and fret, especially about time. Every task had a deadline, and we were never, ever late for anything. She almost worshiped punctuality. Most every day, we could sense her concern about our being late for school or church.

Mom worried, too, about the grades we got, how hard we worked, what we saved, about our sitting still in church, how we looked, and other bits of life where she had well-developed standards. She demanded excellence and also a reverence for God.

Mom and Dad wanted good things for us and for themselves. We all had to work for what we got they said, and sometimes take risks, made bigger by the uncertainties of farming.

FOUR

WHERE'S THE MONEY, THE POOR FARM, AND BUYING A TRACTOR

[Wamego Reporter – October 19, 1939] **TOURED IN SIXTEEN STATES** – Mr. and Mrs. Floyd Funnell returned home Friday from a five week motor tour through sixteen states. They traveled in the northern and north eastern states. Their tour covered over 6,000 miles and it was a most enjoyable trip along the way with fine cities and scenic wonders.

WHERE'S THE MONEY?

"...you tell me that, John Burgess! How are you going to pay for a rubber-tired tractor?" Veda said with fire in her eyes. She was upset. And frustrated. "Just where is nine hundred dollars coming from?"

"And, what about the F-12 you and Alfred bought two years ago? What about that?" she asked. "Why in heaven's name do you need a new tractor?"

"I don't want to go in debt!" she said with force. "We'll go broke and end up on that Poor Farm. After all we've been through, I can't stand the thought of going into debt!"

Finally, squeezing her hands together, she said, "We're always struggling!" She looked away, her eyes watering.

Yes, the young couple had struggled. Their six years of married life had brought little farming success. The Depression economy and the Dust Bowl years almost wiped them out. Grasshoppers ate much of the crop in 1936 and 1937.

"Veda, honey," John said, "calm down and think. When we move to Aunt Maggie's place at Hartford, things will get better. This is a real break for us."

"Anyway," he said, smiling, "we'll have a problem trying to use the F-12 at Alfred's and also 95 miles south at the same time, won't we?"

"Maybe, we could cut it in two, like the Solomon story in the Bible. That way Alfred could use half and I could use half," he said, hoping he could make Veda laugh.

"Yep, that's it. We'll just saw the F-12 in half. Wonder if I should claim the left side or right side?"

His grin broadened, and his wife calmed down...slowly. "I know eight or nine hundred dollars is a lot of money, but it will pay for itself in time," he said. "We need to take the chance."

"Oh, alright smarty pants, but I hope you know where you're going to get the money?"

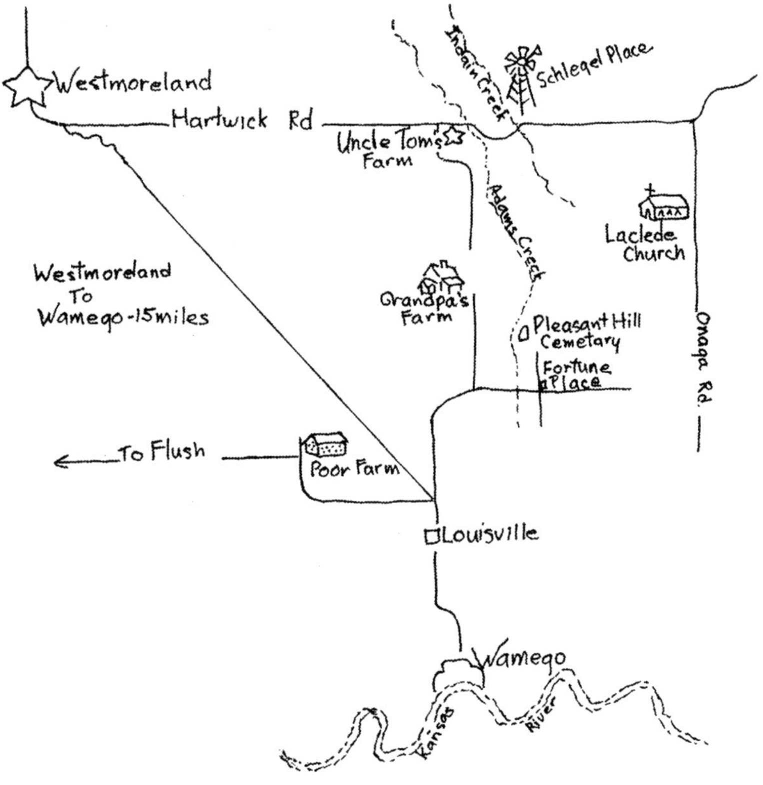

"We'll just have to find a way," he said, "other people do, you know."

"There should be some corn to sell," he said looking toward the bottomland along Indian Creek. Rows of silky-tan cornstalks fluttered in the breeze, each holding a yellow ear or two. A few dry days and he could shuck it.

Veda calmed for a time, and looked out into the morning sunshine of this early fall day. Puffy, high clouds contrasted against the blue Kansas sky. Chickens scratched in the yard, and in the background, the battery RCA radio played station WIBW in Topeka.

"And, after I give Oscar Krause five of those Hampshire shoats for thrashing the wheat, I'll still have one for us and 15 or so to sell. And, there are nearly 300 bushels of wheat, too."

"With what we sell, and if Alfred can pay for my share of the F-12, we might have four or five hundred dollars," he said. "It won't be enough, but maybe we can borrow some from the bank or from Dad. We can find the rest somewhere."

"Oh, John," she said sighing, "why is it when we get a little money, we have to go spend it? What about the other things we need? The boys don't even have decent clothes. Oh, we're just never going to make it, are we? And you work so hard, John. Must we go into debt? We'll never be able to pay it back," she said, her eyes watering again.

"I can't stand this!" she said. "I just know we'll end up on that *Poor Farm*!"

THE POOR FARM

Veda worried herself sick about being poor. She loathed the idea of defeat, and most of all, she hated the County's most tragic and graphic symbol of failure...the Poor Farm.

When her thoughts piled one on the other, her frustration grew and she sometimes felt like giving up. Then images of the Poor Farm changed her mind.

Living there would be awful. Those poor people, she thought. They look so sad...bedraggled. Oh, I don't want to live like that.

Only the hardest of the hard-up lived at the Pottawatomie County Poor Farm. It was the last resort for those down on their luck, those who could not make it on their own. It was the only help—except perhaps from an equally poor relative—for the rural destitute.

The penniless families raised livestock and grew enough food to live...with the county paying the bills. With this help went the stigma of being inept and that labeled them failures for a lifetime.

"If we end up on the Poor Farm, people will look down on us forever," Veda said after a bit, "I couldn't stand to hear them make snide comments that we couldn't make it as farmers."

"Now Veda," John said with a smile, trying to head off another attack of frustration. "Being poor keeps some people from getting into trouble. They have less, so they make fewer bad choices...and they don't have much to fix if something breaks. Why I could see how the Poor Farm has lots of advantages."

"John Burgess...you just take the cake. How could you think of living like those poor families? They have no hope. It's so sad. Oh, I hate the thought of that farm."

§

So, anytime we drove near the County Farm, just a few miles from where we lived on Indian Creek, Mom worked hard to convince us we'd end up there if we didn't watch our money. So we bought only important things...most of the time. And so did most of the neighbors.

Everyone wore a lot of hand-me-down clothes, brother to brother or from cousins or neighbors. Some kids wore made-over parents' clothing, especially coats and heavy shirts. So did our relatives, and very few had new things of any kind.

Some did get new clothes, in a way, by sewing cloth from feed and flour sacks into dresses or shirts.

§

"My, that's a pretty new dress, Helen," Veda said to her sister-in-law, Helen Gordon.

"Thanks. I sewed it from fifty-pound Betty Crocker sacks," Aunt Helen said. "Of course, I washed out the flour first. Didn't want it pasting my arms together, did I?"

"You know, these violets and daffodils look quite good together, don't they?" she said, striking an overstated pose.

"Yes, they do. And, now you look just like Louella Ethel Brockman. She's got that same dress."

"Oh, good heavens. Why I had no idea someone would wear this very same frock. My goodness. I'll have to find a new dressmaker," Aunt Helen said, tossing her head with mock indignation. "The thought of someone with the same outfit. How inconsiderate."

"Helen, you're a case," Veda said, smiling. "Anyway, I like your dress."

"Well," said Aunt Helen, "at least the material didn't come from hog feed sacks."

Feed sack dresses came from the red and white checkerboard Purina Hog Chow, something most farmers couldn't afford. Most home dressmakers used Betty Crocker's flowers or poke-a-dot patterns. Still, any material coming along free with a purchase was like finding money.

"I got this new dress cheap, and that's what counts. And, maybe if I don't wash it too often...it will darken down some and not look like anybody else's," Helen said. "Yep, that's just what I'll do."

"I can wear it for years," she said, chuckling, "unless I get too fat."

Feed and flour sack dresses did last for years, being used, reused, and used. Like most everyday clothes, they were patched and repatched, and became quilting scraps in the end. Socks were darned and redarned, sometimes containing more darning thread than the original.

The boys' mom was a meticulous darner and

patcher. She turned the edges of the tear under and sewed in a patch with the garment inside out. This neat method came from the Home Demonstration unit, so it had to be right.

"I can't stand seeing kids with patches on the outside of their overalls or shirts. And some, poor dears, have patches on their patches," Veda said.

Then she turned to her husband and said, "I know those families have lots of worries besides clothes. How do some of those poor folks make it? You know how we agonize over buying things. And now we need a tractor...."

After days of discussion, the boys' mom stopped fretting and gave in. There would be nearly 500 acres to farm at Aunt Maggie's huge place near Hartford. And a rubber-tired tractor could make the 190-mile round trip south to the edge of Coffey and Lyon counties in the fall to plant winter wheat.

Now what tractor was best? It was time to find out, an exciting event for any farmer...and in this case...for his sons as well.

WHICH COLOR DO YOU LIKE?

The boys' dad walked up the hill toward the house, watching them play with the cat. Sweating from fixing the pasture fence on that humid, muggy morning, he soon stood, washing his hands in the enamel basin on the back porch. A hint of a grin turned up the left side of his mouth. This is the day, he thought, I'm ready to check out tractors. "Well, boys, why don't you get ready to go to town. It's time to see about buying that tractor. You don't mind if the boys go with me, do you, Veda?"

"Well, I guess they can go..." she said. "That'll give me a few hours of peace around here. But, you boys need to wash up first, and comb your hair. Here, let me check your teeth. And put on your clean overalls," she said, calling overalls...overhalls...as everyone else did. "And don't forget to brush your teeth."

§

On those few occasions when we went with Dad alone, you'd have thought we were going to see Santa Claus. We always felt butterflies in our stomachs. And in this case, maybe we could help decide which tractor to buy, or maybe Dad would buy us a bottle of pop—both equal value events to us.

We washed our faces and brushed our teeth. Then we jumped into our overalls with the fewest patches and ran to the car. It was about 11 a.m. when Dad headed the old Chevy—still wearing scratch marks—toward Wamego. We giggled about everything, and Dad simply smiled back.

§

"Are you really going to buy a tractor today, Dad?" Freddy asked, above the engine noise and the door rattles. The car jostled through some rain-filled ruts as two mourning doves flew up from collecting muddy road grit to land on a telephone wire.

"I'm not sure, but maybe. I've looked around quite a bit, but I haven't decided which one fits the bill. Which one do you think we should get?"

Freddy shrugged his shoulders. Why not get a green one like Tessendorf has, he thought, or something red like the guy next to Uncle Tom's place? Maybe a yellow or orange one would do? He just didn't know.

On the other hand, George lost interest in tractors and started thinking about his suddenly empty stomach. Why didn't he eat more cereal at breakfast? Maybe he did have a tapeworm, as some folks said. Wonder if we'll get to eat in town?

Fighting ruts and slippery roads all the way, they finally headed down Wamego's main street…officially

Lincoln Avenue...dotted with daubs of mud dropped from the fenders of passing cars and trucks. Rain during the night created the mess that made the street look like it had warts.

The early September day brought farmers to town, kept from their fields by the weather. They loafed around, walking in knee-high, mud-covered rubber boots, alternating between looking for bargains and chewing the fat.

The old car rolled to the south end of town toward the muddy Kansas River—called the Kaw by the locals—on the rise from the rains. In front of the Holton Tractor Company, the engine chugged a few seconds before it died, but all eyes were on the brand spanking new Farmalls behind the big glass window.

Once through the door, they saw salesman Ernie Brockman—Shorty's cousin—leaning against the oil-stained parts counter. When the boys' dad turned toward the new tractors, Ernie grinned and walked over as if he had mental telepathy.

"What can I do ya fer?" asked Ernie, trying to act helpful, yet not wanting to scare off a potential customer by being pushy. "It's time you had a new tractor, ain't it?"

Getting no immediate response, he said, "Give me a holler if you need me," stepping back a half step to give his customers some breathing room.

The closer tractor was a new Farmall M. It looked as big as a D-6 bulldozer and had 38-inch rubber rear wheels. Rated a three-plow, it looked very up to date with its round-styled hood and gas tank. It was some tractor!

"John, at the end of the season like this, I can let you have that M for about eleven or twelve hundred dollars, give or take a few bucks." Ernie again leaned on the parts counter, picking at his teeth with an oily splinter.

§

Dad seemed to ponder Ernie's statement, and stared at the M without speaking. Then shook his head side-to-side, almost without motion. He moved toward the smaller, less expensive, two-plow Farmall H. Now this tractor could do the job and was closer to his price range. For long, long minutes, he stared at the H.

Then suddenly, as if inspiration hit, he turned, mumbled a short goodbye to a surprised Ernie, and we headed on foot for Eddy's Allis Chalmers dealership a block away.

Inside Eddy's sat two new orange 1939 WD's. However, Dad passed them by and walked directly to the lone remaining new '38 WC. A smile came over his face. He eyed its exposed radiator and unstyled gas tank, the fenders, the tires, and the crank. Slowly, he hoisted the two of us into the WC's big, holey steel seat. What a feeling! Was this the tractor?

§

Freddy pretended to move the steering wheel and drive along in road gear. George made sputtering engine noises and heard some noise in his empty stomach as well.

Their dad stared at the tractor for a long time and then decided not to decide…at least just then. He would think about it some more. Much to George's relief, it was time to move from buying tractors to buying food.

"Are you boys hungry?"

"Yeaaaaaaah! Where are we going to eat?"

"Well, we could go home…or we could go to the diner. But you know what's a better idea? We'll just walk over to Ince's and get something."

Once at Ince's Save Way grocery store, "Home of Baby Beef," they walked to the meat counter in the rear. The chiller case was full of mouth-watering cold cuts and cheeses.

The boys' dad nodded a hello to Robert Ince behind the counter. "Why not give us six slices of that baloney and a half pound of that Longhorn cheese?"

The grocer understood that in local lingo, the question was really an order. He turned on his slicing machine and tossed on a 20-pound bologna.

The rotating blade slid back and forth, back and forth. Zip, zip, zip, zip, zip, and zip. Slices plopped down in an orderly pile onto brown butcher paper from a mammoth roll. The zips repeated on another big block, cutting through both cheese and wrapper.

Mr. Ince then set a speed record wrapping the meat and cheese in separate packages. Flip, flap, flip…tape. Flip, flap, flip, tape. Incredible. He smiled, and with one motion, tossed the packages onto the countertop with a nod of thanks.

Turning away from the counter, the boys' dad said, "Freddy, you go get a loaf of Rainbow bread, and we'll meet up front. George, come with me and we'll get something for dessert. Any ideas?"

"Have you ever had one of those Snoballs?" George asked. He pointed at the coconut-and-frosting-covered, baseball-sized delights. He had dreamed of them since he was a kid….

"Yeah, those sound good to me. Hand me a couple of packages. Let's go up front and pay for everything."

Handing the clerk the money, he said, "We'll go back to Holton's and the car and eat. We can sit on the running board."

They walked to Holton's with the boys slapping at each other playfully and grinning from ear-to-ear. Eating a store-bought sandwich in town was exciting—but there was more to come.

"You boys thirsty?"

"Yeaaaaaaah."

"Here are three nickels, go inside and get us each a bottle of pop. Bring me a Nehi orange. Now, hold those bottles tight when you slide them out of that pop cooler."

With orange sodas for George and their dad, and a

Grapette for Freddy, they returned to the slap, slap, of baloney and Longhorn sandwiches being made. They began to eat on the running board, in front of a tractor dealership, with the damp smell of the muddy, fast moving Kaw filling the humid air.

§

> ***T***here we sat, three 'men' enjoying our sandwiches and pondering some of the questions of life. Why did store-sliced lunchmeat and cheese taste so good? Why did soda pop fizz, and why did people get so hungry when they were in town?
>
> And, why did town store clerks wear neckties? Why did Ernie pick his teeth with a splinter? And of course, why did new tractors look so great and smell so good?

§

"What color are you going to buy, Dad?" George asked. "Will it be orange like your bottle of pop?"

"Well, I don't know. I know I do like orange."

Dad must be partial to orange, we thought. That had to mean he liked the Allis Chalmers. If he liked the red Farmall, wouldn't he have had strawberry pop? He was going to get an AC.

HORSE-TRADER LINGO

In the end, color was only one small factor. Salesmanship was another. The owner of Eddy's Allis Chalmers first asked questions and listened to the answers, and then he used a lot of horse-trader lingo to explain how the orange AC brand would do the job. And, Abe Eddy aimed his pitch to Freddy and George, all the while making sure their dad heard every word.

"You get a little older, you fellas will be plowing in road gear. This tractor can run like a racehorse. And, listen to that engine. Isn't it the sweetest four-cylinder you ever heard?"

He paused, and then said, "This AC will run forever. You boys will still be driving it when your dad decides to quit farming and spend all his time fishing."

"It's mighty powerful, too. Why, just the other day, Bill Maser over by Laclede was in here bragging how his AC could out-pull a Farmall F-20 hands down." More proof.

After a few minutes of this lingo, he turned away from the boys to get the real buyer's opinion and to probe for seriousness.

"Are you going to need this for fall plowing?"

"Well maybe...if I decide to buy. One of these days, maybe, one of these days."

§

Dad replied, not answering the question directly. It was a long, drawn-out process for him to commit to this purchase, or anything else that cost a good bit of money.

He ended up pondering the idea a good while, making several trips to compare brands and models, and to check out the seller for honesty and reliability. Dad didn't want to get taken by some fast talking salesman.

Maybe Dad rejected the John Deere, because the salesman seemed a bit too slick. But, what else could you expect? After all, the dealership was in the big city of Manhattan some 15 miles west of Wamego. Our 30-year-old Dad said that city folks, like those in Manhattan, just didn't understand the farmer's situation. "More interested in making a sale than getting me what I need," Dad said, after a long conversation with the John Deere man.

So, Dad eliminated the John Deere, narrowing the possibilities to the orange AC and the red Farmall offered in Wamego. Which one would it be?

§

Although the boys' logic had been faulty, their guess about the orange color proved correct, and their dad bought the 1938 model WC Allis Chalmers. He made a good deal buying last-year's model, for price was the final consideration.

Wow, was it a beauty! The shiny new tractor was bright and its fresh-paint smell imprinted on the boys' brains forever.

THE MODERN TRACTOR

The AC was a modern tractor with rubber tires, two 14" row-crop tires in front and giant balloon-like Goodyear's, 13" wide by 24" high, on the rear. Skeptics questioned those tires when compared to steel wheels. Could the AC match something like the shovel-lugged Farmall F-12?

Put to the test, the AC and other rubber-tired tractors worked well in all but the wettest soil. And, tires made for fast road travel when compared to the old steel lugs. Rubber tires worked, and for some, made tractors look modern.

"Oh John, I'm so glad we went ahead and bought that tractor," the boys' mom said, now convinced they made the right choice. "It looks so nice and up to date. And, you are so handsome driving it."

The boys' dad did look good driving his rubber-tired tractor, and he tended to show off when he had an audience. He drove most of the time, standing beside the seat, and when people watched, he puffed out his chest and exposed his clenched teeth. Though looking straight ahead most of the time, his eyes shifted to watch the audience admire the new tractor.

The AC had huge rounded rear fenders where the boys could ride facing their dad. Those fenders came off after a few weeks, however, for they trapped straw and dampened gumbo soil. A ball-up meant stopping to unclog the mess and wasted time.

The hand crank—no electric starter or lights—stuck out of the protruding front end. It also housed the steering gear, and gave the AC a unique 'nosey' appearance.

§

For the first time in our young lives, we were aware that there were choices out in the world. We felt like foxes in the chicken coop, thrilled with pondering between green, red, or the orange tractor Dad bought. Like new fishing lures that catch more fishermen than fish, we were hooked by the color, the smell, and the glitz.

That new tractor quickly became a symbol of family pride and success, and in the fall of 1939, Dad used it to plant a wheat crop on Aunt Maggie's huge place. We moved there a few months later, to a land of more opportunity.

Aunt Maggie became our landlord...and often...a source of hard to believe entertainment.

FIVE

AUNT MAGGIE'S BLUE JAYS, THE GHOSTS TURN GREEN, AND BUMBLER BEES

[*The Hartford Times* – March 17, 1939] **DR. EWING DEAD** ~ This community was surprised Saturday evening, March 11, 1939, when the word was spread that Dr. H. Z. Ewing had passed away at 4:45 o'clock, at his ranch home one mile north of Hartford following a stroke of apoplexy. Funeral services were held in the Methodist church Tuesday afternoon....Relatives and friends from a distance attending the funeral were: Mr. and Mrs. Richard Beach, Mr. and Mrs. Alfred Burgess, Miss Dorothy Burgess, Mr. and Mrs. Wm. Wilson and daughter...and Mrs. John Burgess and sons....

A MORE THAN ORDINARY AUNT MAGGIE

"Yikes, Aunt Maggie is coming this way!" George whispered.

"Shsssh...be quiet...she'll be mad if she catches us sneaking around on her," his brother said. "She's heading for her car."

George's fear increased with each step that their dad's widowed, 63-year-old aunt took as she came from her big house toward the car shed with an arm-pumping stride. She wore no makeup—that cost money, something she loathed parting with. At the shed door, she frowned; her face reveling more lumps and valleys than the badlands. Her puckered brow gave both boys goose bumps. "What if she sees us? Oh man!"

"Shsssh."

§

Above Aunt Maggie, we perched high on dusty two-by-sixes in the farm shop's rafters, smelling the mountains of harness, garden tools, a couple of small implements, and cans of grease, paint, and oil. The wall below held coils of rope, hand tools, and an old inner tube.

With our faces pressed against the wall cracks, we looked into the shed. Along the west wall stood a tired workbench. On one end sat dusty tools and coffee cans of rusty nuts and bolts and, on the other, a white Leghorn hen nested in an oil-stained wooden box. Next to the bench, stood Aunt Maggie's car.

We assumed our Great-Aunt was headed to Hartford, for she wore her cotton-print church dress over a work dress. The dark underdress protruded an inch or two below the light-colored top dress. Her baggy, tan wool stockings reached a few inches above her weathered high-top men's shoes, unlaced, as always.

An early 1930s hat creation—the one she usually wore to town on business or to church—covered much of her unbrushed grayish brown hair. On the hatband, a pair of faded, felt blue jays peeked at us from a cotton and wool nest. This hat contrasted with the ragged stocking cap she often wore on the farm, although in frigid weather she did switch to an ear-floppy corduroy cap. Today, however, it was the bird hat's turn.

Watching Aunt Maggie was a show. For one thing, her penny-pinching approach led to many entertaining events. This day, she seemed to squeeze the life out of the dark, and worn, leather pocketbook. No one would get that purse out of her hands—or a red cent from it—without the fight of a lifetime.

When she stepped into the shed, she terrified the Leghorn, and it exploded from the bench—flying, squawking, and flapping. There'd be nothing in the box today; no egg for Aunt Maggie to collect, as she did regularly, much to Mom's disgust.

Mom's free-range hens picked their own nesting sites because open chicken houses allowed that, though why this misguided Leghorn singled out the shed baffled us. It was just as baffling why Aunt Maggie gathered up the daily egg.

"That's one of our hens," our mom said. "It lays in that box because it likes it. Anyway, why does she need one egg? And she's got all that money. She just makes me so mad sometimes."

Sure enough, when questioned, Aunt Maggie suggested the Leghorn was her hen. Unlikely we thought, for her flock consisted of Buff Orpingtons and Rhode Island Reds. We didn't think she had one white chicken in the bunch.

"Anyway Veda, I don't think that hen hardly ever lays an egg. It's just the broody type and likes nesting in that box. She's just setting on an old spark plug." That was Aunt Maggie's final answer.

Now, the hen flew the coop—as they say—and this time, across Aunt Maggie's car, kicking up dust and sparrow droppings on the fabric top. As we watched the protesting hen flap away, our eyes turned to the ancient vehicle, with snap-on windows, wooden-spoke wheels, and tires with little tread. Equal amounts of black paint and brown rust camouflaged the hood, fenders, and doors.

Then we looked at Aunt Maggie. It was time for the next act of her show to begin.

First, she checked the tires and the radiator. Then, glancing all around to make sure no purse-snatching hobo lurked about, she placed her purse—crammed with money we supposed—on the seat.

Was she aware she had an audience? Maybe, for despite all her quirks, she liked most kids, and for some reason, the two of us and our cousin Kathleen in particular.

§

"Shsssh, don't let her see us! She's going to fire it up," Freddy said as Aunt Maggie advanced the spark lever and pumped the gas pedal a few times. Then she pulled out the choke knob, set the throttle, checked the hand brake, and put the gearshift in neutral. Since she never got the starter repaired—an expense—she walked around, stepped over a wooden linseed oil crate, and started spinning the hand crank.

Whirrrr, whirr, whirrr. On about the third crank, the engine started firing. Ker-snort, ker-pot, ker-snort, ker-rumble...prumble...rumble.

She returned to the driver's seat, adjusted the spark lever and the choke until the idle smoothed out. Her next act made Freddy grin and George cringe.

She stomped the accelerator hard to the floor...revving the engine wide open for several seconds. Dark blue smoke billowed out the exhaust pipe. The deafening roar vibrated the boards where the boys hid.

"I'm hiding my eyes," George said, slumping lower.

"Yeah, listen to that. Is it going to explode? Oh, boy, listen to that!"

At that moment, Aunt Maggie dropped the engine to idle—just before it blew up Freddy thought—pushed on the clutch, and ground the gears into reverse. Without a glance, she backed out of the shed.

"Oh no, she's going to hit the side of the door!" She almost did....

The boys scrambled down to watch her leave out the rutted lane. On the main road, she revved the engine wide open again—panicking a flock of side by side blackbirds on the telephone wire—ground the gears twice more, and drove the one mile into Hartford.

In the tiny hamlet on the other side of the Neosho River, the Aunt Maggie show continued. How she acted was quite unconventional—even eccentric—though very predictable.

"Every trip, she pulls up to the curb or double parks in front of the bank, the post office, or Major's Grocery Store...and starts honking," eye witness Ora Ruddinger said. He'd seen Aunt Maggie do this many times. "Yeah, she just honks and honks until someone comes out to help her."

"Everyone in town knows her, and someone finally decides to help her rather than listen to that horn. Mr. Majors would rather go outside and take her order, than hear her rant and rave if she has to come inside the store. She might be harmless, but you'll have to admit she's a little odd."

"I just don't understand Aunt Maggie," Veda said later to Margaret Wilson. "You know she owns half of Kansas, but won't spend a dime. John says she doesn't trust banks, and won't use one except to cash a check."

Aunt Maggie

Margaret shook her head. "Bill and I've talked about how she hoards her money. She won't spend anything she doesn't have to either. Do you know how she sleeps in the wintertime, Veda?"

"Not really, except that she doesn't heat much of her house. She says she doesn't want to waste money on coal. I wonder if she lived that way when Dr. Ewing was alive?"

"I don't know, but Bill says she sleeps fully dressed in front of her kitchen stove, on an old door propped across two kitchen chairs. That way, she doesn't have to heat a bedroom," Margaret said with a grin.

"She's worse than Scrooge," Veda said. "When it was really cold, did you see how she kept her feet warm? She had on men's shoes inside of unlatched, four-buckle overshoes."

"And don't forget that heavy, man's coat and the wool mountaineering hat with droopy earflaps," Margaret said. "I can't help but laugh about her wearing so many dresses. When the dirty one comes off, she still has two or three to go."

"Don't you sometimes wonder if...."

§

The irony was that wealthy Aunt Maggie could have lived in comfort had she chosen to do so. She and Dr. Ewing acquired several farms around the state, including the one Dad and his cousin, Bill Wilson, farmed as tenants during World War II.

With her quirks, Aunt Maggie Burgess Ewing presented several challenges as our landlord—beyond the disagreement about the white hen's eggs. She did things we never saw before, and though she was Grandpa Burgess' sister, we considered her mighty unusual...though plenty smart.

She lived alone in the big house on the first farm north of the Neosho River, beside the main road passing through Hartford. The Wilsons, Bill, Margaret Burgess Wilson, and their daughter Kathleen lived in a smaller house nearer that road and we lived in a tiny, three-room house on the other side of the farm structures.

Aunt Maggie's brick house was huge, and had a wide porch and a parlor with a piano—we'd never seen one in a house—and a large rounded window that looked out on the lane. The downstairs furniture was fancy—except of course the old door-bed by the kitchen stove. The house had a basement, a second story, and an overhanging roof. And, to our shock, we'd learned the house had something else—*ghosts*!

Soon after our arrival at the farm, Aunt Maggie sat both families of us down on her porch and lectured us to follow her many landlord rules. Most involved how to share the farm, the workload, and the buildings. Some, however, pertained to how the folks and the Wilsons should treat her, and of course, what was off-limits for us.

We all paid attention, with only a flock of geese at the bayou south of the house making noise. She explained her sharecropping rules, and then talked about her house.

§

THE GHOSTS TURN GREEN

"Now, I don't want people traipsing all over, especially upstairs. I don't want anybody up there for any reason whatsoever. I told the kids about the ghosts up there, so it's just better to leave well enough alone."

The adults looked at each other, fighting back snickers. Later among themselves, they'd laugh about Aunt Maggie's ghosts. Still, they honored her request for over a year, until Aunt Maggie needed to be gone for a few days.

She said she was going to the Emporia Hospital—the reasons were vague—for a few days, and before she left, she did a curious thing. Maybe not trusting her renters, she sent bus fare to the boys' Aunt Helen Gordon so she could come down from Wamego to watch over the big house and feed the array of cats.

A couple of days after she arrived, Aunt Helen began to complain. "You never saw such a mess in all your life. There is junk everywhere, and that piano hasn't been dusted for years."

"You know," Margaret said, "Why don't we take this time to clean it up for her? It will never happen unless we do it. Let's do it this afternoon."

A couple of hours later, Helen, Margaret, and the boys' mom met to organize the cleaning jobs. "I'll start sweeping and airing the parlor," Veda said. "Margaret, do you want to get going on the kitchen? That way Helen can do Aunt Maggie's bedroom."

"What about the upstairs?" Margaret asked. "Should

we go clean it?"

"Not me," Helen said, shaking her head. "I don't want to go upstairs, and I don't want to meet any ghosts. So far, I've stayed downstairs and let the ghosts stay upstairs."

"You don't believe that tale of Aunt Maggie's ghosts, do you?" Margaret asked.

Helen motioned toward the stairway, and said, "Well, I tell you what, I have been sleeping with one eye open for two days. I wasn't about to tangle with any spooks."

"That's a bunch of nonsense," Veda said. "You know how she exaggerates. She just didn't want us snooping around in her stuff up there."

Margaret grabbed a broom and headed straight to the stairway. "Let's go see what we find. Who knows, we might find a ghost, or maybe some treasure."

"Okay," Veda said. "Three ladies like us should be able to handle a ghost or two."

They looked up the stairs into the dim light. Nothing moved, so Margaret crept up several steps, with Veda following. With a sigh, Helen inched up behind them. No one spoke, until they reached the landing.

"Let's look in here," Margaret said. With caution, she opened the first door on the right and the trio looked in to see, not ghosts, but piles and piles of grimy clutter. Boxes, trunks, bags, used suits and dresses, stacks of papers, old magazines, and medical books were crammed around the room and into every corner.

An easel, still holding paint brushes, stood near the door next to a sewing machine, a mannequin, and several pieces of old dusty furniture. Nails in the walls held more things, including a stuffed squirrel suspended by wires.

"No wonder she didn't want us up here. Just look at this place."

"Do you suppose the ghosts messed it up like this?" Helen asked, her heart still pounding.

"Ghosts? Do you think a ghost would live in this

place?" Margaret asked. "What a mess. Where in the world do we start?"

"If you want to begin sweeping, Helen and I can stack these boxes and papers," Veda said. "We'll move the furniture for you when you need to sweep around it. Then we can dust."

After about five minutes of stacking and restacking, Helen let out a yelp. "Well, would you look at this!" She was shouting.

"What?"

"Over here. Come and look at this...this money."

Helen had pulled old newspapers off the top of a three-gallon galvanized bucket full of money. Lots and lots of cash.

"Can you believe this?" Helen asked, fingering the rolls of bills, mostly fives and tens. "There must be hundreds of dollars in this pail."

"There's money in these buckets, too. Let's each take one and see just how much money we come up with."

"The hair is standing straight up on my arms," Veda said. She flipped through the money in her bucket a bill at a time.

"I've got three hundred and eighty-eight dollars here. How much did you get?" Helen asked.

"I've got three hundred thirty-seven," Veda said.

"There are four hundred and twelve dollars here," Margaret said, shaking her head.

More looking uncovered four more buckets, each with several hundred dollars in it. "I can't believe what I'm seeing," Veda said. "We'd better put these buckets back like we found them. We don't want to make Aunt Maggie mad, or have her think we stole something."

"Come on, let's get out of here."

Downstairs, they paused and looked at each other. "Now we know why she didn't want anyone up there. The only ghosts we saw up there were of the green variety," Helen said, with a grin. "But we better not tell her we saw them."

The others laughed and decided to only clean the

downstairs. While they worked, they chattered about Aunt Maggie's quirks and strange ways. When Veda and Margaret turned to leave, Helen said, "Well, I'm glad we went up there. Now I can close both eyes when I sleep. Ghosts, my foot."

So...Aunt Maggie's house had no ghosts. However, it did have cats, a few mice, spiders in the unused rooms, and lots of flies—fly-paper strips hung in several places—and outside in the brick wall, resided a hive of bees. Those honey bees lived undisturbed—well, until now.

Unfortunately, nobody bothered to fill Freddy in.

THE GREAT BRICK AND STICK EXPERIMENT

About six feet off the ground, the honeybees came and went through a single crack between two bricks. They visited sunflowers, alfalfa, and in particular, the large flowering pecan trees in the yard. They buzzed around and did their little dances, fascinating Freddy, who studied them many times.

One humid Saturday morning, he realized he needed to know why bees did the things they did. He watched a while, and decided to experiment to test bees' reactions.

Reaching up, he prodded the crack with a small stick. The bees responded with increased activity. That's what I figured they'd do, he thought.

Maybe I should try something larger.

He looked for a larger stick or a board, with no luck. Finally, he noticed an old brick lying beside the house. He tossed the brick toward the opening. The bees' activity increased again, though about the same as with the stick.

Maybe a harder toss, he thought. This time the brick smashed the house just below the crack, bringing more action and more bees. This was fun.

One more toss—a bull's eye—and the bees went crazy. A horde of frenzied sentries stormed from the hive looking for the enemy.

They impaled his heavy corduroy cap, the earflaps, and his coat. As Freddy stumbled away, one highly accurate dive-bomber buried its stinger just above his left eye, near the bridge of his nose.

In a wink, his left eye puffed shut and the right eye became a swollen slit. He looked like a battered boxer after a 15-round loss. The experiment was over, and he'd learned two lessons: bees responded to stimuli and bee stings hurt.

At the house, his mom gasped at her swollen-faced son. "Goodness, what happened to you? You look like you were stung by a bee!"

"Yeah," Freddy said, sighing for sympathy.

"How did it happen? Did you do something to make the bees mad?"

"I was just watching those bees at Aunt Maggie's house...and this one came out and just stung me," he said.

"Well, you know better than to mess with them. Good heavens, you're a sight. Here, hold this damp cloth on the swelling. You're just a sight."

For a few days, Freddy squinted through his eye slit, looked for pity, and ended up blaming his problem on Aunt Maggie. Why didn't she spend money and get those bees out of her bricks?

He never admitted to anything, but later he watched other bee research that added to his learning.

BUMBLER BEES

In the hayfield that summer, Bill Wilson designed a little bee experiment that began as a practical joke. Ground dwelling bumblebees harassed the haying crew and their horses several times. One team had a near runaway.

"Hey, look at ole Slim fight with his team on the buckrake. That bay horse acts like it just got stung by a bee. Yippee, look at 'em go. Hope he gets 'em turned before he hits that fence."

Across the winnows—called wind rows locally—Slim Colglazer ran behind his team, cussing and sawing on the reins. The horses bucked and hopped toward the setting sun. At the last instant, they slowed and Slim turned them back toward the stacker. A minute later, they stood shaking and lathered beside the crew.

"Those dad burned bees nearly cost me a horse and some fence," slow thinking Slim said. "When ole Harley stepped on that nest, five or six of them stung him on his legs and belly and he just took off."

Bill jumped into the conversation and said, "Yep, those bees sure are a menace. We ought to go get rid of them. It's an easy job if you know what you're doing. A couple of guys could knock them off in no time at all."

Long on stature, but short on uptake, Slim wasn't sure. He had just dealt with mad bees and panicked horses. "Not me, I ain't messing with no bees. I don't want to get stung by them big bumbler things," he said.

Always full of answers, Bill said, "Slim, Slim, you don't seem to understand. Why those bees would hardly see a person like you, being skinny and all. I doubt you'd even get one sting."

"Yeah, Slim, you're jist the guy to go after them things. You and me could do the job in a couple of minutes," a grinning and ornery Russell Laws said.

Slim still had doubts, but asked how this marvelous feat could be achieved.

"Why, all you and Russ would need is a couple pieces of this," Bill said, holding out a discarded wooden shingle.

"Sure. What we can do is jist go swat them bees when they come out of their hole," Russ said. "Dead bees can't sting, now can they?"

Displaying great confidence, he took the shingle from Bill, broke it into four narrow pieces, and handed two of them to Slim. Together, they headed across the meadow toward the nest.

"Now, let's be sure to work together on this. We'll have to swat pretty fast at first until we get rid of the first

5 or 6 of them, then it will just be, whack-a-whack, whack," Russ said, demonstrating his technique to the worried Slim.

They sidled up to the nest and Russ gave it a kick. The bees came boiling out. Russ disliked the mission and ran off...leaving the other frustrated bee slayer alone.

Slim didn't miss Russ at first—he focused on the bees—and swatted and cursed, and cursed and swatted, with incensed bees swarming around him. His shingles flew...up, down, behind his back, over his head, and against his pant leg. Remarkably, only one bee stung him when he ran from the hive at last. Perhaps, his slim stature did help.

The haying crew howled and Slim scowled. For the next few days, Slim seemed especially put out with Russ and Bill. Like Freddy, he had learned a valuable lesson about bees—don't provoke them!

The story of Slim's bee whacking became local lore, and after a while, he began to tell his own version, including how he swatted for fifteen minutes and killed between 500 to 800 bumbler bees. The pile was so big, he insisted, it caused a permanent knob in the hayfield. Yep, he had learned a lesson.

Like Slim, the boys also learned much about Aunt Maggie, her car, and Leghorn eggs. They also learned about life on the farm and bees, and about haying and friends.

Through it all, George sometimes lagged behind his older brother and his approach to things. However, there were times when he couldn't drag his feet any longer. And those times proved to be pretty exciting, like his time at milking school.

SIX

FIRST DAY OF MILKING SCHOOL, CHICKENS ON THE ROOF, AND FACE TO FACE WITH A GHOST

[The Hartford Times – October 24, 1941] **THE LARGEST FLOOD SINCE 1928** ~ This part of the Neosho valley is now experiencing the worst flood since 1928 caused by heavy downpours upstream Sunday and Sunday night. Most of the people in the flooded territory have moved from their homes and highways north and east of town were closed to traffic.

THE FIRST DAY OF MILKING SCHOOL

"This is as good a morning to start as any. It's time, George, that you did your share of the milking," his dad said. "Start with Claudette down there next to Freddy. She's good and gentle."

Me? Milk? George thought. Butterflies stirred in his second-grader stomach. He gulped, then cringed, when Maggie's tail whapped Freddy in the back of the neck.

George didn't know how to milk—and he didn't want to learn. In the past, he'd let his dad, Freddy, and his dad's partner, Bill Wilson, do all the milking.

Most often, he spent milking time leaning against a hand-hewn post watching barn swallows swoop the cats or spiders capture flies. He could help herd cows into their stanchions and feed them, but that didn't make him a milker, did it?

Those cows are huge, George thought. The way they shift around...I'll get stepped on or whacked with a tail. How do you milk anyway? Do you pull, then squeeze, or squeeze and then pull?

"There's nothing to it, even with this funny looking cow," Freddy said, settling on his stool, milking Maggie, the odd looking hump-backed Jersey.

"Yeah, she's a strange looker," Bill said from where he milked one of the Holsteins. "I bought her over at Strong City. Guess one rodeo bull broke free and spent the night with a local farmer's Jersey cow."

"Now we have a mixed breed called the Jersey-rahma. Ole Maggie there gives good milk, but don't ever lay a hand on her back.

"She's pretty goosey, and if she feels weight on her back, she thinks some cowboy's trying to ride her. And then her Brahma streak comes out and she starts bucking and stomping.

"Too much of that churning around, and she gives off nothing but butter.

"We named her after Aunt Maggie, though neither one of them much appreciates the honor."

George didn't hear the words, or see Bill and his dad grin at each other.

Nor did George see anything to grin about. He slow-stepped toward Claudette, the farm's most gentle and easiest milking cow, and held his breath.

How can I pull on *those things?*, he thought, feeling mortified. He tried blocking the word, teats, from his head. Was he even allowed to say that word? His face turned deep red when he stared at Claudette's big bag with four dangling nipples.

"What if I can't do it?" George asked his dad.

"Ah, you'll do just fine. I'll help you get started."

As he approached Claudette, George breathed in the fly spray on the cow's hide. He coughed and sneezed. Can I breathe that spray for very long, he thought? What if it makes me sick...right in the milk pail? And, how can I hold a bucket between my knees and balance on a one-legged stool? My legs are too short.

George picked up the shortest stool and a two-gallon pail. With caution, he moved up to Claudette's right flank. She turned her head to eye him, but kept on eating.

I hope she likes me, he thought, staring at her cocklebur gnarled tail and then at her splayed, cloven rear hoof almost at his toes.

"That's it," his dad said. "Just move your stool in close to her side. Now sit down and put your head against her side for balance."

George bent his knees and dropped his rear end toward the seat. Oops.

The stool skidded one way and he fell the other, headlong into the startled cow, the empty pail banging off the wooden floor under her body.

This kind old cow, which never flinched when his dad or Bill or Freddy milked her, bolted forward into the stanchion and then lurched back against the closed metal bars. Her hindquarters almost dancing, Claudette moved left, then right, and gave a mighty kick toward the helpless George lying beneath her.

The kick missed, but sent his pail clanging across the floor toward the Holsteins, Alma and Louise. They, too, started to dance, using a high-stepping routine. Louise dumped the startled Bill from his stool, and sent broad, white sloshes of milk high into the air.

Meanwhile, the panicked George scrambled to emerge from the other side of Claudette, and charged square into Freddy and Maggie.

George braced himself on Freddy's shoulder and the cow's back. That caused her to react on cue and join the dance. She bucked and jerked and hip-rolled Freddy across the floor, drenching him with milk.

While Bill cussed and Freddy yipped, the boys' dad threw down his fly sprayer in disgust.

George? He ran from the barn shouting, "I hate these cows! I hate these cows! Let me out of here!"

Freddy's howls trailed him all the way to the house. Bill joined the laughter and his dad just shook his head. Would that boy ever learn? Maybe he was better off at the house.

The last laugh? The barn cats descended on the spilled milk like an army of ants, lapping and licking their fill.

The cows, on the other hand, were harder to coax into the barn for a few days. Over time, however, everyone—except for George, and maybe Claudette, Maggie, Alma, and Louise—tended to forget the incident.

And of course, George learned to milk, and he, too,

could later laugh about the dancing cows at his first day at milking school.

It was easy to laugh in this the third year at Aunt Maggie's place. Both the Wilson and Burgess partners were making and saving money. However, just two years before, their opportunity had been in doubt when disaster struck, as a giant flood shook the entire community and almost destroyed Aunt Maggie's farm.

In 1941, the house where George took refuge from his milking lesson, and the surrounding land, endured the flood of the century. The Neosho River overflowed to record highs, with the torrent moving brush, logs, and whole trees down stream. Some buildings and houses floated away or the water and debris crushed them. Others filled with mud and silt.

Nothing in the path of the river escaped damage, including the family's tiny home.

IN THE FLOOD PLAIN

The house, like many in the Middle West, including rural Kansas, rested on a flood plain, whether of the 10-, 50-, or 100-year variety. Families near rivers or creeks could expect floods, small every 10 years, more severe every 50 years, and a whopper every century.

"You know, Veda, our house is built in a pretty strange place," her husband said. He sat on the stoop reading the *Hartford Times* while the warm morning sun filtered through the box elder trees. Heavy rain a day earlier meant no field work. It did provide excellent mud for his sons to mold barns and livestock in their play.

"What do you mean, a pretty strange place?"

"The paper says people who build farms next to rivers, in the flood plain, face the chance of being flooded out. But, they still do it, because farmers like the rich bottomland soil."

"It sounds crazy," Veda said, "but I guess we're doing the same thing. With all the rain lately, I wonder if we'll have problems with flooding?"

"If it rains much more, we could," John said. "You can see over to the west how the Neosho bends south and then curves east around us. We're only a quarter mile from the river.

"If we get hit here at Aunt Maggie's, Hartford will get it too. Hopefully, the steel river bridge won't wash out. That would be a mess."

"If it flooded, what would we do?"

"Aunt Maggie said we should come over and stay at her house. That part of the homestead is higher. Bill, Margaret, and Kathleen would come over there too.

"Unfortunately, our house sits in the lowest area." Shaking his head, he pointed out how the land sloped down to them from Aunt Maggie's house and her near buildings. "I just hope the rains stop pretty soon."

The rains did not stop, and within a few days, the newspaper and radio broadcasts said flooding was inevitable. Water pooled all across the fields.

SWIMMING IN THE FIELD

"Mom, can we go play in the lake?" Freddy asked. He looked to a low spot in the field west of the house, filled with eight inches of water.

"Oh I guess you can," his mom said. "But, take off your overhalls and go in your under shorts. That way I won't have so much to wash. And, don't worry, George, no one will see you this far from the road."

The boys—George a bit bashful at first—ran out the door yelling. Freddy, of course, did a sit down dive into the sun-warmed field pool, churning the water and sending tadpoles sloshing over the sides.

Next came a tadpole rescue—mercifully to a nearby pool—and then the building of a stick and board navy. There was plenty of mud, and later, when they devised a slippery water slide, the mud seemed to multiply.

"Oh, mannnnn...," Freddy yelled as he skidded down the two-foot mud ramp. Water flew in all directions. Now George came running, jumped on the ramp, and landed behind his brother, with more muddy water flying high.

"Hey, this is fun. Let's do it again. I'm going to run from way out there before I hit the slide."

"Maybe we can splash the pool dry!"

Freddy tore toward the shallow pond at full speed, jumped in the air, and landed...not on his rump...but on his feet and headlong into the water. Water flew, followed by a sputtering, coughing face. He had overdone it again!

That ended the 'swim,' and since George's teeth were chattering, they headed to the stoop where their mom poured warm water over their heads. With the worst removed, the boys had a real bath together in a big, round galvanized tub.

For many days during sun breaks between rains, the boys played in the pool. Since the ground could absorb no more water, the pool and others like it filled until little trickles from them turned into rivulets, and then into streams that poured into the river, the huge flooding river.

§

HERE COMES THE FLOOD

The Neosho continued to rise, and each day we'd go with Dad and Bill to examine the angry water, fast approaching flood stage. The river rose for nearly a week, finally edging over its banks, to creep across lower fields and some low spots in the roads.

Our daily walks became shorter and shorter until we stood at the edge of the feedlot, muddy water swirling at our feet. The cattle stood near us, heads cocked, and eyed the roiling water.

Aunt Maggie thought maybe this was a 10-year flood, and it wouldn't rise higher. However, the radio forecast more rains and said the river might crest at a record flood stage in the Hartford area. That meant we'd be in trouble.

§

"Bill, do you think it's time to move the livestock?" the boys' dad asked. "The flood might not get to the barn, but we can take the guesswork out of it if we move them to the higher pasture up north. If we get marooned here, Slim Colglazer said he'd milk the cows."

"I think you're right, John," Bill said. "We won't have use of the road if we wait much longer. Water is already a few inches deep in some places."

"We'll have to chance it with the hogs though. Later, we might have to hoist them up into the corncrib. At least, it's a couple of feet higher. Our chickens should be okay on their roosts or in the trees, don't you think?"

The boys' dad nodded in agreement, and soon the eager cattle, horses, and mules hurried out the lane behind Bill on the pony. The family car moved along behind them. The herd hurried past water-filled ditches—trickling across the road in spots—and soon turned into the hilly north pasture.

§

The radio now warned us when to expect the highest water in the Hartford area, for the Neosho and its largest tributary, the Cottonwood—they drained thousands of acres of Southeast Kansas—would crest together.

"John, do you think this will be a 100-year flood?" Mom asked. "If it is, how high will the water be here at our house?"

"How deep would it be? Nobody knows, but probably it will go bluff to bluff across the valley. In a day or two we'll find out!"

The next morning, we hadn't been out of bed long when Dad came through the kitchen door after leaving his muddy rubber boots on the stoop. The sky was overcast, and dark, though it was not raining. In the distance, a pair of redtail hawks circled, watching for rodents fleeing the waters.

"The water is a couple of inches deep across the lane and is rising fast," he said. "We need to get out now and go to Aunt Maggie's house like we planned. It sits eight to ten feet higher than here. The Wilsons will join us there."

What would happen if the flood entered the house, we wondered? Would it ruin everything? Would our house float away?

"The best we can do is to stack the furniture from our three rooms as high as we can. Maybe the water won't reach it."

"We'll put the sofa, the two living room chairs, and the kitchen chairs on the kitchen table. Some of our few clothes can go on top of that. Let's lay the cupboard flat on the kitchen stove, and just leave the pots, pans, and dishes in it."

"What about the beds and the bureau?" Mom asked. "Should we put them on top of the cupboard?"

"Right," Dad said. "And, we'll put the cream separator and other things in the screened-in porch on the workbench.

"That will have to do, Veda," Dad said, surveying the stacked furniture one last time.

"Hopefully, everything is high enough. Remember it takes a lot of raindrops to raise a river this wide as much as a foot. Maybe things will be safe where they are. If not...."

"We need to get going, it's rising pretty fast out there," he said, looking through the kitchen window and then shaking his head.

"Leave the rest of those clothes. It's time for us to move."

Out on the stoop, Mom looked toward the chicken coop. "Oh, John, what about the hens?"

§

CHICKENS ON THE ROOF

Fifty feet away the chicken coop, with its door wide open, had floodwater a foot deep swirling around inside it. Hapless Leghorn hens perched on their roosts, now only a couple of feet above the rising flood.

"The water trapped them during the night and they didn't make it to the trees. You three wait here," he said. "I'll go toss them on the roof."

Wading to the coop in the deepening, chocolate-colored water, he grabbed two or three hens, stepped outside and threw them, one at a time, up on the slanted roof. Each fluttered and scratched, trying to gain balance. In turn, they climbed to the peak and settled down as if they now had hope.

Hen after hen flapped its wings and clawed at the shingles, until one ill-fated hen lost her balance and slid backward. Down the roof she scratched and flapped, then hesitated for an instant, only to plop into the swirling, fast moving water.

No one could do anything. The hen spun out of reach, wings stretched wide, moving away in the heavy current. The boys' dad shook his head, while the rest stood in shock, watching the poor hen get smaller and smaller, bobbing and spinning away.

How sorry they felt for the hen, for she would surely die. If only....

Still, about 30 hens did survive the next three days, though frightened and hungry, perched on the roof. During that time, the flood covered their roost. They'd been rescued—except for one.

THE WADE OUT

The floodwater lapped, knee deep, at the stoop's

top step as the family left the house and chicken coop behind. The boys' dad lifted five-year-old George on to his mom's back and then picked up seven-year-old Freddy. In single file, they trudged across the yard, wading into the face of the oncoming current.

§

> ***M**om, holding her skirt above her knees, struggled against the water. Dad moved up to steady her as they turned left on to our short lane, visible just a couple hours before.*
>
> Where was the lane? Where were the ditches, now waist deep with water? Thank God for the fencerows, for the strong current hit their right sides, trying to push them into the deeper water.
>
> Step by cautious step they walked, with Dad breaking the current on Mom's right. Nothing could have pulled us from where we clung. We had seen the chicken's fate.
>
> What if Mom or Dad slipped or got knocked down by the water? What if a giant log hit us? Could people swim in this water?
>
> Step by step, they moved toward the three-acre mound, holding the barn, silo, sheds, and Aunt Maggie's two-story home in sight. At last, after 50 slow yards, the ground began to rise and the water shallowed out.
>
> We had made it! The wade out was over!
>
> "Oh, thank God," Mom said, with tears in her eyes. "I don't think I've ever been so nervous."
>
> "Amen," said Dad. "By the Grace of God...."
>
> At last, we found sanctuary, completely surrounded by miles of floodwaters. Now we could join Aunt Maggie and the Wilsons and begin the wait.

§

The next day and a half was tense and tiring, for everyone felt marooned. Would they be safe on their tiny island?

"At least if the water keeps rising, we can go upstairs," Margaret said with a worried look. "We should be safe there, shouldn't we?"

"Yeah, unless the flood moves the house off its foundation and we go floating down to the Gulf of Mexico," Bill said. "Say, you know that's a place I've always wanted to see."

Then, trying to ease the tension, he said, "That would be a cheap way to go. We won't have to buy tickets."

"Don't even think of that, Bill Wilson," Margaret said. Her frown met her husband's grin.

"Maybe we should have built an ark." Bill's second attempt at humor drew another sharp glance.

Aunt Maggie looked across the expanse of churning, rolling water and said, "Now don't you worry, Margaret, over the years this house has withstood many a flood. It's as sturdy as a locomotive. We might have a mess to clean up later, but we're just fine for now."

§

> *I*t wasn't long before the two of us and eight-year-old Kathleen forgot the flood. We were in Aunt Maggie's big house, full of rooms to visit and all kinds of furniture, closets, and gadgets to inspect. Our room had a large bed and different, expensive looking dressers and chairs.
>
> The Wilsons had a similar room upstairs. Aunt Maggie said she'd talked to the ghosts, and they agreed to let the Wilsons sleep up there—but, only until the flood was over. That concerned us some, but we kept on exploring the downstairs until it was time to eat.

Our supper together was late in the evening—a pretty sparse meal Mom said—and we soon slept in the room where our folks would join us later, though Dad and Bill took turns keeping watch through the night.

Next morning, we were up before the sun to see that the still rising river now surrounded the windmill and water tank apron on three sides. It had reached the barn's foundation, and slapped at the concrete.

A huge lake surrounded us, with the solitary highway bridge appearing to float between the farm and Hartford. Debris bobbed and drifted everywhere, and giant trees, roots and all, came by and then disappeared downstream. Swirling whirlpools and eddies intrigued us, but then so did Aunt Maggie's house.

§

FACE TO FACE WITH A GHOST

"Let's go upstairs and look at our room," Kathleen said, making sure Aunt Maggie didn't hear her. "Maybe we'll find some treasure in someplace."

The trio slipped away from the adults and the two boys—for the very first time—followed their cousin up the stairs. Would they see the ghosts? If so, Kathleen would run into them first. How about treasure? Would they find gold or money?

In the Wilsons' room, huge pictures stared at them and the oversized bed had posts at each corner. Above the chest of drawers hung the largest mirror they had ever seen.

Beside the bed was a stone pot Kathleen said people used for a toilet. Imagine that, the boys thought. Right in the bedroom. This exploring was fun.

Across the stair landing stood another door. It creaked when George—pushed into the lead by his brother—opened it. With caution, he stepped inside the unlighted room. In horror, he came face to face with a *ghost!*

George yelped and jumped, landing against a large easel. The ghost started to move toward him, as if reaching for him.

"Ghossttt! Let me out of here." George appeared to fly down the stairs.

Hearts pounding, Freddy and Kathleen saw the ghost continue to move, before falling face down on the floor. This was a strange ghost. It didn't have any arms and only one center leg.

Before them lay not a ghost, but a life-size dress making form.

Still shaken, Freddy closed the door. He and Kathleen went downstairs, finding George clinging to his mother. They'd had enough exploring for a while.

§

A*bout noon, the sun peaked through the white and gray clouds, and the rain stopped. Dad listened to the radio, and said, "The crest has passed Hartford and the water should begin falling. Looks like we're out of the woods for now."

A few minutes later, a dead cow, her stomach bloated like a huge balloon, floated to the edge of Aunt Maggie's yard. We watched it hang up against the roots of a giant pecan tree, then dislodge and continue on to its final destination.

Dad said it was probably Mr. Stennis' cow, a neighbor who lived upstream about a mile. We felt sad for Mr. Stennis—and the animals lost in the flood.

Thank God, we were okay, for Aunt Maggie's haven kept us safe. We'd find out, however, that our house was not so lucky.

GRITTY MUD ON THE FLOOR

When the water receded enough—two days later—Dad checked on our house. It had filled with three feet of silt-laden water that stained the walls and deposited 3-4 inches of gritty mud on the floor.

In amazement, he found the water had risen to within one inch of the tabletop! Everything stacked high was safe.

We slept in safety at Aunt Maggie's until we cleaned and dried out our house. It took several days to scoop out the mud and to wash everything and we all worked at this mucky and disgusting job. We knew diseases could infest the silt, so we received typhoid shots at the Hartford School—repeating them every six weeks until the danger was gone.

Thank God, we did not get sick. We, and all our animals except for one unlucky hen, had survived the power of the flood. That chapter was over, and in a couple of years, a new one began.

§

TIME TO MOVE

"You know Veda, things have been good here on Aunt Maggie's place," the boys' dad said one day in October 1943. His hand held the savings passbook showing a balance of $2,344. "With this money, maybe we could get into a place of our own. What do you think?"

The tenant farmer years at Aunt Maggie's place had been fruitful, in spite of the flood. World War II was raging and demand for farm products kept prices high. Maybe it was time to move.

Veda paused and then said, "Well, it would be nice not to have a landlord, especially Aunt Maggie. She makes me so mad sometimes."

"Yeah, we could be our own boss for a change and with a place of our own we could build a real future," her husband said. "And if it was ours, we could keep what we made."

"I'd sure like to have a bigger house, maybe one with a basement where I could store my canned goods. Would we have to borrow money again? You know I hate that."

"We'd need to find part of the money somewhere, but we do have this chunk in savings. That would pay for a lot of it," he said. "We can make it on a good-sized farm if we take the chance. The boys are growing fast. They'll be real helpful soon."

§

As we grew up, we took on more and more responsibilities. If we moved to a new place—our place—we knew we'd have a whole new world to investigate. Exploring to find a farm could be exciting, too.

Over the next few months the folks made several trips—with us along—toward Dad's roots in Pottawatomie County. These were great adventures in their own right, for we spent our time with cousins, aunts, uncles, and grandparents, getting to know them better, and learning about their part of the world.

This turned out to be a prelude to our move back to Wamego...to our own farm...and to a new set of challenges. Would we be ready?

SEVEN

CLEAN HIM UP, FRESH FEATHERED EGGS, AND THE RIGHT DAY TO MOVE WAS WRONG

[*Wamego Reporter* - March 2, 1944] **PRISONER LABOR MAY BE AVAILABLE** ~ During the next week local farmers who anticipate the need of additional farm help next summer and fall, should contact the County Agent. The farm labor situation was serious last year and no bright prospects are in view for 1944, except through the use of prisoner of war labor.

CLEAN HIM UP

His mother held George's forehead as he bent at the waist, coughed, gagged, then let go a stream of upchuck. It doused an orange ladybug on a button weed, the syrup-like liquid washing the bug onto the sand road's shoulder. He gasped and whined something.

"Now just stop your sniveling. You do this every time we go through here. These are easy S-curves. They shouldn't make you sick." Up came another stream.

"This wouldn't happen if you just didn't think about it," she said, wiping him with a towel. "It's all got to be in your head."

Between George's feet, a vile smell rose with the steam from his former breakfast. "I feel awful!" he moaned. More breakfast exited.

His dad—impatient to get going—drummed his fingers on the steering wheel of the idling car and looked straight ahead. Clean him up and let's get going, he thought. That boy....

Feeling weak and ashamed, George thought, why does this happen every time we come through these Eskridge curves? And why now? The folks want to look for a farm today, and they'll be mad at me for slowing them down.

At last, he turned back to the car, just as he wiped his right sleeve across his mouth. "Don't do that! For goodness sakes! Here, let me clean you up some more."

"Come on, Veda. Get him back in the car. We need to get going. I just don't understand that boy. For crying out loud, he's seven-years-old!"

A minute later, with all four windows down, the Chevy rolled along the sand road again. George—a pitiful mess—curled up in the back. His mom, feeling his distress, reached into the backseat and stroked his whitish hair. His head and face were colorless.

"You smell awful," Freddy said, sliding to the far side of the seat. "Why do I have to sit back here with him, Mom?"

"It isn't my fault, it's the road," George whispered, swallowing back the urge to heave again. Only the wind from the windows saved him. Somehow it calmed his stomach and cooled his sweaty body.

On this Saturday morning in 1943, the family drove north on another farm hunting trip. They traveled the 85 miles from Hartford to Wamego, then north through Louisville and on to Adams Creek Road.

They'd stay at Grandpa Burgess' farm for a couple of days, and while their folks looked at property, the boys would play and eat with the cousins down the hill and across the road at Aunt Helen Gordon's.

§

> ***A***t long last, we arrived at Grandpa's place, eight miles northeast of Wamego. He had lived alone—Grandma died in 1941—since his unmarried daughter, our Aunt Dorothy, moved to Topeka to live and to work for the Episcopal Diocese of Kansas.
>
> When we turned left from Adams Creek Road, Dad herded the '36 Chevy up through the ruts and around the protruding granite rocks of the long, bumpy lane. Nothing but dirt—tire spinning, slippery when wet—the entire slope seemed dotted with deep potholes.
>
> As Dad stopped the car at the top of the hill,

Grandpa came toward us from the kitchen door, grinning between the tobacco stains caught in a week's growth of whiskers. Both—stains and whiskers—were Grandpa's trademarks, for he didn't like to shave, Dad said, because he'd only use cold water and Lava soap.

While the adults talked by the car, Grandpa pulled a tobacco plug from his vest and cut a sizable chaw. Our eyes widened when, a few chews later, he spit tobacco juice at a garden spider's web in the fence. It sagged under the spittle and the brownish stuff oozed to the ground.

Wow, we thought, Grandpa does some strange things. Still, his warm smile and friendly head pats led us to think he must like us...and that, of course, made up for the scruffy-whiskery look and chewing tobacco wad.

Dad said Grandpa Burgess was a God-fearing man and, with Grandma and Aunt Dorothy gone, that he might be lonely in his empty house. At age 68, Grandpa also had some health problems, and that was one reason Dad wanted to be close by—just in case.

In a few minutes, the three adults finished talking and Grandpa headed to hitch up his team for a day of field work. Our car went back down the lane and the folks dropped us off at Aunt Helen's, and then left to look at the several farms for sale in the area.

FRESH FEATHERED EGGS

Aunt Helen—Dad's older sister—and her kids lived in a square, two-story house with a pyramid roof. Her husband, Uncle Houston, was away in Oregon all during the War, building Liberty Ships. This separation made life difficult for the family, but Aunt Helen kept a smile on her face...and on ours.

§

The Gordon boys—Jim, Ben, and Rollie—had plenty to show their cousins. They had hunting knives, BB guns, and some ship models Freddy and George had never seen. They even had big bedrooms of their own...something the boys didn't have in the little house at Aunt Maggie's.

To the five boys, the morning went by in a hurry, and it wasn't long before Aunt Helen called everyone to come to the table to eat. With an empty stomach, George filled his mind with thoughts of piles of delicious smelling food. However, when Aunt Helen put a cracked plate with two lard-fried eggs before him, he hesitated and sniffed at the eggy odor.

"Why Georgie, there's nothing wrong with those. You go ahead and eat them. Those are real good cluckers. They don't come any riper. In fact, they're *fresh feathered eggs!* I had to pluck the feathers off 'em before I cracked them in the skillet!"

"And with this one," she held up a brown Barred Rock egg, "I had to hurry the hen that laid it twice. I finally told her that if she didn't get on with it, she's Miss Dinner. I'll fry it next...as soon as it cools off."

Aunt Helen's eyes twinkled and everyone laughed. It was how she said things.

Next, she walked around the table cradling a homemade loaf under her arm. "You want another slab of this bread, Freddy?" she asked. He nodded yes, and she started sawing upward toward her left breast with a butcher knife, all the while squeezing the heavy loaf between her rib cage and left arm.

"I sure hope I don't cut myself," she said. "This bread tastes better with butter on it than blood."

Of course, she didn't cut herself, and besides, her butter wasn't butter, but some brand of oleomargarine—

she called it ohlee—and full of yellow streaks. During the war, oleo companies saved costs by including a pack of pigment with each pound they sold. It was the customer's job to mix it to look like butter...or not.

Careless hand mixing often left streaks, but omitting the color all together—Aunt Helen sometimes did—meant eating a spread resembling pure lard. Neither streaked nor a lard-look-alike ohlee changed the taste and on that day all the streak covered bread and greasy eggs were gone in a hurry.

With the meal over, Jim left to help out a neighbor, and for the other four boys, it was time to explore. To our amazement, Aunt Helen gave her kids a very loose rein. Her only directives were, "Don't hurt yourselves. And don't get too dirty—as if telling you that will do any good...."

Freddy and George, away from their mother's watchful eyes, could now experience things that were impossible when she was around. And, with the help of Ben—older by a couple of years—and Rollie, who was Freddy's age, they took advantage of this ideal playground—Grandpa's big farm and the Gordon house and buildings.

<u>SQUAB STEW</u>

"You guys like to shoot a gun?" Ben asked, picking up his Western Auto pump BB gun and pouring a whole tube of grayish lead BBs into the magazine. Freddy, who had never held a gun, nodded yes...meaning he'd *like* to shoot one. After all, shooting a rifle in the movies looked easy, and he could do that, couldn't he?

"Okay then, let's go up to Grandpa's barn and shoot some pigeons. We'll get Mom to fix us some bird soup. Yum, yum."

George looked horrified. Pigeon soup? "Dad said the only things pigeons were good for was to eat the cattle's grain and to poop all over the barn. Won't their soup make us sick?" he asked.

"Naw, it's good. Anyway Mom calls it squab stew when she wants to be hoity-toity," Rollie said. "You'll like it, you'll see, but first we have to go hunt some birds."

George and Freddy looked at each other. Would Grandpa care if they shot pigeons in his barn? Was that even legal? What about shooting a BB gun?

The foursome walked up the lane and approached the barn just west of Grandpa's house. The center drive-through opened into the two-story hay maw above. The birds would be there.

"Listen to that cooing," Ben said. "There are pigeons up there for sure. Who wants to go first?"

"I'm probably a pretty good shot," Freddy said, trying to cover up his nervousness. "I haven't had a lot of practice though."

"He's never had any practice," the ever-helpful George said. "He's never shot any kind of gun."

Ben smiled and said, "It's okay. We'll show you how to shoot and you'll get the hang of it in no time at all. Come on."

"Be quiet though," Rollie said, "we don't want to scare them off."

Just inside the barn door Ben pointed up high toward the dimly lighted rafters loaded with birds. They—and their droppings—seemed in great supply.

With uncertainty, Freddy took the BB gun and shakily leaned it against Grandpa's hayrack. As he tried to still his thumping heart, he took aim at the center of a mass of gray and white feathers.

Ker-ping.

"Shoot, you missed it. Try it again."

Freddy cocked the gun's lever, aimed upward a second time, and pulled the trigger. Ker-ping. This time the pigeons stirred a little, but continued their cooing.

Ben whispered some aiming advice about picking out a single bird. Freddy nodded, and with sweaty hands squeezed the gun and tried again.

After another miss, he hit a plump pigeon dead

center and brought it fluttering to the barn floor. I did it! See, that wasn't so hard, he thought, completely ignoring the several misses.

"Good one," Rollie said, tossing the dead bird on to the hayrack. Then he took the gun and in six shots brought down three birds.

Ben looked for George and asked, "You wanna shoot?" In a stall corner, half hidden by harnesses and tools, George shook his head sideways.

"Well then, here, let me have the gun and I'll see what I can do." The boys watched in awe as Ben bagged four more pigeons without a miss. "That should be enough," he said.

On the walk back to the Gordon's house, Freddy explained how it had taken him a couple of shots to get the hang of things. Rollie teased that he could have brought the pigeons down quicker with rocks.

George lagged behind, not wanting to touch the dead birds, and wondering if he could eat that pigeon soup. Would it taste like Cream of Wheat?

At the house, Ben helped his mother dress the pigeons and then she went to work in the kitchen. The squab stew turned out to be a hit—and yes, even George asked for seconds.

§

When we walked down from Grandpa's the next morning, Jim was skinning a muskrat he'd trapped along the banks of Adams Creek during the night. There was blood all over his hands and arms, and the stump that he used for his butcher table. "I get a few of these critters every week," Jim said.

His sharp knife worked the skin from the animal's body. Soon, he tossed the naked carcass over the fence for the crows or a coyote to eat and then held up the soft, furry pelt for all to see. We looked the fur over, and then to cure it, Jim stretched it over a circle formed from a willow sapling.

"After they're dried, I sell these pelts, and sometimes get two dollars for one of them. When I get enough money, I can buy more traps, or maybe a .22 rifle.

Wow, we thought, maybe we should get some traps and make some money. Still, the idea looked pretty disgusting....

Leaving Jim to clean up, we talked about what we'd do next. It was Rollie who said, "We might go look for some arrowheads around those big rocks across from Grandpa's house." He pointed at the massive cluster of boulders—some the size of a house—on the pasture side hill. "There must have been lots of battles there."

The sun started warming the air as we climbed through the fence and crossed the trickling slough between Grandpa's barnyard and the pasture. A pair of rabbits scurried away and disappeared in the clumps of bluestem.

At the boulders, Ben took just seconds to find two sharp pieces of rock. "Here are a couple of flint stone arrowheads. Looks like the Indians had a big battle here."

Examining the worn grass at the base of a truck-size red and gray boulder, we found a half dozen more. Ben said Indians made each arrow tip by chipping away on a rock for hours. How could they do that, we wondered? And why did they fight each other here in the Flint Hills?

"Some of these have busted tips," Rollie said. "Wonder why that happened? They're made of rock."

"Maybe some brave missed his target and hit that boulder instead," Ben said. "Or, maybe they hit a tough ole buffalo."

We felt special, walking there where others had walked, years and years before. What had the hunters or warriors been like? Did they fight from ambush? Did they scalp their enemies?

"Pow, pow." Rollie held a wild plum limb like a gun, and soon, we were mock-battling among the rocks. Instead of ancient battles and weapons, however, we fought each other with pretend rifles and hedge ball hand grenades.

We didn't shoot Indians, but the despised pretend-Nazis that had caused the world war. Many of them fell that day among the hills and boulders in Grandpa's pasture. And, when the battle was over, we four boys went back to the Gordon's house—dirty from head-to-foot as Aunt Helen expected—for supper.

There Mom, and our aunts Helen, Dot, and Dorothy—up from Topeka—were cooking a special Saturday night meal.

While the roast cooked, Aunt Helen took center stage—yet again. As she spoke, she'd lean forward and flick her elbow toward her audience or slap someone on the knee. When everyone laughed, she acknowledged it with a couple of nods, and then all would laugh some more. She energized the grownup jawing to the point of leg-slapping laughter.

§

"Lyle Brockman stopped by last week," Aunt Helen said with a smile. "Just about noon, right in time for dinner…as usual."

"He always does that, Helen," Aunt Dot said. "He's an old bachelor you know…always looking for a decent meal. I heard all Lyle eats is bacon and eggs and boiled potatoes."

Aunt Helen—with a little help—launched into another tale. "Maybe. But, all I can say is that he has some curious table manners." She paused for the audience to ponder Lyle's ways.

"I cooked up a mess of peas, which he liked, but he ate them kinda funny. Used his fork, which was okay…to scrape the peas onto his hunting knife…which was strange. When I saw that sharp knife with a dozen peas on it heading toward his mouth, I jumped up and headed to find a towel! To mop up the blood in case he cut his lips! How he got 'em down, I'll never know."

"Still, I really don't think he came just to eat. My guess is he thought Dorothy was visiting, and he came over to catch a glimpse of her, don't you?" she asked, nodding toward the others. "His being not married and all, I think he came looking for a wife."

"Why, I wouldn't marry that ole galoot for all the tea in China," Aunt Dorothy said, frowning and crossing her arms.

"But he has such a nice farm across Adams Creek," the boys' mom said. "He might be a great catch."

"And he could teach you how to eat peas, Dorothy."

"And he can sing to you, too. He sat right there and sang: 'I eat my peas with honey, I've done it all my life, it makes the peas taste funny, but it keeps them on my knife!'"

"Honey, on peas?"

"No, I didn't give him honey, and he doesn't have much of a voice either."

"Oh I declare..." Aunt Dorothy said.

There would be no wedding. But the family would get together often and laugh and tease. No wonder the boys' folks wanted to move back to the rolling Flint Hills of Pottawatomie County.

Still, buying a farm in the area, or anywhere else, was a huge investment. They looked at farm after farm, hoping to find just the right place.

TO BUY OR NOT TO BUY

While the boys enjoyed Aunt Helen's humor and her fresh feathered eggs, and played with the cousins, their folks visited many farms around Wamego, Louisville, and

Westmoreland. At last, they found the Anderson place three miles west of Louisville—population about 150—and about six from Wamego—with about 1,500 residents—and about eight miles from Grandpa's.

Bordered on the north by ever-flowing Rock Creek, it had 100 acres of cropland and 85 acres of rolling pasture, a soft-water well that never went dry, an Aeromotor windmill, and a two-story white-frame house.

The house—most houses looked large compared to the tiny house at Aunt Maggie's—had two bedrooms upstairs, and another bedroom downstairs, a living room, a dining area, and a large kitchen.

One door from the kitchen led into the pantry and a second opened to the unfinished cellar below. A large concrete porch wrapped around part of the north and west sides, and held a small milk separator room near the kitchen door. White posts decorated both the front porch, as well as the wooden back porch, that would later hold the washtubs and scrub board. A garden patch lay a few feet beyond the back door.

A spacious barn—most important to the boys' dad—sat just north of the house. It had a milking parlor, two double horse stalls, corncribs, and a huge hayloft. To the east stood a big cattle shed, with grain bins and a shop on one side. Next to the house perched a fine smokehouse atop a large storm cellar, and beyond that a small garage.

About 50 feet from the house, in the shade of a large hackberry tree, stood an unpretentious one-family, two-holer outhouse. In the heat of summer, everyone gave it wide berth, except when it was a necessity.

The farmhouse would have no running water or indoor plumbing until Freddy was a junior and George a freshman in high school. That would be four years after the Rural Electrification Agency brought electricity to the farm. But for now....

"Oh I'm so excited," the boys' mom said. "This place has everything. It's just wonderful. And, I can see the country for miles right out of the kitchen window. See how beautiful this is?"

"We could like it here, Veda, provided you're willing to live without electric lights," her husband said. "It may be years before the war ends and the REA gets lines out this far."

"Oh, John, we can use lamps like lots of people do, and the boys will like it so much. Let's buy it."

"Well, I like it too, though I hope we don't end up on the Poor Farm," he said, sending a tender tease toward his wife. "But, I guess if Mr. Funnell is willing to loan us the money, it must be alright. He seems to think we're good for it."

§

The next day, Mr. Floyd Funnell, owner of Funnell's Lumberyard in Wamego, did loan Dad $6,000, with the farm as security. With the additional $2,000 saved while at Aunt Maggie's, the folks purchased the Anderson place for the sum of $8,000 in early 1944. Once they finished the paperwork, we had a new farm, a big mortgage, and lots of new challenges and responsibilities.

The weeks dragged by, but in mid-March, the time came to leave the security of Aunt Maggie's farm. It would be an interesting—and memorable—move.

TO WAMEGO AT NINE MILES AN HOUR

Can you imagine our Dad driving a 1938 Allis-Chalmers tractor over 85 miles of sand roads to Wamego and then 6 more to the new farm. All in one day? In cold Kansas, in March? Can you imagine pulling an old hayrack, converted into a rubber-tired farm trailer, loaded with farm machinery? All, at the amazing speed of nine miles per hour?

Since American farmers fed the armed forces

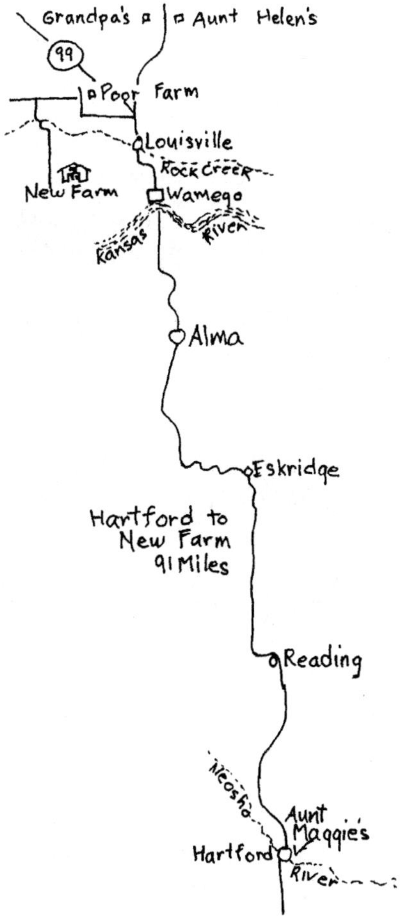

and much of the world at that time, Dad wasn't affected by fuel rationing. He was able to take a couple of extra gas cans on the trailer while he traveled through Neosho Rapids and Reading, then west on Kansas 170, and finally north on Kansas 99.

He went through the tiny towns of Admire, Eskridge, and Alma, and during the trip crossed the lines of Coffey, Lyon, and Wabaunsee counties. Once across the Kaw River, he also passed into the southern edge of Pottawatomie County.

Dad used every bit of daylight for the more than 10-hour trip—the tractor didn't have lights—as it purred along in road gear hour after hour, toward the new farm and the family's new life.

Uncle Alfred drove Dad back to Hartford, arriving well after dark. He stayed overnight and helped load the hard to find civilian trucks in the morning. That was the day we'd be on our way.

THE RIGHT DAY TO MOVE WAS WRONG

Moving day tiptoed in with fine mist and

muddy, slimy footing. Instead of a bright March morning, water dripped from every leaf and dark clouds seemed to bounce along the ground. But, rain or no rain, the move was on, and just before 7 a.m., two huge trucks arrived.

Minutes later, Russ Laws and Slim Colglazer came to help Uncle Alfred, Bill Wilson, and Dad load the cattle and hogs, crates of chickens, some machinery and hand tools, a small grinder, and the household goods. When the last hog went up the ramp into the big Ford, the chilling mist turned to light rain.

We left Aunt Maggie's place for the final time, just as the cheerless weather became a gully washer that tested the windshield wipers for the next couple of hours.

Rain drenched everything except the canvas covered household goods. Wet cows dripped water from tufts of red and black hair and from low hanging noses and tails. They swayed back and forth, and above the motor noise, we could hear the hogs grunt with each jolt of the truck.

§

"How come the hogs make that noise?" Freddy asked. "Are they mad at something?"

He rode in Uncle Alfred's Plymouth just ahead of the livestock truck. His folks and George led the procession in the family car.

Uncle Alfred smiled, and said, "Those hogs don't like being penned up in the back of that truck, Freddy. I guess animals don't like getting squeezed and jolted either. Your Dad sold all but those 5 Hampshire sows, most of his cattle, and his team of mules so he wouldn't have to haul them."

"If you look back now, you can see the livestock shift around when the truck hits a bump or follows a bend in the road. See how the stock bunches on one side going around this corner. The other truck doesn't rock much, does it? It has an easier job than the one with the animals."

Easy or hard, both trucks rocked some under their overweight loads. Both were underpowered, too, and struggled at a snail's pace on each hill and curve.

"Your Dad had a hard time locating those trucks because of the war. They came all the way from around Lebo or Wakefield," Uncle Alfred said. Then, trying to head off another of Freddy's questions, he added, "The stock truck is a two-ton cabover Ford and the other one is a ton and a half Chevrolet. They're quite a sight, aren't they?"

To Freddy, just 10, it was a sight. The trip and the move were great. Eight-year-old George, however, brooded in the backseat of the family car. He was moving away from the known, cozy life in the tiny three-room house at Aunt Maggie's. There the four of them shared a bedroom. Now the folks would have their own room, Freddy would have one, and so would he. Was he ready for this?

After a while, he got so caught up in the events of the day, that he forever broke the curse of his shameful lack of self-control—without even being aware of it.

Near Alma, a few miles beyond Eskridge, he realized that he didn't notice the S-curves, didn't get sick—a first!—and as a result still had his breakfast.

"Hey, Mom," he said, "I didn't get sick today, did I? I didn't puke or nothing."

"Good for you," she said, with a smile. "See, when you don't dwell on it, you don't get sick. It's just like we said."

George smiled. He'd conquered his S-curve weakness at last. He smiled again, all at once interested in the scene outside.

"Mom, why is that pasture burned like that? Did lightning start it or something?"

On this dark and cloudy day, the burned-over bluestem clumps seemed especially black, though grassy new spikes were beginning to peak out.

"It wasn't lightning. Those pastures are burned over each spring just like the Indians used to do. They did it so the buffalo would come to eat the new shoots. It works for cows, too," his mom said. "These Flint Hills stretch all the way to the Dakotas, and you'll see spring-burned pastures all through them."

A half hour later, as the caravan neared Wamego, most of the clouds disappeared—it had rained almost two inches—and now spotty sun gleamed on the new grass, tree leaves, and on the Standard Oil Delivery Truck coming toward them.

It was Uncle Alfred's brother-in-law, Ora Bowman, who stopped when the caravan slowed. After saying hello, the boys' dad asked, "How's the rain been up this way? It rained on us hard most the way from Hartford."

"We've had a lot of rain, too. There is quite a bit of run-off flooding," Ora said. "Some dirt roads are hardly passable. You might have trouble getting to your new place."

The boys' dad shook his head and said thanks. Ora nodded, waved goodbye, and continued on south to make a fuel delivery.

"Oh, John, what'll we do? Won't the roads be a mess?" the boys' mom asked. "This makes me so nervous."

"Yep, Orie says the ditches will be full and so will the ruts. I don't know if the trucks can make it," the boys' dad said, "but, we'll just have to chance it. We need to unload the stock soon. They're getting worn down."

"We could try driving west from Louisville, but I think we should take the county sand road toward Flush and go in from the north," he said. "That way we'll have one less mile of mud."

So the plan formed. The next few hours would test the strength and resolve of this small moving party. Only time would tell if they'd made the right decision.

EIGHT

NEIGHBORS TO THE RESCUE, WATER ON MY PILLOW, AND SHORTY'S DIVORCE PIGS

[*Wamego Reporter* – March 23, 1944] ~ **PRAIRIE VIEW NEWS** ~ A family by the name of Burgess purchased and have moved to the Anderson home place.

FIELDS FULL OF SHALLOW FISH PONDS

Although the downpour had stopped, everywhere we looked there were puddles, run-off flows, and small rivulets. All along Highway 99 into Wamego, the ditches looked full and we could see muddy water flowing across some side roads.

Our caravan of two cars and two trailer trucks stayed on the highway—also the town's main street—north through town and then three miles to Louisville. There we crossed the highway bridge over Rock Creek, full of angry, debris-filled water, and an uprooted tree that bobbed and spun in the current.

A mile later, we turned left onto the road that led to Flush. With the rains behind us, the afternoon sun now peaked through the clouds and light danced on each puddle and pool. All of the fields on both sides of the road seemed full of dozens of shallow fishponds, linked together by water clogged furrows.

"Oh, John," Mom said, "there is standing water everywhere. And did you see how bad Rock Creek looked? The road to the farm is probably covered with water and mud. This is just awful."

"It doesn't look good," he said. "But we can't stop now. We have to do something. Somehow, we have to get through the mud after we leave this sanded road."

The muddy challenge came closer when, three miles later, Dad turned the procession south from the main road. A half mile later, the sand ended at the Romanus Heiger farm. Ahead, we stared at the first stretch of muddy, unimproved road leading up to the rickety bridge of another Rock Creek crossing.

When we stopped, the Heigers listened to Dad's concerns and offered to help if they could. After a couple of minutes, Mr. Heiger said, "Why don't you park the heavy stock truck in my driveway, and send the lighter loaded truck ahead. If it can't make it over the bridge, I'll hook my tractor to it."

Dad nodded and then asked the Chevy semi's driver to try to reach the bridge. The truck crept forward inch by inch, with tires slipping and spinning as it doubled the rut size with its smoking duel tires. After what seemed like several minutes, the grinding and spinning had gained just a couple of truck lengths. The hapless truck could go no further. The rise to the bridge had bogged it down.

§

NEIGHBORS TO THE RESCUE

A minute later, Mr. Heiger's '37 John Deere B came popping to the rescue—everyone hoped—slogging through the mud to the front of the semi. The boys' dad knelt in the muck and attached a log-chain from the truck to the light tractor's drawbar.

Mr. Heiger pushed the hand clutch forward and inched the old B ahead to tighten the chain. Then, at full throttle it began poppity-pop-pop-popping like a machine gun and belched a black smoke signal-like puff with each pop. The big rubber tires clawed down to dryer soil, while the tractor spun and yawed, working the truck ahead. At last, it moved up and over the bridge.

Next, the John Deere rescued the heavy Ford cabover with the livestock. Once on the bridge, the driver steered to miss a gapping hole in the planking. About mid-span small bits of rotted wood dropped into the swollen stream below.

The two cars stayed in the truck ruts, and made it over the bridge on their own, stopping at the wide farm driveway of more new neighbors, Louie Riat and his sons, Mark and Leo. From that point, almost a mile of mud remained...and the day grew short. After talking with the Riats, the boys' dad said, "We'll unload the cattle and hogs here. Alfred, why don't you and the Riat boys herd them to our place? The fence at the barn needs fixing, so put them in the cattle shed corral."

The cattle—beef and dairy—rushed out of the truck with the five hogs not wanting to be left behind. They were eager to move and to be away from the swaying ride, although some did stop for a muddy drink, and soon were herded on with ease. They wanted a safe place...and they'd soon have it...their new home.

"Well," the boys' dad said, "it's a cinch this load of furniture, machinery, and crates of chickens can't walk this last mile. We're going to have to get that truck through that mud somehow. I'm afraid Heiger's John Deere is too light to make it up that last hill."

At that point, Louie Riat offered a suggestion.

"If we can get that old tractor of mine started, it might do the trick," he said. "It's got steel wheels that can get a better grip in the mud."

"I don't even know if it will run though. It's been a few years since we used it," he said, nodding toward the forlorn looking McCormack-Deering 15-30 Gear Drive tractor parked beside his machine shed.

The old gray tractor looked squat, tired, and unloved sitting with last summer's dead weed stalks caressing its undersides. Some paint had chipped away and areas of rust stood out against the remaining paint. It looked like a candidate for the junkyard. Would it ever start?

"We need to get her ready," Louie said. "Here John, you add some gas and I'll put water in the radiator. Then he said, "I'll set the throttle and choke, and we'll see if we can crank her up."

He moved around front and cranked and cranked. Nothing. The boys' dad then took a turn and cranked some more, until it fired a couple of times.

"Hey, it's beginning to fire," Louie said. "Keep after it." Two cranks later the engine coughed and black smoke shot skyward for a couple of minutes, then the engine began idling in a regular rhythm. It would run!

"Hook up the chain," Louie said, "and we'll see what we can do. Keep the truck in low and we can work together."

Little by little, the tractor crept ahead with the double rows of three-inch lugs biting through the mud to solid ground. The truck's dual wheels began to spin again, but the pull of the tractor kept it moving forward.

They swung wide around the first corner sloshing water and mud. Groaning and growling at full throttle, the tractor struggled up and over the first low incline. A few minutes later they reached the base of the last, long hill. Here, the long semi couldn't track the slippery right turn and Louie twice dragged the trailer sideways to align it.

That last, steep quarter-mile challenged the tractor. It moaned louder and steam boiled from the radiator. But, with the steel wheels clawing and truck tires spinning, the two vehicles climbed the hill and crept into the driveway of the new farm.

§

We followed behind the truck in our car, spinning and jostling along in the freshly plowed ruts. After what seemed like an hour, we made it to our new yard! The ordeal was over—at least the moving part of it—and we watched big globs of mud drop from the vehicles, to later become hard lumps when they dried.

There before us like a welcoming committee stood the white farm house, the red barn and the windmill, the paint-less cattle shed-shop-granary, the free standing garage, the white smokehouse—and the two-holer outhouse. A now radiant-orange setting sun highlighted the scene like a precious painting. How welcome we felt. Thank God!

The two of us pitched in to help unload the semi, carrying in pots, pans, and some of our clothes. The Riats, Mr. Heiger, and both truck drivers helped Dad with the stoves, the furniture, and large household items.

Meanwhile, Uncle Alfred watered the animals, and gave the cows hay and the pigs corn. They were now under cover—new rain clouds were building in the northwest—at the cattle shed. Locked in the barn's empty corncrib, the chickens received grain and water. Most everything was out of the weather…or so we thought.

Darkness settled around us as the last machinery rolled from the truck. Dad thanked the drivers for their roles in the difficult moving job and gave each a check. Louie watched, in case his tractor was needed, while the empty truck inched along toward his driveway and the other waiting semi.

When the truck stopped at Riats, Mrs. Heiger drove by the other way, bringing her new neighbors a huge pot of ham and potato soup plus fresh bread, a much-appreciated and needed meal. Everyone acted as if they hadn't eaten in a week, particularly the two of us.

"Veda, those boys of yours must have hollow legs!" Uncle Alfred said with a smile, though most were too tired to laugh.

The lantern on the kitchen table—now low on fuel—flickered as the new neighbors prepared to leave. These great people had come to our rescue, and had pitched in to help, unasked. Louie Riat's comment summed it up, "We're just being neighborly."

Mom and Dad thanked everyone and Uncle Alfred in particular. "We couldn't have done it without you," Dad said to his brother. And he meant it.

Later, the folks thanked God for helping with the move, and then prayed for our new neighbors. No doubt, the neighbors prayed for us, too. And we needed their prayers, for more concerns awaited us here on our new farm.

§

WATER ON MY PILLOW

It was past nine o'clock and dark by the time everyone had gone. A half hour later, the kitchen utensils were organized and some of the beds were set up.

The only job left was milking the cows. George had fallen asleep, so Freddy and his parents picked up milk buckets and headed for the cattle shed. When they reached the gate, lantern light lit up Freddy's exhausted face.

"You look tuckered out, son. You've had quite a day, haven't you?"

"You look just about done in. Why don't you go on back to the house and go to bed. Use that mattress on the floor in the dining room," his dad said to the ten-year-old.

"Mom and I will do the milking tonight."

With gratitude and relief, Freddy walked back to the house by cloudy starlight. Soon he slumbered, clothes and all. His folks soon followed—milking four cows didn't take long—and they, too, soon fell into an exhausted asleep. The challenges were behind them. Or were they?

What felt like just a few minutes later, George bolted

upright from where he slept on the divan. Something was wrong. His head was wet and water dripped on his pillow!

He jumped up, wondering where he was and what was happening. Heavy rain pounded on the roof and drops of water splashed on the divan and on the floor in several places.

"Mom, Mom, there's water coming in. My pillow's all wet. What should I do?"

"Stay where you are 'til I light this lamp," his dad said from another room. "It sounds like the roof is leaking."

"Dad gum it," he said, holding the lamp at arm's length. "Come here, Veda, and help me put pans down to catch the worst of it. There must be 4 or 5 places that are dripping out in the kitchen."

He sighed, then said, "It's too dark to do any roof fixing tonight. We'll just have to wait 'til morning. Let's move the divan so George can sleep dry. We'll set up his bed tomorrow."

George dropped off to sleep again in just seconds. A couple of minutes later—so it seemed—he awakened to whisperless quiet. Why the quiet? He scooted off the divan and glanced out a window. The whole world glistened in a soft white blanket lit up by the early dawn light.

"Hey, everybody," he exclaimed, "look at the snow!"

Sometime during the night, the rain had turned to snow and now two inches covered everything. Each flake sparkled yellow and orange in the just-rising sun, while posts, trees, and clumps of grass created long, dark shadows.

The family, groggy from fatigue, looked outside. His dad shook his head. "That's all we need, isn't it? Now we'll have to do the chores in the snow."

He began to pull on his warm coat and overshoes, then said, "Come on Freddy, you can help. We might as well get to it."

"Wait a minute, John," the boys' mom said. "I've got

the kitchen stove going and the coffee is about ready. Here, you can have some hot chocolate, boys."

"George, you can help me empty these rainwater pans and pots. When the snow melts, it will drip some more and they might run over. We've got to keep this house as dry as we can."

George did as he was told, though after a couple of minutes, he took a good look out the front door at the quiet scene. His eyes widened. He took an excited breath and smiled. Wow! The new farm sparkled everywhere in its soft, white blanket. His eyes moved from the cattle shed to the smoke house, and then to the barnyard.

"Hey, there's Pep!"

"He's playing 'King of the Hill' on that big mound in front of the barn. See, he's looking around and sniffing," George said, watching Pep's brown and gold Collie coat contrast with the white snow and the red barn. "He must think this is his territory."

"Mom, this is a great farm! Can I go outside and look around? Maybe I can help with the cattle...and er...maybe the milking."

"All right, go ahead. I'll cook breakfast while you are gone," she said. "Then your dad is going to have to see to this roof as soon as the snow melts off."

"I guess there'll always be something to fix on this place. Some things have been let go for a while."

The new farm did bring plenty of challenges and things to fix. That first snowy morning, however, was a blessing. The snow and the cold froze the top layer of ground and made it easier to feed and milk and mend the barnyard fence so the cattle could be held near the windmill water tank.

However, the sun warmed things up, and by late morning, the snow began melting and by midafternoon it was gone. While the kitchen stove dried out the inside, the roof received a few temporary shingles.

Around the farm, all manner of things needed fixing and mending. In time, doors got new hinges and the huge manure pile at the barn—Pep's kingdom hill—

became field fertilizer. A couple of broken windows received new panes, and as planting time neared, some machinery needed to be reworked from horse drawn to tractor drawn.

FIX IT UP AND MAKE IT WORK

"Okay boys," their dad said a few weeks later, "it's time to get to work. Let's head up to the shop and change over that two-row cultivator so we can pull it behind the tractor. We can't sit here and dawdle all day."

"John Burgess, you can at least let them finish their breakfasts," the boys' mom said. "George needs to eat. He's skinny as a fishing pole. Just look at him."

George frowned. I'm not a stick of wood and I don't catch fish, he thought. With resolve, he dipped a spoonful of rich cream covered Cream-of-Wheat and brought it toward his mouth. Man, I hope I don't gag, he thought, as he pulled a half-bite off from the spoon with his lips. Ugh.

While George played with his food, both parents fidgeted. They'd watched him poke and play with his meals before. Maybe he'd have to stay skinny.

His dad became impatient and broke the silence. "Let's go boys. If you're going to be farmers, you'll have to learn to fix things and to find ways to make things work. No one is going to do it for you."

§

We pushed our unfinished cereal away and dashed from the table. At last we could escape and go do some farm work with our hero. Working with him was exciting, at least most of the time.

We pulled on our ball caps and walked toward the shop in the warm, spring air. It was damp and the early sun made it feel sticky. Leaves, dripping with dew, shone a shining new green. At the granary shop, sparrows twittered and flirted with each other.

"Freddy, get the saw and the hammer and the chisel. I'll find some bolts and nuts to attach these iron tongue brackets," Dad said, while he sorted through a couple of coffee cans filled with old hardware.

Next, he bent over the ten-foot tongue of a two row, horse-drawn cultivator. As he concentrated, we watched big drops of sweat fall from the end of his nose to make dark spots on the weathered, gray wood. He laid the square across the tongue, scribed a mark with a nail, wiped away the sweat, and started sawing the long beam in half.

Kerplunk. A five-foot piece hit the ground, bounced a couple of times, and he pushed it away with the side of his foot. Using the heavy iron hitch—made by the blacksmith in Louisville—as a pattern, he marked the two boltholes.

"Now, hand me that brace and bit," Dad said with a nod toward the workbench. "I'll drill two holes in the end of the wood."

Soon, he pushed the two large bolts through the iron and wood. A few turns with a crescent wrench fastened the hitch in place. Modifying the cultivator tongue had looked easy.

"Now we have to do something about the levers. They're used to raise and lower the cultivating shovels. If a farmer sat on the cultivator's seat, he could reach them easy, but they're the wrong way for the tractor."

Dad became inventive again—he'd put rubber tires on the hayrack before pulling it from Hartford loaded with machinery. He studied the levers a minute and then started unbolting them. He reversed them—extended full length—to point forward.

"There, let's see how this works. When I back

the AC to the hitch, drop this pin through the hitch and the center drawbar hole. We'll test it with a couple of turns around the garden patch."

"Hey, that worked pretty well," he said a few minutes later. "I can just reach the levers. Sure beats getting off and on the tractor at the beginning or end of a row. Pretty hard for a farmer to be two places at once."

§

A few weeks later, Freddy and George saw an example of that getting on and off method. On the way to school, though a meadowlark called from a fence post and somewhere a windmill squeaked, they ignored the sounds to study the cultivating process of another new neighbor.

"Hey, isn't that Shorty Brockman?" Freddy asked, nodding toward a cornfield across the road. "He's fixed his cultivator for his tractor, too. Guess he didn't fix the levers though, did he?

"See how he has to hop off his tractor at the end of a row and run back to lift up the shovels?"

"Yeah, I see that," George said, watching Shorty remount and drive his old Farmall F-20 to the next row. "Now he's getting off to lower the shovels again."

"Boy, he's doing a lot of running," a grinning Freddy said. "Wonder why he didn't change over the levers?"

"Maybe," George said, "he's not smart, like Dad."

"Yeah, maybe he's not."

After school, the boys again saw Shorty—who was not mechanically gifted—cultivating the same field, but this time without stopping. His solution: His wife, Louella Ethel, rode in the cultivator seat to raise and lower the shovels.

"Look at that," Freddy said. "And, Louella Ethel's wearing a feed-sack dress, too. Oh-man-o-man, that's funny. What a picture."

Afternoon sun filled the scene as Shorty, under an

abused straw hat, drove his slow moving steel-wheeled F-20, with his wife riding in the rusty horse-style cultivator seat. Her white dress had measle-like red spots, and hung down to brush the tops of the very young corn. It was a sight…and a two-person job.

The boys came to realize Shorty Brockman, a first cousin to peas-on-the-hunting-knife Lyle and oily-splinter-toothpick tractor salesman Ernie, had his own way of doing things. This neighbor, though not always efficient or practical, did seem to make a go of it on his small farm, though he often hired out to earn cash.

Shorty—so the boys heard—also had an eye for bargains and sometimes turned junky things into profit. Sometimes, however, he did not.

SHORTY'S DIVORCE PIGS

Shorty rented the farm where he and Louella Ethel lived. It consisted of some 20 acres of pasture, 40 acres of corn ground, a garden area, and a small house and barn.

He planted a pretty good garden and—Shorty had a weakness for fresh side-pork—they raised at least a couple hogs each year. He bought 35-50 pound weaner pigs and fed them in his barn until they reached butchering weight…about 200-250 pounds. Shorty and Lulu—she disliked the nickname—kept some pork at home, with the rest at the frozen food locker plant in town.

He often bought pigs from neighbors, but sometimes at the livestock auctions in Manhattan or St. Marys. He was at the weekly Manhattan auction the day after he finished cultivating.

Shorty hadn't planned to go to the auction that day, but hard rain during the night meant no field work. Along with other farmers, he used the wet day to gab and visit, to check prices, and to look for bargains passing through the ring.

This bargain idea is what got Shorty in trouble…again. While the auctioneer rattled away, he sat high in the bleachers with the familiar smells of sheep, hogs, and cattle around him. Without much interest, he watched a couple of groups of weaner pigs sell.

What happened next grew into a legend around Wamego for a long time. Into the straw-covered sale ring walked 17 active looking weaner pigs. The auctioneer, Buck Barkmore, started the bidding at $10 apiece. The crowd remained silent. No one nodded a head, moved a muscle, or even blinked.

In typical fashion, Barkmore stopped and said, "Come on fellas, let's buy some pigs."

High up in the bleachers a fellow from near Junction City hollered, "I'll give you two bucks a piece for 'em." Several people chuckled and a couple of the pigs made a funny kind of snort and coughed a bit, as if they thought they were worth more.

"I got two, a-two, a-two, dollar bid," Barkmore said, bellowing. "Do I hear three, a-three, a-three, three...."

Shorty's eyes bugged out. These were fine Berkshire shoats with pug, turned-up noses like the ones he'd once seen in his high school Ag book. Since they'd been pictured in a book, he guessed they'd produce good side pork and lots of lard, both of which he was rather fond.

Almost not meaning to, Shorty nodded his head. Barkmore, glad to move on, hammered his gavel and pointed the handle right at Shorty.

"Sold."

Hey, I got them pigs real cheap, Shorty thought. Hot dog, I'm gonna make some money on this bunch.

Half an hour later, Shorty helped an auction-yard hostler herd the new pigs down the ramp into his faded blue Chevy pickup. They seemed glad to be heading out of the auction barn, for they were snorting and clearing their nostrils as if to say, "Good riddance."

When all 17 'Berkshires' crowded together in the truck, the snorting and wheezing seemed quite intense. Shorty's stomach felt funny.

Could something be wrong? They had sold pretty cheap. Shoot, you don't suppose they're sick, he thought?

As the hostler turned to leave, he said to Shorty, "If them pigs was mine, I'd stop by the vet on the way out of town."

Dr. A. W. Stubblefield confirmed Shorty's worst fears. His pigs had something called rhinitus, a chronic nasal passage disease that distorted their noses and breathing passages. The turned up noses were not from Berkshire lineage, but from the nasty, though non-lethal, infection.

"What you need to do is give each pig a shot of this every day." Dr. Stubblefield handed Shorty several syringes and a bottle of injectable medicine. "It's best to shoot them up high on the front shoulder. That way, you won't damage the hams or bacon."

Later, at his barn, Louella Ethel—home from her part-time job at the high school cafeteria—helped unload the pigs. Shorty could only give a strained smile when she stared at him.

"What in the world did you buy 17 pigs for?"

"Got 'em at a good price," Shorty said—which was true, in a sense. "Guess they'll need some tending though."

"What do you mean, tending? What is this medicine for? Are these pigs sick?"

"They've kinda got stuffy-type noses," the vet said. "Tomorrow we'll need to give 'em shots."

The next day, the pig doctoring began, but first, somebody had to catch one of the 35-pound piles of muscular obstinacy. Snorting and wheezing, the pigs refused to be cornered, until Shorty finally grabbed the right hind leg of Number Seventeen. With its remaining three legs digging forward, the young pig, blessed with a spectacular set of vocal chords, squealed loud enough to knock the cobwebs from the barn walls.

Inch by inch, Shorty dragged the jerking, fighting pig toward where Lulu stood sneering, hands on hips. This was going to be some day.

"What do you expect me to do now, Mr. Genius?" she said. "I surely ain't giving no shots!"

“Okay, okay. You hold ‘em and I’ll shoot ‘em just like the doc tole me.”

“And how am I supposed to hold that? It just keeps jerking and jerking. And look, it’s crapping. What a mess!”

Clinching his teeth, Shorty drug the pig away from the newest poop—there were plenty of other piles around—and said, “Maybe the best way is for you to sit on ‘em. Here, I’ll flip this one down and you straddle it.”

“Oh, my God!” She had to scream to be heard for between her legs the violent pig shrieked and squirmed. Her faded blue housedress crumpled about her and bare knees rested on the manure covered dirt floor. “Oh, my God!”

Meanwhile, Shorty hurried, fumbling with a syringe. He jabbed at the squirming pig a couple of times, and at last injected the shot under the hide. Hoping to take the edge off her ‘mad,’ he helped Lulu up.

“Only 16 to go.” Shorty was trying to be funny.

§

The long and short of it was that this story got better and better. It was retold at the feedstore, along main street, or across many a fencerow. Soon Shorty’s purchase became known as ‘The Divorce Pigs’ for Louella Ethel had, on each of the 10 days of pig shots, given Shorty notice. In the end, Lulu didn’t quit Shorty, but we heard her complain many times about her husband not having any more sense than his stupid pigs.

To us, Shorty’s approach to life was funny and at times made us wonder. The mental picture of Louella Ethel astride a squirming shoat was good for many a laugh. In the end, Dad said, Shorty’s $3 pigs cost a whole lot more, when you added in the vet bill and the extra feed the nasally-impaired hogs required.

Of course, we didn’t say anything to Shorty

about the story, for he was a trusted neighbor—though as Dad said, "Not with my money."

We came to realize we learned a lot from our neighbors, by the way they farmed and helped others. Of course, we also knew we'd need a whole lot more education than we could get from these good folks.

And, we had just the place for that learning, at our one-room school called Prairie View, District 82. It was just across the hills.

NINE

FRIED EGG SANDWICHES, RATTLERS & COW PATTIES, AND FIT FOR A KING

[*Wamego Reporter* – November 23, 1944] ~ **RED CROSS NEEDS WORKERS** ~ Wanted: Women to sew or knit for men in our armed forces and in our hospitals. For details call any of the following: Mrs. Katheryn Robson, Mrs. O. W. Noe, Mrs. Ann Guilfoyle, or Mrs. L. L. Vilven.

FRIED EGG SANDWICHES

"Arrgh, there's gotta be fried egg sandwiches in there!" Barney Gava said, as he posed on the prairie path to the one-room Prairie View School. His audience—his younger sister, Barbara; his classmate, Freddy; and George—stared when he brought the back of his right hand hard against his up-tilted forehead.

"I hate egg sandwiches. Why do I have to eat 'em? They are just crapola. Yuck!"

Now holding a brown, grease-stained lunch sack at arm's length, his round, somewhat chubby face exhibited intense disgust. His nose flared in and out with each breath. Italian flamboyance—inherited from his long absent father—equipped Barney for an emotional performance. His eyes rolled back and he stood statue-like dangling the wrinkled, grimy sack.

"Can you smell that? I'm going to throw up."

With that, Barney reached into the sack and extracted a wax paper wrapped sandwich, placing the crumpled sack under his left arm. With both hands free, he gripped the two pieces of bread, and with the grunt of a discus thrower, flipped out the offending saucer-shaped egg. It sailed away into the prairie wind…round and round…to float down amid clumps of uninterested prairie grass.

This showy gesture complete, he returned the bread to his sack—he had to eat something—grinned for his audience, and repeated the process with sandwich number two.

"Uunggh! And…good riddance!" he said, his black eyes flashing.

To complete his performance, he rolled his lunch sack, now containing only four slices of chewy homemade bread, into a mush ball and played catch with himself. Always the philosopher, Barney pronounced advice as his final line of the performance.

"You only get to be here once…so don't cough up no hairballs."

Huh?, the boys thought, missing the meaning of this profound remark. What does that have to do with throwing away fried eggs?

One could never be sure about Barney; for sometimes he carried the egg sandwiches all the way to school, and there used them in his oft preformed lunchtime show. It began with moaning from his back row desk, where he held an egg sandwich near his mouth. Then, he'd gripe and complain until his schoolmates turned to watch.

Now, with attentive spectators, he'd broaden his nostrils, sniff the sandwich, and bit by bit move it toward his quivering lips. Without hurry, he'd open his mouth to flash large white teeth, and then gnash off a huge chunk. He'd sit in silence while the smell of lard and sulphurous egg filled the room and yellow, gooey yolk oozed down his chin.

"I can't stand it! It's a plot by the enemies of our noble lands," he said. "I hate egg sandwiches more than a case of the boils!"

These lines delivered, Barney sat stock-still while the yolk started to harden on his chin. At last, he'd toss his coarse, black, Rose Hair Oil covered mane, and with a dramatic sigh he said, "The Gestapo must have invented eggs to torture people. I vow-eth to not eat-eth an egg sandwich again!"

Then he added, "Never give your life an even chance!" in a philosophical whisper, before bowing his head and closing his glistening eyes.

§

We found Barney's philosophy, while making no sense most of the time, interesting and his performances entertaining. Still, we marveled at the waste. How could anyone throw away food? There were people in the world going hungry; yet before our eyes, eggs flew into the wind or the wastebasket.

From our parents and our church, we had learned the 'waste not, want not' adage. Dad taught we shouldn't copy the unsuitable actions of others, for he said, "Just because someone jumps off a bridge, that doesn't make it right for you."

For Barney, these egg sandwiches were often the only food his loving grandmother, Mrs. Cotton, had to send as his lunch. With gratitude for her giving him a home—plus probably fearing her wrath—his egg-tossing happened out of her sight.

No doubt about it, we marveled at Barney...and his fried egg sandwich drama. We also marveled at many other events that we experienced during our treks to and from school. Much of our route took us along the path across Cotton's big bluestem pasture, and this became the stage for most of our mysterious and entertaining adventures.

We learned during these walks...and wondered.

THE PRAIRIE PATH

What created the path through Cotton's pasture? Had school-bound students of the past done it? Or, we wondered, had that path been tramped out by herds of Herefords, walking one behind the other? Or buffalo?

Perhaps, the prairie path was an old Indian

trail made by moccasined-feet and unshod ponies. The Kansa and Kaw Indians, according to our social studies book, *Four Centuries in Kansas*, had roamed the area before the white man came. The Pawnee, Wichita, Kiowa, and Osage sometimes visited, too. Had they crossed this piece of virgin prairie?

Had the Indians hunted deer and buffalo here with willow or Osage Orange shafted arrows, the kind they tipped with flint rock arrowheads?

Had there been wars?

At Grandpa's farm a few miles away, we had found arrowheads and broken stone axes. These convinced us a great Indian battle had taken place there among his pasture's granite boulders. But, along Cotton's pasture path, none appeared. Why?

We often enacted our own battles, and in the process missed appreciating the rolling hills and dales of this pasture and the nearby area. They were formed—the social studies book said—by a huge ice-age glacier that stretched from Hudson's Bay to near our farm. Had the melting glacier really created the hundreds of valleys and ravines? And, did the glacier really leave a zillion rocks?

Everywhere laid the numberless red granite stones, the size of buildings down to baseballs. They were smooth and rounded, ground down and polished under the weight of the glacier. The name Flint Hills came from these rocks.

Now, we moved over one of those hills, following the meandering path as a guide to our feet in both good weather and bad. And, as we walked near the end of the school year in early June, nature was at its finest all around us, had we paid attention to it.

Lost in thoughts about more everyday things, we took for granted the yellow petals and winking eyes of showy black-eyed susans, and paid little attention to the drooping mauve-colored petals of the purple coneflowers. We even ignored the many-headed sunflowers—our State Flower—that flashed in the high Kansas sun.

We walked oblivious, through acres of big bluestem grass that swayed in the slight breeze, and seemed to twinkle with reflected aqua light from jointed stalks. Though we overlooked it, the sky was a vast dome of blue, dotted by almost motionless red tail hawks, and a few cottony thunderheads far to the east.

When we left the Cotton's corral heading to school that spring morning, a meadowlark filled the fresh, sweet-smelling air with song from the top of a fence post, and the brilliant red of a cardinal flitted in the wild plum thicket.

The movement of a pair of western bluebirds hunting insects, and barn swallows dipping and darting to catch rising lacewings the cows kicked up did catch our eyes. Yet, we saw only a portion of the scene.

§

"Hey, Freddy," Barney said, "Look at this ole turtle. It looks like a brown helmet, only it's half-sized. I wonder where it's going."

"I don't know, but it might be headed to Laclede. Turtles always seem to walk to the northeast for some reason," Freddy said.

"Look over there. Isn't that a coyote with a jackrabbit in its mouth sneaking up the draw? She must have a den over there somewhere. Wanna try to find it after school?"

Before anyone could answer, George had something to say. "You guys...look over here. Here's some coyote sign," he said, pointing at a small brown pile on the path.

"That's just poop," Barbara said.

"Yeah," George said with a grin, "It's a sure sign some ole coyote's been here."

"Oh, you're teasing," Barbara said. "I know what poop is."

"But it's more than that. It's an animal sign like rabbit pellets or the bundle of bones and fur that owls leave on open ground. You know, like the tracks of a coon along the creek or when the cows wander through dewy grass. The Indians were experts at recognizing animal and human signs.

"They could tell something's been there. Like a horse's track or a dog's. Every animal leaves a sign."

"Worms leave them after a thunderstorm and snakes wiggle in the dust," Freddy said. "You can even tell George's been here by the notch in his heel from where he whacked it with the corn knife."

The signs the boys and their friends saw somehow told them what was happening in their place in the universe. They felt secure on these daily walks with familiar sights and smells. Their lives seemed full, although they still had plenty of questions.

"How come those cottonwood trees stand so close together?" George asked. "They must be a 100-feet tall."

"They might be half that size. They're growing near the springs by the Cotton's house," his brother said. "Listen to the leaves rattle in the breeze. I'll bet they're hundred years old."

"I wonder why the willows crowd along the banks of the slough. They sure droop down over the water, don't they? Minnows like to hide under their shadows."

"The redbud trees are my favorite," Barbara said. "...and the dogwoods, when they are all white with blooms."

"Look at how many trees we can see around us. Along the road there are elm, black walnut, and hackberry trees, and over on the side of the hill are locust trees."

"Why are there so many hedge trees?" Barbara asked. "And why do they have thorns? I don't like them at all. They hurt."

"Oh, those are Osage Orange. Farmers planted most

of them before they had *bob-wire* fences. They sure keep the cattle at home," Freddy said. "They make good fence posts, too, though they look kind of crooked. Dad says they can last for 30 years or more."

"Did you ever try to drink milk after the cows ate some of those knobby green hedge balls? It's bitter," George said. "The squirrels and quail eat them in winter, after they're ripe."

"Well, I'm no animal so I'm not going to try them," Barbara said, and walked on.

So, from each other and from observation, during their prairie walks, the boys learned many lessons about creation. And sometimes, these lessons came in dramatic fashion.

RATTLERS AND COW PATTIES

The walk to school during cold, and/or snowy winter days, meant the boys and their friends found out about Mother Nature's harsh elements. However, the warmer months were a different story, for the daily walks could be interesting and educational—especially for two very attention-grabbing perils.

Longer spring days came with more sun, new grass, a sense of nature restarting its cycle—and two on-the-path hazards. Whether walking alone, or with Barney and Barbara, the boys learned to watch where they stepped.

Woe to the walker whose foot landed on—or into—a sunning *snake*...or a steaming *cow plop*.

Menace Number One, slithering sunbathers, warmed and wiggled in the bright sunlight. Menace Number Two appeared when grazing cattle over ate the new, light green grass, and—in the end—produced large, liquid, and foul-smelling cow patties.

For reasons mysterious, both hazards nestled in secret, coming into view as if by magic, only inches before impact. Oops, too late...a writhing snake...or a squishy cow pie.

By instinct, the hikers assumed—in error—that

every snake they encountered was a rattlesnake, although they never, ever saw one in Eastern Kansas. However, they reacted as if every snake could kill them dead—on the spot!

"Hisssssssssssss, pfssst!" a huge bull snake hissed in anger. From the middle of the cow path it threatened, with its heat seeking tongue lashing the air.

"Yikes…arrrrh…eeek! Look out…rattler!" George said. "Uhhh."

The snake, coiled like a rattler, hissed again with the same spine-chilling public statement that inspired George's grandiose athletic feat. He had responded, as always, with a violent knee-jerk reaction, jumping sideways and up, cracking his neck.

His heart pumped as he stared at the threatening snake. It stared back, tongue probing. George bobbed left, then right. So did the snake's head, then all motion ceased.

"Hisss, pfst," the snake said, this time with less intensity.

They both stared and then as if saying…"I guess I told you"…the snake turned away little by little and disappeared into the tall grass. It headed east, and George, after several shallow breaths, circled west.

Whether black, gopher, bull, garter, or blue racer, such snakes always got the same reaction from the boys. While never harmed by a single one, they did learn a number of dance shuffles when they stumbled onto a snake.

"I thought I was dead; I think my neck is broken," George said to Barbara, Freddy, and Barney as they cautiously watched for other dangers.

"That was some snake. Must of been six-feet long."

"Yeah, six feet at least," Barney said, glancing over his shoulder and moving out of last place in line.

§

Though snakes caused panic, the cows, or

rather their byproducts, were more offensive. After eating dry hay and grain all winter, each spring cows relished daylong meals of new grass, as if trying to fill all four stomachs at once.

Through observation, we concluded this diet was similar to eating large masses of chilies or pinto beans. Every day, the cows deposited loads of the slow drying, liquid-green substance in huge patties—right where we wanted to walk.

Any 'cow-pattie-on-shoe' incident brought on our teacher's wrath and a day in stocking feet, with our shoes banned to the outer hall. Even then, a subtle aroma from a kid's shoes the teacher missed, floated near the ceiling of the single classroom. Once the manure dried, shoes were dyed with a greenish cast for all time.

We certainly didn't want the slow death from a rattler bite, or...cow smell on our shoes, so we tried hard to avoid them. And we did pretty well, most of the time.

However, out on our prairie walks, we found there was another peril that wasn't so easy to dodge, and that was the weather.

BLIZZARDS AND LIZARD BLOOD

The weather hazard was far more risky than snakes or cows. Slogging home in heavy snowstorms could be down right dangerous. Every winter, when the wind howled and drifts piled high, somewhere in Kansas someone froze to death, either because they weren't prepared or got lost in a blizzard.

On some snowy days, we left school early, trying to get home before the wind chilled us or the drifts got deep. Those cold, miserable walks brought on thoughts of freezing to death, and the empty feeling that no one cared about us. Surely, if our parents loved us or our teacher cared at all, we wouldn't be abandoned like this.

In the movies, we had watched Arctic explorers fight the high winds and blowing snow. We felt as if we were in their midst, struggling step by step across the frozen tundra, crevasses, and ice-covered mountains, while icicles and frost formed around our faces. Why would men—and us—suffer so?

On our prairie, we felt alone and exposed to the elements, for little stood between us and the North Pole. Just a few low hills, a handful of trees and knee-high bunches of last summer's grass. Howling winds, off the arctic ice above the Canadian plains, made a Bee-Line straight for us. All around us, wind-whipped drifts formed in the brown grass.

Luckily, even in near whiteouts, our feet could follow the half mile of the well-worn path with confidence. However, it wasn't until we reached the Cotton's barn that we could find shelter from the chilling wind.

§

George suffered most from the cold. No matter how he dressed, it drove through to his skinny frame. When a blizzard started, he dreaded the walk home with the wind full in his face; for as one friend put it, his veins ran with lizard's blood.

On this particular day, he wondered why it was that people would torture him with this death march. Maybe I'll just die out here, he thought. No, I'll probably never get home. Would people be sad if I died? Yeah, and do you suppose they'll make a movie about me? At that moment, his cold-induced dreaming ended when he realized he couldn't feel his toes. Just where were they?

Freddy spotted Cotton's barn first, for George, trying to stay warm, walked head-down with his hands crammed into his pockets. Freddy shouted over his shoulder, "Follow me through the gate. I can see the barn!"

Out of the wind, the air seemed much warmer. The worst was over. The boys knew the rest of the trip, across the slough bridge, west to the mailbox, and a quarter mile north up the road, had some shelter and seemed easy by comparison. Provided they had the energy.

FIT FOR A KING

On a really bad day in early February, Freddy, George, Barney, and Barbara struggled against snow and wind for what seemed like hours to George. Several times someone pulled him, shivering, from behind a grass clump on into the northwest wind.

"Ah go on…just leave me here to die," George said, copying a line he heard in the movies. "I just can't make it."

Together, Barney and Freddy grabbed George and dogtrotted downhill. Piles of snow slowed their progress, but at last they struggled through two huge drifts and reached the barn, to find Frank Cotton there to meet them.

He hurried all four to his house and out of the wind. Though Freddy said they needed to go on—George was too cold to think—Mrs. Cotton insisted they stay long enough to warm up and eat something. In five minutes, she had fried up some eggs—yep, in lard—and fried some ham and some sourdough bread, also in lard.

"This is a meal fit for a king," Mrs. Cotton said, setting the warm plates before them on the kitchen table. "This will cure whatever ails you."

§

> ***W***e could only agree, for we each ate three of the notorious lard-fried eggs, and Barney ate four with no ill effects. As we warmed next to Mrs. Cotton's wood-burning kitchen stove, we sensed

eating kept out the cold or at least part of it. And we needed that because we still had another half mile of cold to face.

Frank told us Dad called earlier—we were glad someone cared—and had him watch for us when we came over the hill. Now Frank could report we were safe.

He went to the wooden wall telephone and cranked four short times: br-inng, br-inng, br-inng, and br-inng...our number on the party line.

"Hello, John? Your boys are here. They got pretty cold...but they made it. With this wind piling it up, some of the drifts are getting deep."

"Maybe you should come get them with your tractor."

Dad agreed, and twenty minutes later, we heard the Allis-Chalmers driving up.

We dreaded facing the cold again, but bundled up, thanked Mrs. Cotton and Frank, and hopped on the AC's drawbar for the slow, cold ride home. Dad plowed through drift after drift in second gear, about two miles an hour, but it still beat walking.

When we got home—cold all over again—our noses followed the aroma to the kitchen. Mom had cooked us a thick homemade beef stew. Off came our hats, mittens, coats, and overshoes, and we dug into another feast. Ahhhh.

§

COLD HANDS ON COLD UDDERS

Fortified with eggs, ham, and fried bread, and thick stew, the boys once again put on their heavy clothing and headed into the cold. Outside, the evening chores awaited, as they did every night at the milking parlor, the granary, and the hayloft.

Freddy went to hand milk the five cows in the dairy

herd—cold hands on cold udders. Inside the closed, but unheated barn, he sat atop a milk stool with his head pushed, in turn, into each cow's right flank, welcoming her warmth. The wind drifted powdery snow under the barn door, while little white half domes of frozen milk clung to sides of his tin milk bucket.

Meanwhile, George and his dad fed the beef cows, pigs, chickens, and horses their evening ration of grain or hay…or both. They chopped through the ice on the tank and troughs, so the animals could drink. Within hours, these holes would freeze shut again.

With the animals fed, watered, and the milking done, the boys got out of the cold for the night. It'd take an hour for the sting of the cold to work out of their cheeks. They took off their shoes and massaged their feet and toes, to bring back warming circulation.

The day had been demanding and a struggle at times. But they stood up to it. Days such as this toughened them and the other farm kids.

That mile-long walk between home and school, with its fair and foul weather lessons, turned out to be their *right of passage.* It helped prepare them for later challenges of life—and there would be many.

TEN

THE WRONG COLOR CALF, TRYING TO FLY A ROCK, AND THE POWER OF POISON IVY

[*Wamego Reporter:* March 15, 1945] ~ **WAMEGO OVER THE TOP** ~ The annual drive for money for the War Fund Campaign of the Red Cross was held in Wamego last week. With the customary liberality of the Wamego folks, the drive was conducted without too much effort on the part of any of the workers. The Chairmen, Glenn Stewart and Gene Larson, want to thank all of the contributors, large and small, whose gifts ranged from 25c to $100.00.

THE WRONG COLOR CALF

"So boys," Uncle Alfred asked Freddy and George, "what do you think you'll do when you grow up?"

The three sat around a table in St. Luke's parish hall enjoying cookies after church, the boys with milk and their uncle with coffee. He reached for another oatmeal-raisin treat, and asked, "Are you going to be a farmer like your dad?"

George also reached for another cookie, paused and then his face brightened. "No. I'm going to play for the Brooklyn Dodgers and be like Dixie Walker."

The nine-year-old knew all about baseball—or so he thought. His dad played town team baseball in his 20s and talked a lot about old time players like Honus Wagner, Ty Cobb, and Babe Ruth. "You can come to some of my games, and if I'm a good player, maybe you'll get in free," George said.

Uncle Alfred smiled, then asked, "What about you, Freddy, are you going to be a ballplayer, too?"

"I guess I could, but I don't know. Maybe I'll play ball, or maybe I'll be a farmer with Dad. That would be great, and we could get a new John Deere, maybe a B or even an A. Maybe we should buy a big Case that would pull three 16-inch plows, 'cause we'd have lots of land."

"So, you and your dad are going to farm wheat, huh? What about cattle?"

"Yeah, we'll plant wheat on a thousand acres, and have a big herd of white-faced cows on a giant ranch. I'll get a palomino horse, like we saw at the Strong City Rodeo and ride out to check on the cattle every day."

"Sounds like you'll be a regular cowboy. Does that mean you want to be in the rodeo? Maybe be a Brahma bull rider or bust bucking broncs?"

Freddy's face clouded and he hesitated.

Ever helpful George answered for him. "He doesn't like rodeo much, Uncle Alfred. He tried it out by our barn and got bucked right off Maudie's skinny brown calf," he said, grinning while Freddy frowned.

"He didn't last more than two jumps—a couple of seconds. You should of seen him come in for a landing...just crashed down head first. It knocked the wind out of him and bent his glasses. An' he had stuff all over his head."

"But, maybe he just needs practice. Or, maybe he tried the wrong color calf."

"Well," Uncle Alfred said, his eyes twinkling, "You boys have a lot of time to decide. And remember you'll have lots of good choices, so ponder on them. But, be sure to get through high school first, or you might have to ride cows for a living."

§

On the way to school the next day, we talked about different jobs and there seemed to be a hundred choices. Could we help build liberty ships on the west coast like Uncle Houston or work in the woods like Uncle Luther in Michigan?

Or, would we live in town and sell new tractors or maybe have a grocery store? How about being a teacher or even a priest like Father

Davies? Maybe we could be an officer in the Army and lead troops in battle.

Army and other military troops were in everyone's thoughts those days, for World War II—still raging in Europe and the Pacific—reported the deeds of these men. They flew bombing runs, commanded ships, and led troops and patrols. Many times our play—when we weren't trying to rodeo—involved mock skirmishes where we imitated real life fighting men.

§

FAKE BULLETS FLEW

The low March sun was short-sleeve warm that Sunday afternoon when the boys went off to pretend war, along with the cousins, Danny, Denny, Dean, and Dwight Burgess—called the four 'D's for obvious reasons. After considerable discussion, Freddy and Danny both became squad leaders with Dwight, their only private. Denny and George—the same age—commanded younger Dean. The next issue was to decide which side would be Americans and which were the Japanese?

Since no one wanted to be the enemy, the winner of a BB gun shoot-off would get to choose his team's role. Freddy shot for his squad and hit a not too distant dried buttonweed pod three out of five shots. Denny hit it four times.

"Hey, that's nice shooting Denny. You knocked that buttonweed pod right off. You can be the Americans and we'll be the Nips. But, leave the BB guns here, we don't want to put out an eye," Freddy said.

§

At that, our patrols moved out in opposite directions to roam what we called the Canyon—a gully about 15-feet deep and a football field in length—south, down the road between the house and the mailbox. When we spotted the enemy, fake bullets flew as we battled back and forth with our sunflower stalk M1 rifles and willow limb Thompson submachine guns.

We patrolled in an up-and-down, over-and-back pattern that included much crouching behind brush or in eroded trenches. When the coast seemed clear, we'd dart from cover and often encounter enemy fire. This constant, high energy motion—a kind of unwritten rule—provided plenty of targets for both sides.

§

"Bang, bang, bang," Dwight said, pointing his sunflower stalk. His high squeaky voice sounded a bit metallic.

"Rat-a-tat-a-tat-tat," went Danny's willow limb submachine gun with a fine curved-branch handle, "Rat-a-tat-tat." Though bullets flew everywhere, every wound seemed to only be a scratch. And, those that did go down recovered—as if by magic—the instant the shooter's head turned away.

"Bang, bang, bang. Hey, I got you. You're dead, Dean. You gotta lie down. I got you right in the heart!" Freddy yelled from behind the pile of bush at the head of the canyon.

Half way across the open canyon floor, Dean shouted back, "You missed me. Anyway, you're out of bullets by now."

"You're cheating!"

"No I'm not. Besides, you can't be the one who shoots people all the time," Dean said. In the confusion, George and Denny dashed across to find protection in a shallow ditch, and Dean, wounded or not, escaped the other way.

The long battles continued with give and take and the occasional debate, until both patrols grew tired and dirty. Unlike real war, the boys called 'King's X' and headed back to the house to drink cold milk and eat cherry pie.

The patrols were only play—thank God—but they did learn what war was all about. No question, the war news, movies, stories, and other unusual events did affect the way the boys and others thought. One unexpected event that happened on the way home from school gave George a dream that, in time, transformed his life.

THE YELLOW AIRPLANE

The week after the canyon patrol, Barney and Barbara joined the boys on the way home through the Cotton's pasture on a clear, crisp spring day. The domed, bright blue sky hovered above and only a soft breeze stirred.

About ten minutes later—they were dawdling along—a steady hum reached their ears. The noise grew louder, and they scanned the sky for its source. Finally, George glanced over the trees to the east. "Over there…above Scully's place...look at that!"

A slow-moving, bright yellow airplane flew toward them. When it was almost overhead, it circled clockwise and eased lower and lower, with the pilot looking through his side window at the easy slope of the cow-path hill.

He circled around again, turned into the slight breeze—indicated by the smoke from Mrs. Cotton's chimney—and slipped still lower. Just above the ground, the engine and propeller noise dropped to a whisper and the landing gear touched down on the grazed down grass—a perfect three-point landing.

The plane slowed to walking speed and taxied toward the foursome. When it stopped, the pilot—wearing a giant white cowboy hat—cut the engine. The propeller spun a few more times and then quit turning.

"Wow, look at the size of that thing. It's huge," George said, walking toward it. "Man, those wings look heavy, and they're even too long to fit in the barn. How can they make it fly?" he said to no one. "And the propeller's made of wood. Wow, look at that!"

Next, his eyes examined the windshield. It appeared tiger-striped with oil streaks for some reason. Why is that?, he thought. Then his thoughts turned to the cowboy-dressed pilot, who dropped the side door and climbed out.

"Howdy, kids. Hope you don't mind me landing here, but I've been losing oil and figured I better stop and try to fix the problem. It could be that if I didn't the engine might freeze up."

With his long white teeth gleaming between his grinning lips, he added, "It's no fun flying with a dead motor. That makes flying really tough."

"What happens if the motor conks out? How do you get down?" Freddy asked.

"Let me tell you, son. It's like trying to fly a big rock with wings...an' the only direction is down. It can be like dropping a big hunk of coal off a bridge, though sometimes you can glide in like a paper airplane. That's why it's usually best to set her down early and fix the problem. Smart pilots do it that way if they can."

Then, studying his rapt audience, he said, "Of course, there was the time at the air show over to Rossville that I waited too long, an' I got in a world of trouble. I'm mighty lucky to be alive."

"What did you do? Could you glide down to land?"

"Well, sir, there were too many ditches and trees so I thought I'd crash for sure. Then, I seen this farmer pulling a big wagon load of hay with his tractor, so I lifted up the nose a bit to match his speed and then just settled down on the hay...and we kept on going at the same speed. That is, 'til the farmer saw me. He darned near wrecked us both before he stopped."

"I wouldn't recommend you try that, though. It's pretty tricky," he said, his blue eyes twinkling under the brim of his hat. "No sir, I wouldn't do that again."

"That wagon might have been going the wrong way, don't you know."

With that, he unhooked the engine cowling and started tightening the leaky oil line. As he worked, Freddy, Barney, and Barbara walked around the plane and wondered about the story.

George, overcome with both awe and curiosity, stared and stared at the plane. "Can we look inside?" he asked.

"Sure, take a peak. This is a Piper Cub. See the stick and those pedals? That's how I steer the plane. And those instruments help me keep track of things…though they don't help you much to find hay wagons."

Everyone marveled at the cowboy pilot's story and at their first close-up look at a real plane. But, it was George who was excited. He ran his hands over the long wings and the tail. Then he stared into the cockpit and had private thoughts.

How could a big machine like this land on a wagon or even in a pasture? Why did the bright yellow paint smell that way? What kind of person piloted an airplane? Could a farm boy learn to do that?

George stopped his daydreaming when the pilot finished his repairs, wiped the oil off the windscreen, and clicked the heels of his cowboy boots together. With a kind of bow, he climbed back into the plane and started the engine. After it warmed up for a few minutes, he waved goodbye, gunned the engine, and took off for points southwest.

George's heart pounded when the plane's yellow faded, little by little, into the sky's blue. He had been bitten by the flying bug and from that day started collecting airplane pictures from magazines.

Years later, he did learn to fly and became an Air Force pilot. Maybe it was all because of the real life experience with the yellow Piper Cub…for many such events changed people's lives.

A HOP TOO SLOW

Just a week later, Freddy, too, had one of those life-changing experiences. It must be said, however, that he never saw an adult do what he was about to do. He was showing off—as usual—when he received a dramatic lesson in animal behavior. While it didn't inspire him to be a zookeeper, it did provide a good lesson for future decision-making.

That afternoon, Barney, Barbara, and the boys were again in Cotton's pasture, almost to the barn. While a bobwhite called along a fencerow, the western sun gave the barn a big, dark shadow from which came an ambling skunk.

"Hey, look at that ole skunk," Barney yelled. "It looks like a stripped kitty, with a pointed nose."

The animal headed north around the barn, going where skunks go when they look for mice, worms, or even chicken eggs. "Man, those things give me the willies."

"Good grief, Barney," Freddy said, "She's just a skunk. They won't hurt you if you play your cards right. Here, watch this."

To make his point, he started bouncing clods alongside the skunk, testing what she would do. The skunk ignored them, though she may have walked a bit faster.

"I'm going to see where she goes," Freddy said, bold as usual. He hopped toward the animal. The skunk, of course, raised its tail and focused its rear end toward him. Freddy hopped back. The skunk hurried on.

Still curious, Freddy hopped forward again—closer this time. The skunk faked a tail raise, shrugged, and kept going.

"She's ignoring me. She doesn't care about me at all." He grinned, and again hopped close and then back.

The next hop must have been too close, and that's when it happened!

In the wink of an eye, Ms. Skunk's tail came up, and

from under it sprayed the most foul smelling, greenish liquid in God's entire world.

Freddy had been a hop too slow.

Bull's eye.

"Dang, dang, dang. She hit me in the belt. And, then she squirted my pants' legs and shoes," Freddy said, gagging on the overpowering stench.

George, Barney, and Barbara stood in shock while the skunk hurried into the taller grass along the fencerow. When it disappeared, Barbara did too. She ran toward Cotton's house with Barney right behind.

George, shook his head, laughed, and covered his nose, before heading for home at a trot. Freddy stood alone next to the barn for a couple of minutes, sorting out what went wrong, then began a slow trip north. Maybe the liquid would dry and the stench would go away on the trip home, he thought. It didn't.

Once home, he stepped through the kitchen door—smell and all—right into his mom's wrath. "Oh, don't you come in here like that. It's going to smell up the whole house. It makes me want to gag."

"Just how in the world did this happen? Don't you know better than to play with skunks? You do some of the dumbest things, John Frederick Burgess. Now, go around to the back porch this instant, and take that smell with you."

Moments later, she cracked the back door and handed Freddy a Mason jar of home canned tomatoes, some homemade lye soap, and a bucket of warm water from the back of the kitchen stove. "Here, use this to clean up with and leave your clothes out there."

"And, don't you come inside 'til you're rid of that smell."

Wrinkling his nose for the hundredth time, Freddy took off his shoes and stripped down to his underwear, tossing his skunky overalls and shirt on the edge of the porch. He scrubbed and cleaned—himself and then his clothes—until only a slight, lingering odor remained. Everything was clean…or so it seemed.

The next morning—again scrubbed with lye soap and in clean clothes—Freddy went to school as usual. When he entered the tiny building, however, what happened was not usual at all!

Mrs. Draper grabbed her nose, and with a look of obvious disgust said, "Whatever is that horrid smell?"

"Oh, that's Freddy's shoes," George said, again offering to help explain things. "Purdy bad, isn't it?"

Everyone stared and wrinkled their noses. George felt compelled to contribute to additional understanding.

"He had a test race with a skunk last night. And lost. Maybe he shoulda cleaned his shoes."

The unwashed shoes had waited on the back porch all night. In the morning, Freddy noticed a lingering smell, but figured the walk to school would fix that. Again, it didn't.

This poor bit of reasoning brought sharp words from gentle Mrs. Draper, and meant he'd spend the day in stocking feet...all because of his need to check Ms. Skunk's reactions.

It seemed for the boys, there was always something to test, from skunks to snakes to calf riding. And sometimes, they had to live with the results of an experiment gone badly.

Like Freddy and George, some adults in the area had interesting learning experiences, too. Some involved life and death situations.

DOING WHAT WAS NEEDED

March turned into April and with it came the showers. Lots of rain made the walks to school slick and sometimes miserable.

Rain was falling the Wednesday morning when the boys headed out, although it quit as they neared Cotton's farm. The sun broke from behind the clouds, and its brilliance highlighted the trees, greening grass, and wildflowers.

"Look where the cows walked through the wet

grass," George said. "You can even see trails in our pasture where the horses are, too." He pointed toward where the big draft horse Prince rested, while his mammoth teammate King grazed nearby.

The next morning, Prince was still not standing, and when the boys returned from school, King was at the barn alone. Something was wrong. Time to investigate.

They found Prince mired on the pasture slope that was full of boggy, seeping year-round springs where watery potholes lurked between giant clumps of almost inedible slough grass. His front legs seemed pointed straight down, for when he struggled to free himself he must have worked them deeper and deeper. With his back legs curled underneath him, he couldn't push away.

He was stuck and hungry. In a circle, as far as his neck could reach, Prince had eaten the vegetation, including the tough slough grass. Someone had to get him out and that meant them, for their dad was in Kansas City selling cattle.

At first, they tried to push Prince from the rear, hoping that would give him enough strength to free himself. Their efforts were feeble on the 2,000-pound horse. He was too big, and they just got themselves muddy.

"Let's go get the tractor," Freddy said. "Maybe if we pull on him, he can work himself out."

They hurried back to the shed and grabbed a spade, some rope, and a halter. They attached a 20-foot log chain to the Allis-Chalmers drawbar, and drove to the edge of the mire.

After some difficult digging behind Prince's front legs, they circled him with the rope and connected it to the chain. Would this work?

Third-grader George inched the orange tractor forward and Freddy pulled on the halter he'd attached to Prince's head. The big horse struggled and struggled, then using the taut ropes as anchor points, his front legs started working free.

Prince bucked and struggled in the mud with lots of

snorting and groaning. Little by little the tractor moved ahead, until Prince lunged forward on to his front knees.

For long moments, Prince stood shaking with black ooze dripping from his legs and belly. At last, he walked stiff-legged to the slough for a drink of clear, cool water.

In the end, Prince recovered, thanks to a pair of resourceful boys who learned by watching others and by testing life themselves. More practical lessons awaited the boys as they grew—some not as serious as a mired horse, but perhaps just as educational.

Take for example Freddy's encounter with poison ivy.

THE POWER OF POISON IVY

For some reason, Freddy's body didn't react to the evils of poison ivy like most folks. Normal grade schoolers dreaded the blistering the plant inflicted. Anyone finding the low growing 3-leafed menace—it grew about everywhere in Eastern Kansas—gave it a wide berth.

All, that is, except Freddy. In fact, he seemed to have an immunity that allowed him to touch it without harm. He even picked bouquets with which he teased girl schoolmates. And of course, he enjoyed bragging about his special, God-given powers.

However, as often happens in real life, Freddy got a little too creative, or at least overestimated his gift. And this would change him forever.

"I can even eat poison ivy," Freddy said to Maxine and Louise Straub and a couple of younger kids, as they prepared to leave school for the day. He held several branches high above his up turned mouth, much like a carnival sword swallower, as if he would gobble down the leaves.

The audience watched, not saying a word.

"This stuff doesn't affect me in the least," he said, and then he shook the bouquet and pretended to salivate over the ivy's delicious aroma. "Are you ready? Watch this."

Little by little, he lowered the poisoned salad into his mouth, and ground it with his teeth to demonstrate his appreciation for the flavor.

Mistake!!

Almost at once, Freddy started to itch, and threw down the weed. A rash formed on his lips and inner mouth. He scratched and rubbed and scratched. Soon, his reddened face resembled a baboon's butt.

His spellbound audience stared in silence, and then one by one turned and headed home—smiling. He'd finally got a dose of his own medicine. What would he look like tomorrow? It wouldn't be pretty.

Freddy's special powers disappeared that day as fast as one can say Calamine Lotion. When he reached home, his mom doused him with enough of that remedy to turn him pink forever.

Many days of itching, scratching, and scabbing followed. Which was worse, the itching and scratching or the merciless teasing heaped upon him?

While his test with poison ivy had flopped, he finally did heal—and learn! Unfortunately, it would take many more tests, in many more areas, before he'd learn real responsibility.

Lighting the school stove one winter day would prove to be another of his major challenges...with Freddy again 'learning the hard way.'

ELEVEN

HARD TO BEAT CENTRAL HEAT, MY BRAIN'S A-FRYING, AND THE CHAMPEEN GAS PASSER

[*Manhattan Mercury:* August 15, 1945] ~ **JAPAN ACCEPTS TERMS ~** The world entered a new era of peace today. Along the enormous battlefronts of the Pacific and Asia the mightiest forces of destruction ever assembled rolled to a victorious halt around the prostrate, vanquished empire of Japan. President Truman announced Japan's capitulation at 7 o'clock; Eastern War Time, last night. The act marked the beginning of a truce that will last a few days until General of the Army, Douglas MacArthur, as Supreme Allied Commander, can accept formal Japanese surrender.

HARD TO BEAT CENTRAL HEAT

At last, World War II was over—since May in Europe and August in the Pacific—and the world now knew peace. A sense of calm prevailed across the nation, though not so one could notice at Prairie View School, District 82, that frigid December morning.

"Hurry up, it's freezing in here-re-re," George said, his teeth chattering and his breath looking like puffs of smoke. He huddled between the one-room school's unlighted stove and the wall. "It's colder-r-r in here than out in the snow."

Emptying the coal bucket into the stove, Freddy said, "Time for kerosene and I'll light it up." He poured in a generous amount from the two-gallon can, and for good measure, added more. He shivered—he needed fast results—and sloshed in a third splash.

When Freddy added more, George got nervous. He'd learned the danger of too much kerosene. Last week—overcome by temptation—he lit some in a coffee can. Flames had balled upward, singeing his eyebrows, he'd dropped the can, and a patch of grass caught fire.

"That's gotta be enough! Put too much in and you'll burn the school down," George said, regretting their job of preheating the single 25-by-30 foot, one-room school before classes started.

"Aw, a little kerosene never hurt anybody. Besides this is a big stove. Nothing is going to blow it up," Freddy said. He poured in more kerosene.

"That ought to do it. It'll catch the first time for sure.

"Hand me six or eight of those," he said, nodding toward the large box of Diamond wooden matches, resting as always, on the end of the chalk tray along the wall.

Man-o-man, eyebrow-less George thought, he's going to burn us up! I'm getting to the far side of the teacher's desk. Then remembering the careless miner from last Saturday's movie, he said, "The explosion is going to blow you straight up...maybe through the roof!"

As usual, Freddy wasn't listening. "Ok, here goes. Stay down." With that, he struck the whole bundle of matches on the cast-iron stove, tossed this firebrand into the coal-gorged maw, slammed the door, and jumped for cover.

Baroovmp! Barooymp-uump-uump! Rattle, rattle, shake kabump, bump, screech!

The concussion rocked the stove. Noise thundered inside the closed room like the howitzers at Fort Riley.

Freddy, down behind the fourth row of seats, swallowed hard. He watched the oversized stovepipe rattle and pull apart high up where it formed an upside down letter L. Black soot spewed out, and then slowed into a gentle, downward dusting-fall.

"Man, oh, man," Freddy said with a grin. "Now that's the way to light a stove. That was some boom! Yeah!"

"That baby sure took right off when I flipped that match in there. Look at her go! It sure is hard to beat central heat."

Bright flames flickered behind the silica-paned door and licked at the remaining kerosene and the big chunks of anthracite. The blaze seemed to warm the room at once, but what about the soot?

George watched the black soot settle down. It dusted the floor, the teacher's desk, and everything in that end of the room. "Oh boyyyyy," he said with a low moaning sound. "What do we do now? How are we going to explain this? It's a mess. And, what about the smoke, leaking from that busted stovepipe?"

"Let's put the stovepipe back together first..." Freddy directed, "before it gets too hot to handle. Then we'll open the doors and let the smoke out."

He climbed on the teacher's chair and wiggled the black pipe back into place. More soot snowed down, so he handed George—still shivering and disgusted—the school's broom. Freddy then opened the school's front and back doors. This let the prairie wind—it ruffled papers and spun midget cyclones of soot—collect smoke on its way through.

The black soot presented a bigger challenge, for it resisted cleanup. It seemed sweeping and dusting encouraged it to seek out the wood grain of the floor and the desk. Still, after long minutes, the room looked almost normal. Most of the smoke had hurried outside, and with the doors closed, the room began to warm—at least near the stove.

For some reason, Mrs. Draper arrived a few minutes late that morning and hurried to start the school day. In her haste, she failed to see anything wrong and the boys dodged another bullet, and even received a compliment. "Freddy and George, you boys got a good fire going this morning. It's nice and warm in here, like a regular bonfire."

If she only knew....

§

> ***T***he day we lit the stove was very cold. We'd walked the one mile in ten-degree weather with lots of wind making it seem colder. The light cover of dry snow whipped from one drift to another and the cold made the trees, posts, and buildings seem brittle and fragile. Inside the school, the wooden floor had creaked and

snapped when we walked on it.

Once out of the wind, our faces had tingled and, when the room warmed, our cheeks became puffy. Soon, our bodies felt a sense of calm and safety—once the soot was cleaned up—inside the small, white, wooden school perched on a prairie knoll.

From a distance, Prairie View's sloping roof and bell tower had a certain charm. Charming or not, we knew it lacked many conveniences found in bigger schools. For one thing, our school had only one room, a single teacher, and even used outhouses instead of toilets.

However, our school did have a feature that city schools did not have. It had our central heater, er...stove, that students—appointed for each day—got to operate, either as fire starters, coal-bucket fillers, or damper tenders.

Our stove worked very well during moderate temperatures; however, in frigid weather—near zero or below—it struggled to heat the room from one corner to the other. That meant students in back had cold hands and feet. Their complaints encouraged the damper duty tender to adjust the spring-shaped handle of the flue for more draw.

The cold room also motivated the coal-bucket person into action, so that after several minutes of more coal and more flue, the stove often burned red-hot—roasting the students up front.

The damper tender then narrowed the flue and a cool-down process started. When those in back began to freeze again, the process was reversed. We were too hot or too cold all day long.

§

Whether hot or cold, the stove had a large appetite for coal, so the bucket detail ventured—again and again—to the coal shed-pump room-washroom to refill it.

"Freddy, will you and Bubba go out and bring in more coal?" Mrs. Draper asked, with a slight shiver. "We're just about out."

The two boys left their desks, grabbed the coal bucket, and then walked out the back door. A frigid gust of Kansas wind burst in, filling the room. All learning stopped for a time.

Outside, the bucket brigade walked through the open wall serving as a door of the icy-cold three-sided coal shed-pump room. Irregular lumps of coal—like frozen bodies—lay under drifts of powdery snow, sifting through wallboard cracks and whipping in through the open front.

Freddy started sweeping the drifted snow from the coal pile, while the shivering Bubba pulled out his shirt tail to use as a glove on the coal shovel's metal handle.

"Man, it's colder than a witch's you-know-what," Bubba said. "A guy could freeze his arse off in here." His teeth began to chatter.

"Yeah, and a smart guy would work faster," Freddy said, impatient with Bubba's lack of effort. "Hand me that shovel."

Bubba shivered, handed over the shovel, and stood watching Freddy work. Too cold in the coal room for horseplay, Freddy filled the spouted bucket—some coal and some snow—and headed inside. Bubba and the wind followed.

Again, learning stopped, with everyone waiting for the show. On cue, Bubba grabbed a lump of the snow-covered coal and tossed it atop the burning embers. Hissing and popping sounds from the melting snow erupted to Bubba's delight.

In went the rest of the coal and snow, and still shivering, he opened the damper all the way. That'll get us warm in a hurry, he thought. It did.

MY BRAIN'S A-FRYING

A few minutes later, everyone knew Bubba had been overzealous, for the stove glowed red hot. The little kids at the smaller desks up front began to roast and complain.

The only first-grader, Rayfield Straub, asked with a whine, "Mrs. Draper, can I move to the side table? My brain's a-frying."

The teacher nodded, and Rayfield and his brother Delafield—the only second-grader—took readers and paper to the table along the far wall. The temperature there was 10-20 degrees cooler.

Georgette Talley, the appointed damper tender, cut back the amount of draw and the inferno began to subside. After ten minutes, the red stove turned back to black and the heat evened out—except in the far corners.

Students around the room's edge now felt cold—including Rayfield and Delafield who moved back to the front row. Georgette dutifully opened the flue, and in just a half hour, brains were refried and the stove glowed hot. And so went the day.

Sometimes, another heating concern arose, for sometimes the early morning fire-starters arrived late and lessons began in a cold room. On those days, it always seemed freezing weather or high winds seeped into the not-so-well-weatherized building, and everyone—still bundled in coats, hats, and overshoes, and looking like prairie dogs poking out of holes—shivered around the slow-to-warm stove.

Those were times when wise Mrs. Draper held what she called special discussions. Since no one could concentrate, she diverted their attention by—of all things—making her students think!

UNHEATED GROUP DISCUSSIONS

"Alright children, since we are here around the stove, let's do something fun," Mrs. Draper said, taking minds off the cold.

"Who knows an interesting current event? It could be something you heard on the radio, or that happened at home, or does someone have a funny story to tell?"

The word *funny* somehow triggered the imagination of Louise Straub—older sister of Delafield, Rayfield, and Philomena from George's class. "Maybe I could tell about my mom's baking. Her chocolate cake turned out awful. She started mixing it up from a recipe book and then she got a phone call from her sister. When she got back to the kitchen, she read the wrong instructions and added in ingredients for chocolate frosting instead of cake."

Several 'prairie dog' heads poked out and looked at Louise. Cake was something they knew about.

"She stewed about it a while, but decided not to waste everything she'd put in, so she went ahead and baked it. It turned out ugly black, raised up only about an inch high, and was tough and chewy like bad taffy. The cat wouldn't even eat it, so she fed it to the hogs...and they kept asking for more!"

Several kids chuckled, and Mrs. Draper cleared her throat. Then she asked, "Who has heard of the United Nations? What can you tell us about them?"

Some heads poked back inside, but Freddy's face lit up. "The United Nations is a group of countries that want to work together for world peace. President Roosevelt got it started before he died."

"How many countries have agreed to be in the UN?" Mrs. Draper asked. "And where will the headquarters be?"

"Wasn't it 50 countries that signed up at first?" Freddy asked. "And, the headquarters will be in a new building in New York. I sure do hope we won't have more war."

"Good for you, Freddy. What you said is right, and no one wants war."

§

The war now became the topic for our discussions, and even though both Germany and Japan had surrendered it was something we heard plenty about. We were thankful it was over, for we all knew someone—an uncle, or cousin, or family friend—who had fought in some of the battles. Some had been wounded or killed on D-Day, at Anzio, at the Battle of the Bulge, or in the Pacific.

Iwo Jima, Saipan, and Okinawa were behind us, and bombing runs over Cologne and Berlin were over. We boys still talked about the machines of war, however, fascinated by the P-51 Mustang, the P-38 Lockheed Lightning, and the B-17 Flying Fortress. Tanks, trucks, jeeps, rifles, machine guns, and cannons all interested us. Terms, like AWOL (absent without leave), ASAP (as soon as possible), and SNAFU (situation normal, all fouled up), became a part of our language, and a soldier was a GI (Government Issue) in military lingo.

The girls talked about how the WACs, WAAFs, and WAVEs had served, and how the nurses cared for the wounded. Lulu Brockman had even wanted to be Rosie the Riveter and help build a Liberty Ship. The girls also talked a lot about how movie stars were still entertaining troops at the U.S.O. clubs.

Now, these troops were occupation forces keeping the peace throughout Europe and in Japan. Those war-torn areas were hard to manage, and bad feelings existed between the Russians and the rest of the Allies.

One occupation activity reported about the travels of an imaginary G.I. called Kilroy. His note was scrawled wherever servicemen passed through. It read: *'Kilroy was here!'* Somehow, the phrase even ended up scribbled inside the boys' outhouse.

§

Georgette Talley told a story she vowed was true. She said she'd heard of a man near Belvue who hooked up two milk cows to his hay wagon when his mules got sick. According to Georgette, when the man milked the cows that night, all he got was buttermilk and oleo.

Everyone laughed at Georgette's story, and that encouraged Bubba Brockman, the coal tender and nephew of Shorty Brockman, to share a story of his own.

"Did you hear about Otis McCord over by St. George? One night he was cutting through old lady Featheringil's chicken yard when he stumbled…

"…and his big wad of chewing gum popped right out of his mouth." Bubba paused.

George, always trying to be helpful, poked his head out and asked a thoughtful and sincere question.

"Oh, how did he ever get it back?"

With a big smile, Bubba took a deep breath. "You know, he looked and looked in the dark and never did find his gum…

"…although he thought he had four times!"

Several laughed out loud at Bubba's farmy joke and, though Mrs. Draper frowned a bit, a slight smile appeared when she turned her head. Bubba did well telling stories, even to a cold audience.

District 82 students long remembered the true-life lessons and entertaining stories told around the slow to warm coal stove. The learning events—some good and some not-so-good—made the one-room schoolhouse, there in the heart of the Kansas prairie, a special place.

THE PRAIRIE VIEW FROM PRAIRIE VIEW

Any person who ever attended a one-room country school, knows that the experience—privilege!—provided learning far beyond the usual. With it came an appreciation of the natural world, and in the boys' case, their school's name—Prairie View—had been picked for a good reason.

§

From our school's concrete steps, the Kansas Flint Hills' prairie stretched—and moved—in all directions. The grass moved, the wild flowers moved, and the wheat fields moved, ebbing and flowing like an ocean. Even the continuous rows of Osage Orange fence posts—to us at least—seemed to be on the march. One after another, up and down the hills in single file, they separated one farmer's cows from another's.

Peaceful trees, large and small, lined the roads, and milkweed and buckbrush clogged the fencerows. Plants and grasses sparkled in the brilliant sun beneath the bright blue of God's great high-canopied sky.

Wintertime snow turned the clods and clumps of grass into miniature white beaver mounds, and drifts built sculptured ledges. These filled in the ditches and furrows as if two giants pulled the landscape smooth from opposite directions.

Winter embraced the now barren trees, stark against the white backdrop, while lonely brown stems of prairie grass poked through the soft blanket in golden-tan contrast to the sun-reflecting snow.

In truth, our eyes saw a peaceful charm. And at Prairie View, our ears heard dozens of melodies as well, especially in warmer weather. Crickets, frogs, grasshoppers, and all sorts of birds sent vocal music into the air. Children frolicked, with boys yelling and—for reasons known only to God—girls screaming, as they played tag, or ball, or jostled on the teeter-totter. Visual and audio appeal seemed everywhere.

Most people marveled at the vastness of the prairie, but Prairie View School was often described as little. We laughed at that comment and said our schoolhouse wasn't little, it was tiny. The classroom appeared just a bit larger than a good-sized chicken coop. Tiny it was.

Perhaps, this smallness made us defensive, for in some ways, we envied kids who attended, what we thought at least, huge grade schools. Places like Wamego had maybe 300 students and the county seat, Westmoreland, with maybe 60. Even little St. George, about five miles away, had about 35—if you included its high school.

Prairie View School did not measure up in size, but we had something other schools could not have, for we had them—the greatest teachers in the world. No one could have been better than Mrs. Draper or later, Mrs. Straub.

Our schoolmates, the 11 to 13 others—depending on the year—from neighboring farms, ages 6-14, were the best, too. We got along most of the time, even though we had students in at least six of the eight grades nearly every year.

City schools, in our opinion, lacked our unmatched playground. We had acres of outdoors carpeted with grass instead of blacktop or gravel. We had jackrabbits and sparrows and meadowlarks instead of cars and houses. And, we had the quiet peace of the prairie with only the laughter of children, the sounds of the wind and wild animals, plus an occasional neigh of a horse or the moo of a cow.

We did not believe city schools lacked advantages. They no doubt had janitors—we didn't—and had consistent heat in winter. They probably had more learning aids and playground equipment, while we had only a mushy softball and a wounded bat with a flat side.

Kids in the city probably even had more than

one set of clothes for school. And, we were pretty sure that parents kept city kids' clothes and their bodies a whole lot cleaner than some farm kids.

§

A NOSE FULL OF SMELLS

Farm kids, with only one set of school clothes, faced some unique situations. For one thing, body odor, or b.o. as everyone called it, could be a nuisance. During warm weather—or if the stove got too hot—the b.o. smell could grow intense.

"Ugh, did you smell that Bubba Brockman today?" Maxine Straub asked during recess. "I wish he'd take a bath."

"He needs a good scrubbing with lye soap," her cousin Louise said, laughing. "Maybe my mom can loan the Brockmans some. It'll cure b.o."

"We could always give him a bath—you know—down at the pond," Freddy said. "We'd need to take off his clothes though. Who wants to do that?"

"Ugh…not me," Maxine and Louise said at almost the same time. "I'm not touching him…ever," Louise added for good measure.

The last of the quartet of fifth-graders, Georgette, smiled and said, "You guys leave him alone. Maybe the Brockmans just don't know any better. And besides, I've had to stay upwind of the three of you on a time or two," tall Georgette said to the other members of the school's only four-person class.

That ended the b.o. discussion; however, body odor was only one of the several smells that could waft through Prairie View School. Some good and some bad, each sent a special message to ponder and catalog.

Another odor needs a bit of mention—in delicate terms of course. Bubba Brockman was the biggest offender, although others made random contributions. For some reason, however, Bubba had the unique ability to break wind very indelicately.

Perhaps it was a family characteristic, or perhaps it was a type of deformity, or maybe just a fondness for beans. For without a doubt, Bubba was Prairie View School's 'champeen gas passer.'

To his credit, Bubba had the good sense and the ability to foul the outdoors and not the indoors—thank God—most of the time. Without a doubt, in the confinement of the classroom, many living things could have died.

§

Other smells, including the fragrance of the farm, were ever present. They increased when winter coats warmed up, and we suspected Mrs. Draper ended some discussions around the stove for that reason. Some lunch sacks on the hall bench smelled of burned hamburger or charred onions, or even of lard-fried eggs. We even knew that the sickly smell of Life Buoy soap seemed to grow stronger when the pump house-washroom neared freezing.

In contrast, we knew good smells as well, including books, and chalk, and paste, and paper, and of course, the smell of freshness of the great outdoors—when Bubba was being good. Maybe these smells stimulated us and in some ways encouraged our learning.

Did we get a good education? The answer was yes. We learned the Three Rs and how to live and work together. We also learned a couple of the basic lessons of life, about having fun and taking risks, and even about swinging like Tarzan.

TWELVE

ME RIDE LIKE TARZAN, THROUGH THE OUTHOUSE DOOR, AND GET HER SOME BLOOMERS

[*Westmoreland Recorder* - June 13, 1946] **LOCAL NEWS ~ LACLEDE** ~ by Mrs. Milton Rightmire - No church services next Sunday, June 16. Merle Max Osborn returned from Wichita, Saturday. George Wayne Walker attended the 4-H club State Round-up at Manhattan last week, returning home Friday. Mr. and Mrs. Edgar Ault and Mrs. Leslie Schwandt were in Topeka, Monday. Ronda and Judy Kolterman are visiting relatives in Wamego.

RINGING THE BELL AND UP THE FLAG POLE

No one knows when it started, but each morning at eight o'clock, Prairie View's giant school bell scattered birds and startled cows with its donging and bonging. Every day, someone pulled the long rope dangling through a small hole in the hall's ceiling—again and again.

A slow rhythmic pace from the steepled tower—dong, dong, dong—signaled an older girl had the assignment. Dong, dang, dong, dang, dong, dang—a fast chain of tolls—suggested an older boy. They said when Jim Scully was an eighth-grader, he pulled so hard it flipped the bell over, a practice now outlawed.

Donging the bell—a prized assignment—presented a challenge for lightweight George. He needed help to start the big bell rocking in its giant frame. However, after some bigger person gave the rope a couple of pulls, George would grab on and go for a bell rope ride. Up and down, up and down, as if he and the rope were one. His feet never touched the floor. Bell ringing made his week.

"Me…swing on grapevine. Me…swing uppppp… toooo tree…," he said in a whisper. "Me ride like Tarzan…me…go save Cheetah…!" In his drama, he mentally directed himself to save a monkey, never once feeling any reason to save Jane, a detestable female.

On and on he flew, clanging and tolling, grapevining toward the sky, until one of two things happened: Mrs. Draper sent someone to stop him or his hands began to give out.

Even then, he'd make the ride last as long as possible, relaxing little by little while the bell lost its energy. With a forlorn expression—as if reluctant to leave Cheetah—he'd let go, look for blisters, and then go to his seat to await another bell ringing day.

§

***A**ll boys relished the noise and the rope rides from bell-ringing, and we were no exceptions. On the other hand, girls rang the bell with less enthusiasm, always aware of the potential of boys peeking up their skirts. Perhaps some boys, being boys, did enjoy peeking, but certainly all boys enjoyed showing off, as they sometimes did outside at the flagpole.

Someone always seemed willing to risk his or her neck trying to climb it. No one ever made it to the top because of its slick metal surface, but someone tried it nearly every day.

After all, the flagpole was considered part of our playground equipment, along with the softball, the flat-sided bat, the teeter-totter, and the hitching rail. That was all there was, so Prairie View students had to try climbing the pole—because it was there. Some could climb well, some a little, and some not at all, and so turned to other pursuits.

We marveled at Bob Riniker who—he couldn't climb the flagpole—could walk the teeter-totter, balancing the seat board horizontally while standing with pride at the center. We believed he would one day be a circus high-wire walker.

Besides pole climbing and teeter-totter walking, other outside activities included softball, tag, and chase games. But before playtime, on fair weather days, we carried out a solemn duty. Gathered around the flagpole, we stood at attention while a couple of students hoisted the Stars and Stripes to the top.

§

"Freddy, it's your turn to raise the flag today," Mrs. Draper said. "Watch out for the wind, it is pretty gusty out here. We don't want the flag to get away from you and fly into the fence."

Hence, the ritual began. With Barney Gava at his side, Freddy connected the first clip. The breeze snapped at the red, white, and blue banner, unfurling it in the wind.

"Hang on, she's blowing today. Got the other clip? Good, I'll let her go," Barney said, then stepped back, hand over heart, feeling very patriotic. Freddy pulled the rope and the flag inched up the pole.

So Freddy, or George, or Rayfield Straub, or Delafield Straub, or Louise Straub, or Maxine Straub, or Philomena Straub, or Pauline Straub, or Rita Straub or one of the Waggoners, or Barney, or someone else, each day solemnly—maybe not Bubba Brockman—ran the flag skyward. The Kansas wind might blow and gust, but the students stood tall and watched Old Glory whip and flutter from atop the shiny metal flagpole.

Everyone now said the Pledge of Allegiance, outdoors when nice and indoors when cold, rainy, or too windy. The salute over, Mrs. Draper gave an order that started another ritual.

§

IT'S TIME TO GET STARTED

She did this every day, the same way, over and over again, until with smirky faces we'd mouth the words when she said, "It's time to get started, boys and girls." We guessed she liked routine.

At her direction, we moved to the hard wooden seats of our hard wooden desks—sentenced as captives, like we sometimes felt—for the rest of the day. In truth, lots of breaks came our way: recess, lunch, recitation groups, and even trips to the blackboard to do math problems. The more creative enjoyed self-initiated diversions as well, like trips to the outhouse, to the pump for water, and some even visited the 12 or so books on our library shelf.

Still, the hard desks, held together with long black bolts, lacked comfort and provided plenty of togetherness. They stood fastened four in a row on a pair of long two-by-four runners. Five columns totaled 20 desks—we only needed twelve or so—and each had a wooden flip-top with storage space below for books, pencils, crayons, and paper. A pencil groove and an inkwell hole decorated the downward slanting top we used as a writing board.

A filigreed, black iron frame secured the desks, with the back of the seat of one, becoming the front of the desk behind it. The smaller seats were in front with the largest in the back and the hard wood and iron made our desks almost indestructible.

Almost is the operative word here. We never saw anyone break a desk, except for a few seat hinges, but they weren't resistant to all forms of punishment. Bubba, a self-styled woodcarver, found a way to modify a back row desk top with his pocketknife.

To our surprise, he carved his full name in the desk, "Bubba Bleford Brockman, Jr.," seven times—in letters more than two inches high. We assumed what limited the number of 'signatures' may have been the unfortunate length of Bubba's name.

He outlined each letter with pencil marks—plus a spill of tomato soup—that gave the block letters depth and character. The desk turned out to be a sort of school landmark we could show off to the right kind of visitor.

Prairie View School did, indeed, have some interesting features, and that included our lunch storage area—sometimes known as the lunch treatment facility.

§

HOT AND COLD LUNCHES

Each day, students left their lunch sacks or pails in the eight-foot by ten-foot entry hall under the bell tower. In the warm weather of early fall or late spring, the hall warmed and without refrigeration, so did the lunches. This provided a hot noon meal of sorts.

Wintertime lunches, on the other hand, presented problems if the temperature stayed below freezing. Many eaters faced a lunch of frozen sandwiches. "My sandwich is hard as a rock," Bubba said, bonking his desk with three laminated baloney slices welded with frozen mustard between two slabs of bread.

"Mine, too," said George, trying to pry bread from his meat with his pencil, which broke and left a lead mark trail across the white bread. "How am I gonna eat this?"

Sandwiches to George, frozen or not or filled with

farm grown beef, pork, or chicken, were huge, lifeless creations. The meat—the best in the world—stacked between thick slabs of homemade bread and dredged with mustard, didn't fit his mouth.

"I hate these sandwiches. They're as hard as a sledgehammer. You could break windows with them."

Prairie View students just learned to live with what they had, lunches, weather, desks, or school. So George, Bubba, and everyone else made do with what they had, for they problem-solved, adapted, and learned many things in the process—including how to clean outhouses.

THROUGH THE OUTHOUSE DOOR

Schoolhouse cleanup came after school each Friday. Since there was no janitor, Mrs. Draper offered students an unbelievable incentive for each of the many jobs to be done. There were plenty of takers because her reward of a store bought candy bar was a unique treat for just doing a little—in some cases very little—work.

The jobs included cleaning the hallway, the classroom floor, the blackboards and erasers, emptying the stove ashes, and the wastebasket. Someone filled the coal bucket and several helped dust up what the wind had blown in. Over time, even evidence of Freddy's stove-starting disaster faded.

The youngest kids cleaned the chalk-packed erasers by dashing them together outside. That sent some white dust into the prairie sky, with the remainder rubbed across their overalls or dresses. The erasers got clean, but chalk marks ended up everywhere!

George learned Mrs. Draper's body language and knew when she was about to seek volunteers. And when the time came, he was ready. When she opened her mouth, he interrupted.

"I'll go clean the boys' toilet!"

She nodded okay and away he went to use his remarkable cleaning discovery. He had found that a single pail of water would do the job.

Since the outhouse door was hidden from the teacher's view, he'd prop it open and unload the entire contents of the pail in one quick motion. Sploosh—and the job was done. One sweet deal, George reckoned, visualizing a Payday, a Snickers, or a Milky Way.

This dubious—though fast—cleaning technique did have some drawbacks. If he returned too early, it might be a tip off that he'd taken a shortcut, so he'd stay hidden behind the tiny building for a discreet amount of time—staring at his work and smiling.

George's wait had other side effects—dealing with the ugly smells. His solution: hold his shirtsleeve to his nose and watch irregular, but interesting, patterns form as the walls dried.

George's eyes also traced the cobwebs in the upper corners, sometimes spotting a spider preparing a supper of a hog-tied fly. He always stayed clear, convinced that every spider was a Black Widow.

When he felt Mrs. Draper would assume a well-scrubbed outhouse, he'd take his empty pail, and unused broom and brush, back to the pump house. Then he'd get in line for his candy.

"Thank you, Mrs. Draper," he said with a satisfied smile and a bit of a disguised smirk. Victory again, although it was a good thing Mrs. Draper didn't check his work.

George did learn later—in the real world—that hard work and quality control go hand in hand to produce adequate rewards, for not all life is play. But for now....

§

GAMES AND SUCH

Barbed-wire pasture fence surrounded three sides of our playground with a dirt road on the other. The two acres of trampled grass got mowed once in a while by a neighbor on the way to his hayfield or when a school board member—

perhaps trying for re-election—came by to cut the grounds and the ball field.

Our softball field on the east side of the building had a grassless first base path, and a bare spot near the girls' outhouse marked home plate. Girls seemed reluctant to use the tiny house during a ballgame. Maybe, we thought, they didn't like us watching them go into the toilet...or something like that.

On the ball field, some grass survived between first and second, more endured between second and third, and a lot of grass filled the lane between third and home. That was because recesses didn't produce many runs.

Since we could never field two nine-person softball teams, we played workup. It took nine people—fewer if interest was low—at the fielder positions with the other players as batters. When a batter made an out, he or she went to right field, and everyone else worked up one place.

If no one made an out, the fielders held their positions all recess, and some batters, like the older Rita Straub, batted on and on. She had a powerful uppercut swing, and often sent the ball past the boys' outhouse and under the pasture fence in centerfield, to the gully below. Rita could out hit most boys, so they often sought other games.

"Hey, let's play stink today. I'll draw the line," Danny Riniker said, scraping the dirt with his heel. "You five girls be one team and us guys will be the other."

"Don't come over on our side of the line, or we'll tag you good," he added with a grin. "We're gonna have all five of you in jail in no time."

Daring—and speedy—Louise Straub dashed into enemy territory and sped in a circle around Danny. Bingo, he was caught! He wanted to argue, but he'd been trapped fair and square, so off to jail he went. There he'd wait for one of the guys to slap him with a 'get out of jail' tag—without getting caught on the wrong side of the line in the process.

The two ends of the hitching post served as the jail for the sides, and it often came between taggers and jail break attempts—with the whole game a lot of running and chasing…and plenty of arguments.

In the winter snow, we played another game of tag called Fox and Geese. Someone trampled a wheel pattern and soon we were chasing each other around the circle or across the spokes. Dressed in heavy coats and overshoes, we burned up lots of excess energy.

Still, after all the chasing, we had trouble settling down at the end of the recess. Our outdoor games were fun. But then so were the indoor activities.

§

SCHOOL HOUSE CHRISTMAS

Christmas activities highlighted the school year. One big event that led to delight—sometimes anguish—was the drawing of gift exchange names.

"Oh, man, oh, man, I got Rita Straub's name," George said to fellow third-grader, Bubba, during afternoon recess. "Yuck!"

"Dang, that ain't good, Kilroy."

"I'd rather take a beating with a hedge post…then draw a seventh-grade girl's name."

"Man-o-man. What you gonna do? Get her some bloomers?"

Bubba took off with George in hot pursuit, vowing bodily harm. The chase soon ended with both boys leaning against the hitching rail panting…and laughing uncontrollably.

"Yep, that's it. Bloomers are a good idea. Maybe I'll try to find her some with red spots!" George said, with a snort that fired air and other things out of his nose.

"Or maybe you should get her some that are nudie pink." More laughter.

The reality was George—or any guy—did not deserve to draw a girl's name, above all, the name of an older woman. Getting Rita Straub, or fifth-graders Maxine and Louise Straub, or Georgette Talley made a person tease-bait for sure.

"Guess you must be in love with her, huh?" Bubba asked. "Do you do a lot of smooching?"

By this point in the drama, the boys and their buddies rolled with laughter, including the tease-bait George. He'd just have to find a gift for a disgusting female—under the one-dollar limit.

Drawing another boy's name would have been different. That meant escaping the pestering from friends and shopping for something he might want to borrow one day. But, for boy or girl, everyone knew the gift exchange capped off the day of the Christmas pageant.

The pageant—taking weeks of planning—involved every kid in school. Bigger students created the stage by attaching the old black, musty, wrinkled, and somewhat tattered curtains with hog rings to baling wire stretched across the room and along the sides.

The front of the classroom developed into a square stage with small rectangular rooms to either side. The pig rings slid easily to open and close the front curtain between acts.

"Jim, would you please slide the curtains back and forth for us?" Mrs. Draper asked. The biggest boy in school, eighth-grader Jim Scully, moved the curtains through every possible situation. "Thank you, Jimmy. See how well our stage works, boys and girls. We'll have a splendid theater for our pageant."

The makeshift theater consumed a third of the small schoolroom and triggered plenty of holiday excitement. Many giggled, and for some reason, a lot of kids poked each other. Were these signs of nervous anticipation? Silly question.

Classes went on—there were inconveniences—as usual, though the first- and second-graders kept eyeing the mounds of folded curtains that balanced on the wires above their heads. Some class time went for pageant practice, for some had to learn speaking parts, others how to move curtains and props as stagehands, and everyone needed to practice the Christmas carols again and again. Mrs. Draper, using a pitch pipe, led the singing.

Soon it was time for dress rehearsal, and George, wearing a tinfoil-covered oatmeal box for a crown, began to deliver his few short lines with force and a bit of dread. With a bit of flair, he extended his hand toward the first- and second-graders, wearing old bathrobes.

"Greetings, princely Wise Men from the east. Come into my castle and tell me why you have come so far," he said. "I want to know, for I am the great King of Babyland."

"Forsooth, I am the great king, Neville Can Ester!"

Red faced, George knew he'd said Nebuchadnezzer wrong again. Laughter filled the room...directed at him. What if he couldn't say it in the show?

"Mrs. Draper," George said, "why do I have to say that name? Is this really a part of the Christmas story?"

"Just pronounce it, Neb-bew-canned-nez-sor. This person is important to our story. You'll be able to say the name just fine. Just pretend it's the name of your favorite ballplayer."

The man with the long name—at least at Prairie View School that year—was part of the Christmas story. George, with a deep breath, thought about ballplayers Leo Durocher, Joe DiMaggio, and Red Schoendist. Later, he worried and practiced...and practiced and worried.

Pageant night arrived clear and cold with a silvery, half moon sparkling on the frozen snow, as cars crunched to a stop alongside the schoolhouse. A festive mood filled the building while kids and parents crowded into the area in front of the stage.

The room smelled of the cedar Christmas tree holding small paper chains and popcorn strings. The space seemed too small for all the parents, the stage, the props, and all of the actors...plus the teacher-director, turned spoken-line prompter. The old potbelly stove took up room too, standing in the corner and blocking one side curtain.

Half a dozen coal oil lamps cast shadowy light from high shelves with people adjusting to the shadows the way they did at home. A weak glow from a single lamp leaked through a side curtain and marked the spot where Mrs. Draper cued the actors.

Another lamp played a very important role. It illuminated the stage from within, and became an integral part of a campfire that, as if by magic, appeared in every scene.

Some scenes had several actors who told the story or sang together. Freddy had several spoken parts that he wiggled and shifted through. Later, he lost his nervousness when he sang with the choir, and during his solo of *Away in the Manger* when he stood in the middle of the stage all by himself—with no accompaniment—and sang with energy and on key.

"I love thee Lord Jesus, Look down from the sky,
And stay by my cradle, 'Til morning is nigh."

While Freddy sang beside the flickering campfire, his dad nodded in time with the music, a lump rising in his throat. Tears of joy ran down his mom's cheeks, and other parents looked her way and smiled.

In this setting, the cut down blue and red housecoat turned Freddy into a shepherd. Towels, big shirts, and extra big leather belts dressed kings, wise men, and Mary and Joseph. Pauline Straub's China-headed doll was baby Jesus.

§

Our performance—we were convinced—must have rivaled a Broadway show, or at least one put on at Wamego's High School. We had practiced and practiced. Mrs. Draper, our producer, director, and musical expert, somehow kept us singing on key—except for a couple of timid souls, and of course, Bubba who didn't know the meaning of gentle.

When Jim Scully and Bob Wagoner closed the curtains for the last time, the pageant ended to warm applause that sounded like thunder to us. Had we really been that good? Had we put on that great a show?

Of course we had. We had done it, with good singing and some not so good, even with botched lines—yep, someone messed up Nebuchadnezzer again!—and delays to add coal to the big stove, the show had gone on, amid a flickering campfire light and in the cedar-scented room! The pageant was the first event of this special night!

The next activity was when we gave our parents gifts: embroidered potholders for moms and hand-stitched wallets for dads. The many oohs and aahs and thank yous touched us. Wow!

§

Then came the under-a-dollar gift exchange with most presents costing about 30 cents. During this last event of the evening, George gave Rita Straub a teeny bottle of 32-cent perfume from Duckwall's Five and Dime. She splashed on plenty—it must have been good—and its odor soon overpowered the cedar scent, and any lingering body odor from the 30 or so in attendance.

Right on cue—to most everyone's surprise—the lamps flickered and Santa Claus came "ho, ho, hoing" in the front door...along with a rush of cold air. He moved about in his bright red and white costume grinning with a funny smile—he may have had a beer or two on the way from the North Pole—even stopping to sloppily kiss several of the mothers.

Santa presented each student with a small toy and a bag of candy, then turned to leave, saying Mrs. Claus needed him at home. Santa, acting like one of the dads, exited and the evening was over.

The show had been great...the boys felt that for sure...and they now knew music, drama, and staging, too. In truth, through the years, they also gained a good mastery of reading, writing, and arithmetic—enough for Freddy to earn the top score on the Pottawatomie County Achievement test at the end of the eighth grade. This was a grand success for the tiny school, and for the wiggly redheaded kid.

In the final analysis, bell ringing, chasing, softball, cleaning outhouses, singing, and play acting took a lot of effort. Even book learning required strength and vigor. Where did the fuel for these strenuous activities come from? Where could the boys go to find the energy?

THIRDTEEN

IT'LL SUCK OUT MY STRENGTH, BOX TOP TREASURES, AND HAVE TO SELL THE KIDS

[*Westmoreland Recorder* – June 20, 1946] ~ **W.S.C.S MEETING** - at the church on Thursday evening, June 6. The business meeting was conducted by the vice-president in absence of the president. An executive meeting is to be held on the evening of June 21, at the church. All committee chairmen, group leaders, and officers of the society are asked to be present. It is time for our quarterly reports which must be submitted by July 1.

IT'LL SUCK OUT MY STRENGTH

"Uggggh! Mom I can't eat this, I think I'm gonna conk out," George said. "I might have to vomn-a-mit." The skinny nine-year-old squirmed at the breakfast table. "I'm going to gag."

Looking at the lumpy and smelly substance in his bowl, he said to himself, this stuff looks alive. Why do they make cereal so squishy and cover it with cream like that? Maybe it'll suck out my strength? When this Cream of Wheat kills me, that'll prove it's poisonous.

Just then the battery-powered RCA radio started playing the Cream of Wheat jingle. Oh, no, he thought, not that. How can anybody believe that song?

'Cream of Wheat is so good to eat.
Yes we eat it every day;
We sing this song, it will make us strong,
And it makes us shout "Hooray!"
It's good for growing babies
And grown-ups too to eat;
For all the family's breakfast
You can't beat Cream of Wheat!'

He shook his head. The only thing good about Cream of Wheat is that tune. Maybe they made this smell to kill children. He grinned at his weak joke, and then frowned. How could anyone eat this junk—any cereal for that matter—and shout hooray?

Yep, he thought, all cereals are crud: Cream of Wheat and Quaker Oats and Kellogg's Cornflakes and Post Toasties and…Malt-O-Meal. That's the worst. It's just a brown blob. I'm maybe gonna gag just thinking about it.

"Why does a person have to eat cereal? I know it's gonna kill me."

"Why, cereal is good for you. You'll grow up big and strong like Jack Armstrong," his mom said. "Besides, if no one ate cereal, how could there be radio shows? Without Cream of Wheat you'd miss *Big Jon and Sparkie* on Saturdays."

"Maybe I don't want to listen to them or to *Let's Pretend* any more. Maybe I don't want to hear any more about leprechauns and talking animals."

"George David, you quit complaining and eat that cereal this minute…or else." That got his attention. This was the wrong time to think about radio shows, or gagging, or death, or what he didn't like. So, while the speckled light from the low spring sun shone across the kitchen table, he struggled with his problem.

Though somewhere, a white-faced calf bawled and a grasshopper clicked his legs together, George postponed any action. I just can't stand that buttery-tasting cream. Yeah, maybe that's it, he thought, his rambling mind concluding that it was the cream that made him sick.

§

So in a flash, Alma, Louise, Claudette, or some of our other cows became the scapegoats. They produced the whole milk that we cranked through the cream separator twice each day. By some miracle, what went in as whole milk flowed from the machine as one stream of pale, golden cream and a second stream of porcelain-colored skim milk.

The offensive cream—our assessment—that oozed from the top spigot did taste a lot like butter, and seemed most unfit for hot cereal. As our thinking came together, we realized the cream caused our stomach aches and uninvited belches. How could we endure what the folks forced on us and often made breakfast a time of conflict?

Picture the battle scene around the well-worn, oil cloth-covered kitchen table: oppressive grownups in one army and helpless children in the other. Our folks won the battle if we ate and we won only if we avoided the cream-covered, detestable white or brown stuff.

Over time, Mom formed many battle strategies and creative tactics. These included pleas, threats, coercions, promises, bribes, common reasoning, uncommon reasoning, scripture teachings, tears, and even the getta-stick threat.

"Eat your cereal, or I'm going to get mad. And drink your Ovaltine. We paid good money for it. It's highly nutritional, you know," she said, repeating the Ovaltine commercial's mundane sales pitch. To us, when mixed with rich whole milk, it tasted vile. Ovaltine was chocolate-flavored toxic waste.

"Don't you want to grow to be a strong and healthy All-American Boy?"

To tell the truth, we reckoned that if radio hero Jack Armstrong had been primed with Ovaltine, he'd never have been capable of heroics. Further, if the Roman Army had marched into Gaul with rations of Cream of Wheat or Malt-o-meal or Ovaltine on their breakfast menus, the face of history would have changed.

A final plea came when Mom said, "You better eat that food; just think of all of the poor, starving children in China." Most children of the

'40s heard this shallow ploy, and we wondered if Chinese parents pushed fish heads and rice on their children with such fervor.

In the final analysis, the folks' attempts at child psychology seldom worked, for they bred counter-tactics. With great imagination, we learned to avoid eating the very things our loving parents thought they should force-feed us.

§

BREAKFAST TORTURES

On this particular day, whining was a good, though not foolproof, way to avoid breakfast tortures. "Oh, my stomach hurts. I think this gives me die-rear. Can't I just eat toast?" George asked. "Please?"

Then, being blessed with a special ability—he could even use it when he yawned—he filled his eyes with tears. The sides of his mouth turned down to form a sad-looking upside-down 'U' and salty tears came glistening out. His mom looked on with both pain and determination.

So, inside the house, the tension grew. Outside, sparrows chased each other in the mulberry tree. A meadowlark trilled his call from a garden fence post. There was lots of happiness in the winged world. But then, the birds didn't have to face Cream of Wheat bathed in whipping cream.

So, George kept whining and tearing until this ploy lost its effectiveness. Then he turned to Plan B...stalling. He excelled at dawdling.

Like a slow moving snail, he filled his cereal spoon with a dip it, fill it, empty it, and refill it technique. Glassy-eyed, his gaze followed each drop of cream pouring drip by drip from the spoon back into the bowl. His spoon never reached his mouth.

When he sensed one-more-second-of-filling-and-refilling was about to bring on parental wrath, he inched the spoon mouthward and took the smallest nibble, dribbling milk down his chin in the process. His dad looked at him, frowned, shook his head, and turned to concentrate on the morning farm market reports coming over the radio.

Dawdling worked because George was very accomplished—almost professional quality—at moving slow. As he nibbled again, his mother seemed satisfied and turned her attention to his brother. Freddy had been safe while George was the problem, but now he had to come up with his own avoidance technique.

"So, Mom, when you were a girl," Freddy asked, cocking his head to the side, "how far did you walk to school every morning?"

Good one.

"Well, we had to go a long way. It was maybe a half mile, but it was all along the street. There weren't any sidewalks in that part of Bergland, so we had to watch out for cars. Sometimes we'd get splashed when it was raining and the ditch was full of water.

"Your Aunt Annabel got drenched one day and had to go back to the house to change. Your Grandma was so mad at her. She also got a tardy mark on her report card."

Time for another question. "What did girls wear to school in the olden days?" This brought forth information about the clothes his mom had worn to grade school in the years before and after 1920.

"What was it like to walk in blizzards?" Freddy asked, avoiding quick yes or no questions.

Again, his mom felt compelled to reply. She seemed delighted her son wanted to hear about her trials during Northern Michigan snowstorms. "Sometimes the snow was so deep and the drifts so high, they canceled school and we'd stay home all day."

"What did you do when you stayed home from school?"

Again, his mom shared about her past, and explained how she and sister Annabel played as girls. She described her doll with the painted china head that cracked when she dropped it and explained how they changed their dolls' clothes and gave them pretend baths. She was so glad her son was interested.

On a good day, two or three of these questions were worth several minutes of explanations or stories. And, as long as the stories lasted, the spoons stayed at rest.

On this morning, the boys had stalled long enough for their mom's built-in…'you can't be late'…clock to cause her anxiety. As she did every other morning, she stressed over their getting to school on time. "Will you stop playing with your food and eat? It's getting late."

A couple of half-hearted nibbles followed and then she said, "Alright, you've eaten enough. Go brush your teeth and get your lunch sacks. You've got to get going, or you'll be late."

The boys smiled at each other. They'd made it through another breakfast without dying. No made-for-kids cereal killer deaths today. For now, the family war was over, and happily, most other meals were battleless because a table filled with appealing foods ended the need for parental coaxing.

AH, NOW THAT'S MORE LIKE IT

While doing chores the next morning, a welcome smell floated from the kitchen. "Let's hurry up and get to the house, Mom is cooking ham," George said, with a sense of urgency for a change. "Man, am I hungry. I could eat a horse."

§

> **W**ith a real breakfast beckoning to us, we hurried through our tasks without even noticing the tiny dew diamonds dazzling in the just risen sun. Nor did we sense the nighttime creatures going off to hide, while daytime bugs and animals began to stir.
>
> We were even unaware of the robins who,

softly at first and then with enthusiasm, chirped in the trees behind the barn. In our haste, we even missed the chattering sparrows that flew down to help themselves to the scattered chicken feed.

But, like all of God's creatures, we felt the calm and peace of the morning. There was a rightness in the world, enhanced by the aroma calling us to breakfast. The coal burning kitchen range had done its job and from Mom's heavy, cast iron skillet came thick-cut ham, browned on both sides.

Dad had cured the hams right on the farm, stuffing smoke-flavored salt down to the bone in holes made with a sharp piece of shingle. He then hung them, with a certain amount of satisfaction, from hooks in the smokehouse ceiling. The curing hams filled that room with an astonishing aroma that lingered even after they cured.

Breakfasts featuring this ham, or home-cured bacon or unsalted, fresh side-pork along with farm fresh eggs produced no battles. They did, however, include a lot of grease, for in those days, the world thought fat kept out the cold and provided energy.

And, we ate these meals with gusto, for no hot or cold cereal measured up to meat, eggs, potatoes, and homemade bread toast. Yet, while it may seem strange, cereal—with some regret on our part—did have a special kind of appeal. Eating—or at least disposing of it—could lead to wonderful treasures!

§

BOX TOP TREASURES

"Mom, I just think I need some Rice Krispies for breakfast," George said, a couple of weeks later. "My lips are just smacking for some of them."

"Well, imagine that, you're asking for cereal. Will you eat it or do you just want to order some box top treasure from Kellogg's? We're not going to buy you something and then have you waste it."

"Oh, we like Rice Krispies, don't we, Freddy? We like its snap, crackle, and pop. And, you probably should get two boxes. We might need two coupons."

"Yeah," Freddy said, "that's a good idea. I can eat a whole box all by myself. And, we can get the prizes really cheap with the coupons. You'd want us not to spend a lot of money, wouldn't you?"

§

And so the die was cast, because cereal companies, in their wisdom, had hooked us—and most kids—and backed us into a corner. They offered treasures we just had to have...and each required several box top coupons. But, to get those little plastic warplanes, magic capes, a decoder ring, or a Lone Ranger mask, somebody had to eat the cereal—boxes of it.

So, that Saturday night, Dad left Trivett's grocery carrying a sack holding a pair of Rice Krispies boxes. Those two boxes provided just the right amount of coupons to get an amazing decoder ring.

To our regret, our folks worked out a simple, but effective, strategy that caused some light skirmishes between our giant parents and us Lilliputians. The rule was to eat until a box was empty...before sending for any prizes. Then and only then, could we mail the box top coupons and hard-to-come-by money, to the homes of Kellogg's or Post Cereals, in places like Battlecreek or Kalamazoo.

This rule forced us to somehow get rid of a lot of cereal, thick cream and all, in order to keep the peace and to hurry our prizes closer. Through trial and error, we did devise an expert disposal method. We'd fill our bowls to the top and then only eat half of it. The uneaten cereal ended up in the dog's dish. Maybe that was wasteful, but Pep didn't complain.

Nor did we complain about our dinners and suppers, for most of the time, our table groaned with the weight of tasty food. There was plenty to eat and much of it was food we helped to raise.

§

NO SLIM PICKIN'S AT OUR TABLE

"Boys, let's go dig some new potatoes and see if we can find a few peas that are ready," their dad said. The mid-May forenoon, bright with sun, seemed fresh and calm under a sky of cloudless blue. "Those little spuds and fresh peas are the best vegetables there are."

For the past few months, the family's vegetables had come from Mason jars stored in the storm cellar. The diet of canned string beans, canned peas, canned carrots, canned spinach, canned corn, canned beets, and canned tomatoes got old. They craved something fresh, something from the garden.

So, a couple of minutes later, Freddy knelt beside furry green, white blooming plants and groveled half a dozen egg-sized potatoes from a hill, then covered the smaller ones back up. The warm sun felt good as he dug at four more plants. Beside him, a pair of somewhat tame robins watched and listened for worms. The birds had babies to feed.

Meanwhile, George and his dad worked down the 50-foot row of peas, finding a few pods big enough to pick, each holding eraser-sized green dots. What could taste sweeter?

An hour later, a steaming dish of new potatoes and peas in a thick creamy sauce sat on the noonday table. This was a special meal, almost a celebration.

"You know, Veda; this meal is pretty darn good. Maybe the best I ever tasted. Make a note of this café, will you? We may want to eat here again."

The boys' dad complimented the cooking—again—as he always did. Their mom did serve good food, in part because she had a lot of good meats and vegetables, and in part because hungry people are thankful for what they get. Perhaps raising things for the table made them taste better?

§

***W**e guessed farm families like us, being close to God's earth, received satisfaction from a garden that produced well through the spring, summer, and early fall. Mom saved much of that harvest by canning, though some potatoes, onions, and some of the carrots were stored in bins in the cool storm cellar.

Because of the garden, the livestock, and chickens we raised, Mom and Dad spent minimal amounts at grocery stores and saved the money. Early on, Mom had canned chicken and some beef, while pork hung in the open air in the smokehouse to cure. Meat canning ended in the late '40s, when the folks rented a huge—it held a whole beef and a hog—frozen-food locker in Wamego.

We did eat some wild game and fish, but we would have starved if that was all we had. His time was better spent farming, Dad said, than hunting for quail, squirrel, and rabbit, or fishing for catfish.

§

"Look what's happened to these peaches," Veda said. "They are just full of bug holes and bird pecks. They won't be any good to eat…just look at them."

"And what happened to the apples. There were quite a few little ones on both trees last week. Say, have you boys been having green-apple-throwing contests again? If you don't stop, we won't have any ripe fruit this year."

Now was the time to change the subject, Freddy thought. "Hey, aren't there a lot of watermelons and cantaloupes around? We can eat them and maybe have a few wild gooseberries from down by the creek. And, couldn't you make a mulberry pie? That tree next to the garage is loaded."

"You know, Mom," George said, "my mouth is just watering for an orange or banana. Could we get some at the store? Please? I'll help you with the garden."

George offering to work in the garden? Humm. Well...something for something.

Gardening was work, and took special knowledge about when to plant. Potatoes went in first—on St. Patrick's Day, weather permitting—assuring they'd be ready before it got too hot. Peas, beets, and turnips went in early, too. Though the boys' folks didn't believe in the *Farmer's Almanac,* they did sometimes talk about the moon being right for planting.

§

> ***W***e had meat almost every day. In the summer, fried chicken could show up at two meals, and we never tired of it. Mom and Dad ate the white meat: breasts, wings, and the wishbone. The two of us might have liked white meat, but at that point it seemed, God or somebody, had ordained that white meat was only appropriate for grown-ups.
>
> That left us with the dark meat, the bigger thighs to the bigger brother and smaller legs to the younger. The back, heart, gizzard, and liver went to anybody brave enough to eat them.

A VALUABLE LESSON IN FOOD MANAGEMENT

At meals, we passed serving dishes and platters family-style. A well-mannered person took a helping and handed the dish to the next person—with courtesy most of the time. This polite process sometimes turned impolite, when people like Shorty Brockman—maybe there to help hay—used a boarding house reach to stab meat or bread clear across the table.

Mom would scowl at Shorty, or anyone else, who seemed unmannerly. We too, skirted the edge of impoliteness, for as hungry growing boys, we invented some crafty methods to acquire second helpings.

To get seconds—perhaps more than our share—we used a three-step process. Step One: Assess the amount of food left in the serving bowl or on the platter. Step Two: Survey everyone else's plate and estimate how fast to eat our servings before going for any food left unclaimed.

Step Three was when we scooped up available food from a platter or bowl. We did our best to act nonchalant, often laughing at someone's joke while paying more attention to the food situation than the punchline.

Our conclusion: We discovered a valuable lesson in food management, and we often left the table stuffed to the gills.

An important test of this new management skill came when Mom started frying two chickens per meal. Older now, we shared in the white meat, and to assure ourselves plenty, we'd nibble on a piece of chicken, then put it down and grab another from the platter.

Later, we'd return to finish the first piece, thus getting a lot to eat without falling under suspicion, though we should have questioned our ethics. We sometimes over did it and got in trouble. In fact, we did lots of things to cause our parents distress.

§

HAVE TO SELL THE KIDS?

Those times when the boys really disturbed the peace, their dad was the one to air their dirty linen. Neither enjoyed being discussed in public or being lectured 'for their own good.'

When the boys' dad really laid it on, George drank milk. He would hide his face inside his glass and avoid sharp glances. This eased the pain, but as he grew older, his glass fortress grew smaller and smaller.

Once in a while, when the boys were still little and had been bad, their dad came up with the ultimate threat. Turning to their mom, he'd make his infamous remark.

"If these two boys don't straighten up…" he'd say, a scowl crossing his face for effect, "…well, there's only one thing to do…."

"I guess we're going to have to sell the kids."

Oh, no!, George thought, as panic filled his eyes. Don't sell the kids! Please don't sell the kids!

In contrast, Freddy wasn't fazed by this "sell the kids" business. He figured they couldn't sell a kid for enough to be worth the trouble, and besides, who would do the free farm labor he provided?

§

In truth, the folks loved us and were glad we were a part of their lives. At grace before every meal, Dad—sometimes Mom—thanked God for what He had given the family, including us. No wonder we felt loved.

Of course, in our prayers, we asked God to help us to learn to do right. We believed those prayers were answered. We did learn, and moments of conflict or misdeed could soon be forgotten, if we prayed. It seemed as if God loved us and had a purpose and plenty for us to do there on the farm.

FOURTEEN

HARSH UNHOLY HARMONY, FIGHTING SAXONS, AND I'LL TELL YOU A THING A THOUSAND WAYS

[*Westmoreland Recorder* – September 5, 1946] ~ **REAL ESTATE TRANSFERS** - The following deeds were filed during the week ending August 24, 1946: Edward Hartloff, et ux, to John R. Hartloff; N 108 ft of Block 5, Wamego; W.D. $1 love & affec.
Arian W. Birchfield, Guardian, to John J. Willis; 1/3 int. in S1/2 of SW1/4 S & W of RR 2-6-10: Gdn's D. $433.33.
Hazel B. Bretz, et vir, to Ivan L. McGee: Lot 69, Wamego; W.D. $1 and other con.
Leonard Wutherick, et ux to Catherine Irene Payne: Lots 2, 3, 4, 5, 16, 17, 18, 19 & 20, less tract, Blk 23, Louisville: W.D. $2,000.

A HARSH UNHOLY HARMONY

"It's time to rise and shine, gentlemen," the boys' dad said, calling up the stairs. "We have chores to do, and there's a big ole sun peeking over the hedge trees next to the pasture."

George—forever slow and a bundle of sighs—crept from his bed, walked to the nail holding his barn clothes, and struggled into them. Why do we have to get up now, he thought? And listen to Freddy. He's already dressed and skipping down the stairs…singing. The shivering fourth-grader shook his head and rubbed the sand from his eyes, then shuffled down the steps.

"We had a little frost last night so it's going to be nippy this morning. Better put on some warm clothes. Freddy, you do the milking, and George and I will get a load of ensilage for the beef cows. One of us will come help milk if you're not finished."

Here we go again, George thought, pulling on wool mittens and a stocking cap over his corduroy cap. He walked out the kitchen door, and on the porch, a very peppy Pep greeted him. For the first time that morning, George smiled. "Mornin' boy. Want to go get ensilage with us? Come on."

The big, golden-brown collie wagged his tail and ran excited circles around him, and waited behind the shed while the shivering George paused to answer nature's call. Then they both hopped into the back of the old International truck and rode to the trench silo dug in the side of a pasture hill.

Here Pep jumped out and began sniffing brush piles and rabbit runs while George and his dad stood side by side, loading enough steaming ensilage to fill four ten-foot long feed bunks.

Fifteen minutes later, the truck stopped beside the first bunk. "Fork about a fourth of the silage into each bunk," his dad said. "I'll drive along real slow, but you'll have to work fast, otherwise the dominant cows will overeat."

Surrounding the truck and the bunks, the forty-five Hereford cows, plus Maudie, and three Shorthorn cross breeds, pushed and shoved to get to the sweet smelling ensilage. Two flocks of blackbirds fluttered down, trying to join the feast, in spite of saliva slinging head tosses from the cows.

At the barn, Freddy, first pulling and then squeezing Alma's udders, sent rhythmic squirts into the bucket between his knees. "So, Alma, does your bag hurt when it's so full? Maybe you're glad for me to drain it? If I didn't milk you, what would happen? Would you explode?" he asked, smiling at his sorry humor. "Is the cracked corn alright this morning? Well, is it?"

The big Holstein turned her head and looked back at him, sending—so he thought—a message of contentment with her big, brown right eye. Does she understand me, he wondered? Maybe she does. Anyway, she and Louise and the others walk right into the same stanchion every time. They act like they know what they are doing.

While Freddy spent about eight minutes milking Alma, he pondered animal behavior from his perch on the one-legged stool. Finished, he rose and emptied the pail of its china plate-colored contents into a 10-gallon can next to the wall and moved on to the wide Guernsey, Claudette. Sometime during the hour-long process, the barn radio tuned to WIBW in Topeka, played Little Jimmy Dickens singing *The Great Speckled Bird* and something about drinking beer and going to jail. Freddy sang along when he knew the words and kept time with squirts into the tin pail.

I wonder what it would be like to go to jail? Then his thoughts created a comic book-like picture of Bubba Brockman staring at him from behind bars, and as he smiled, the image changed to his brother. Well, maybe that's where George ought to be... sometimes. Ho, boy, that's nuts.

Freddy's daydreaming ended as his dad arrived to help with the last four cows. That hurried the process, and even the radio helped. It played a lively tune by Lulubelle and Scotty called *Keep on the Sunny Side.*

The several barn cats sensed the change and seemed glad that the milking now had a more business-like approach. With two milkers, they'd eat that much sooner.

Meanwhile, George listened to music himself, of a sort, for two dozen half-grown, squealing and snorting pigs sang in a harsh unholy harmony each time he sloshed leftover skim milk and ground corn slop into their feeder. They punctuated their chorus—each in a different key—with grunts when they pushed and shoved each other. Why do pigs crowd each other like that? I wonder if we could teach them some manners? Maybe Bubba could...or maybe not.

Smiling, George left the pigs to work it out and watered and scattered grain for the hens, and for the ever-present, freeloading sparrows. Then he hurried—sword fighting vacant air with a stick—to the house for breakfast.

PARENTAL FEEDBACK AND ERRORS IN REASONING

Feeding pigs, milking cows, and fake sword fighting made the boys hungry. The blessing of regular meals solved that problem most of the time. But, mealtime also provided an arena for—some good and some not pleasant—parental feedback. Frequent comments praised them and produced grins from ear to ear. With praise, they'd have their chests out against their bib overalls, and feel motivated to do more good things.

Quite often though, corrective statements made them grimace. Why in the world did you do that? No you can't. Why didn't you do it the way I told you? Scolding the boys for poor judgment was criticism George didn't like, and he'd want to hide by hunkering down.

"George, why in the heck did you leave that gate unlocked?" his dad asked.

George cowered in front of the noonday meal, and slid a ways down his chair.

"Those darn pigs really made a mess of the garden." Lower and lower, George slid. "Dog-gone-it, boy, you know you have to keep that gate closed."

George got even smaller, and he took a long drink of milk. "You should know better than that!"

While criticism often moved George to fight back tears, Freddy approached it a different way. Everyone makes mistakes, he thought. You don't just have to sit there like George does.

Freddy took an assertive approach to scolding by justifying his actions, often pointing out errors in his folks' reasoning. When questioned, he'd suggest there were several approaches to a task and that he had used the one he could finish in a hurry. His way didn't always work, but it did much of the time, so he'd mention that and promise to do better.

Whether with quiet acceptance or by forthright debate, the boys got the message and did try to toe the line. Their folks had standards, and the boys did, too. Some farm tasks, however, were hard to fathom—standards or no standards—and downright disgusting. One job on just about every summer day had to do with dressing chickens.

To eat chicken twice a day came with a price, for someone had to butcher birds from the family's fryer flock. Most people called this butchering process...dressing. To the boys or to any observant person—plus the chicken—this procedure was a complete undressing. Off came the head, the feathers, and out came the crop and intestines from the opened bird. A very nude, hallow hunk of poultry remained.

"Come hither, ye foul fowl of a Saxon," Freddy shouted, beginning the procedure by raising a sharpened ax above his head. "Thee musteth die now!"

He stood, a young battle-ready Viking warrior, clad not in bearskin and reindeer boots, but in bib overalls and high-top leather shoes. His imagination filled in the blanks, and he lived the part.

"Ahh, yaaaaah, oomph." He screamed like a berserker and swung his battle-ax. The ax thunked through the hapless chicken's neck and into the wooden chopping block. Ker-whack!

"Off with thy head, thou enemy of the noble king and his family!" he shouted at the now beheaded chicken. "Tis thy red blood that shalt flow like a river to soaketh into our blessed soil..."

"...thou shalt be butchered like an animal."

§

> ***A***nd so it was that Saxons fell before the Viking ax, as we did Viking battle against the dreaded invaders to save our cherished kingdom. The drama was one of combat, red blood, and many, many special sounds.
>
> With each resounding thud, a Saxon indeed lost his head and blood flowed red to soak into our soil. Sometimes, our vanquished enemy squirmed and flopped in the throes of dying, splattering us with chicken...er, Saxon...blood. Ugh!

Do you blame us for playing at this disgusting job? After all, whether we called it dressing or butchering, both were repulsive, even when we tried to make a game out of it. Alas, for the chicken, it didn't matter much.

Yes, it was a pretty big stretch to compare chicken hatcheting to defeating Saxons. However, we didn't care, for it proved a good diversion from the repulsive odors and unpleasant gore.

With the beheading over, we plunged the chicken into scalding water for seconds, to loosen the feathers and to make plucking easy though soppy wet. And, with a strong pull, everything inside the defrocked bird came out, guts and all.

As one might expect, we butchered chickens with considerable urgency, and soon presented Mom with 'undressed' whole birds. She singed off the remaining stub hairs and removed any pinfeathers we missed. And with that, the Viking-Saxon battle ended. For a time.

§

The boys were sideline players for other butchering events—a hog and a beef battle every year—and on one cold November day, they watched quite a show that involved Shorty Brockman and Uncle Houston Gordon who helped out for a share of the meat. Bundled in an old red-plaid wool coat—safety pins for buttons—Shorty arrived first. When Uncle Houston drove in, he felt the need to tease.

"So John, are you going to stare this one down?" he asked. "I hear that's a really good and painless method to put them away. The Indians up around Mayetta do it all the time I hear."

"Might be a good idea, Houston, but darn it, I don't know how to do it."

"Guess it's not hard, you just have to have the right color eyes and then do a good job of staring," Houston said. "It takes a person who's got blue ones like Shorty."

"How about doing John a favor, Shorty, and put that steer down for us? Sure would avoid a lot of gore, and John wouldn't have to waste a .12 gauge shell. I hear it's real easy. You just walk into the pen, open your eyes as wide as you can get them and stare at the animal. If you're really calm, it should only take a minute or two with a Holstein-Hereford steer like that one in there. He'll probably just kneel down, roll over, and pass away on the spot."

"That sure would be less of a mess," John said. "I am running low on shells."

As usual, Shorty took the bait and a minute later stood relaxed in front of the steer. He stared and the animal stared back for a while, until Shorty started thinking something wasn't right. He began to fidget and that made the steer restless. When Houston slapped a small 2'X4' against the stall wall, chaos ruled.

The steer kicked and bolted, and that panicked Shorty. Fearing for his life, he hurdled the horse manger—banging his shins in the process—leaving his cap behind in the stall's manure, only to land on his backside in the alleyway.

"Well," Uncle Houston said, "I don't think that was the way the Indians do it. Now, John will have to waste his shell after all because that steer is too shook up to stare down. We need to herd it back in the stall, but first you'll have to get that cap out of that manure. And besides, why'd you make that loud noise? No wonder that calf is scared."

While Shorty fished out his hat with a pitchfork, he thought about the whacking sound that scared him and the calf. Did he make it? He couldn't be sure, but he doubted the Indians around Mayetta would do dumb things like that. Houston didn't seem to think so.

The boys' dad did dispatch the steer with a single, humane shot to the brain, and then slit the throat to let the blood drain. Next, he skinned it the way Indians had with millions of buffalo, loosening the hide on one side, rolling it over, and doing the other side. With a block and tackle, the three men hoisted the animal toward the rafters in the barn's alleyway for gutting and the cutting-up process. And, this time Shorty got it right.

§

A few weeks later, we also watched—a different story without Shorty and Uncle Houston around—when a deceased pig got a hot water bath in an old 55-gallon drum. The scalding water loosened the bristles and made scraping easy. Dad then raised the stark white carcass before drawing the internal organs and trimming away much of the fat.

Later, we did stir big chunks of pig fat while it turned into lard in a huge, black iron kettle heated over the open wood fire next to the smokehouse. That fire's ashes, mixed with some fat, produced the infamous lye soap that both cleaned and reddened the skin.

Butchering…or helping out…taught us that life wasn't quite as pristine as it appeared when standing at the Ince Bros. meat counter ordering the results of someone else's dirty work. We did indeed learn the realities of life, but we also learned that some jobs were just plain fun, in spite of some discomfort. Like making ice cream.

§

WE ALL SCREAM FOR ICE SCREAM

A month later, on a frigid January day, the phone rang just as the two boys, their parents, and baby Judy, born in June, walked in the door from church. "Bring, bring, bring, bring."

"Hello. Oh, is that you, George?" the boys' dad asked. "Yeah, we just got home from church and are going to have a bite to eat, and then the boys say we're going to make some ice cream. Bet your guys would like some, too. Why don't you drive down here for a visit this afternoon?"

"Okay, we'll see you about two. Sure, you can bring some canned peaches. That'll be just right. Bye."

"That was George Burgess. He and Helen and their kids are coming over for ice cream this afternoon. Boys, as soon as you change your clothes, take the tractor down to the slough and bring back some of that ice. And remember, it's slippery out there, so don't get the tractor stuck."

Never mind it was 20 degrees outside. Never mind that it might take a good 10 minutes of cranking to start the cold Allis-Chalmers. Never mind that the boys might get wet in the ice-collecting process. Never mind, because they could run the tractor, have ice cream, and spend time with the four cousins.

The trip started well, for the winter sun had warmed the orange AC's engine, and on the fourth try, it sputtered to life. George, perched on the metal seat, backed up to the rubber-tired wagon, and Freddy dropped in the hitch bolt.

In second gear, George drove the tractor across the frozen, rutted furrows of the south field. The huge clods forced him to wrestle with the steering wheel and jostled the trailing wagon. "Hey, slow down. I can barely hold on," Freddy shouted. "You're going too fast."

George down shifted into low, then turned left to the end of the field and a much smoother ride.

A minute later, between two cottonwoods next to the slough, he stopped the tractor. Here, the cold seemed deeper. Close to the bank, ice had formed into a three-inch sheet. Freddy whacked away at it with a small hedge post, and soon several chunks floated free into the unfrozen center of the stream, collecting downstream against a downed cottonwood limb.

While George watched and shivered, his brother tried to use the post to drag the floes to the bank. When that failed, Freddy stepped out onto the ice edge, which collapsed, of course. He now stood in 8-10 inches of icy water, wanting to curse his luck, but remembering he'd just gotten home from church.

Resigned to his bad fortune, he waded out to the chunks of natural ice that somehow seemed better—and of course cheaper—than summertime ice from the icehouse in town. Soon a bushel of pieces had been tossed up the bank, where the trembling George, poked his face out of his mackinaw and loaded them into the trailer.

§

Ten minutes later, the tractor stopped beside the limestone smokehouse steps where a few hits from the small sledgehammer crushed the ice. Inside, while we dried off and warmed up, Mom filled the canister with sugar, vanilla, and fresh whole milk plus thick cream and nestled it into the wooden freezer.

We stuffed ice around the canister, layered it with livestock salt, and now had our ice cream maker ready to turn the vile tasting cream into our favorite dessert that somehow made us forget the ice-collecting challenges.

With a washtub holding the freezer, the hand cranking began and we took turns with enthusiasm—at first. All was right with the world, we thought. We were making ice cream by a cozy kitchen stove, while that poor fluffed up cardinal sat on a corral post getting covered with large, settling snow flakes. It was good to be in here.

However, freezing was taking place inside, too, for in about 15 minutes, the salt-melted ice began to harden the mixture. Only Dad could turn the crank at this point, so he finished the job. When, at last, we licked the golden-coated paddle, you would have thought we'd died and gone to heaven.

Just then, the relatives drove up and soon we were racing around the house with the 4Ds. We played hide-and-seek until things got too loud. To calm us down, Mom suggested it was time to eat ice cream. First cheering and then silence filled the house, for Dad scooped out one heaping bowl after another.

Helen opened the quart of canned peaches, and Mom offered a second topping of store-bought pineapple. Both choices were tempting, and selection was difficult for little rivaled fruit-covered ice cream.

"You know this is really good," Dad said. "It's too bad though, I've got some peaches left. Maybe the only thing I can do is have a little more ice cream. How about the rest of you?"

Six boys yelled *yea!,* together, and each had seconds, and then thirds. At last, everyone was stuffed and the ice cream was gone. Soon, the adults and boys lounged around the warm-morning stove in the dining room. It was time for a story.

"Did you hear about Shorty Brockman and the electric fence? It was back in September, and it went like this."

I'D TELL YOU A THING A THOUSAND WAYS

"That one little dinky wire ain't goin' to keep them cows to home," Shorty said to Wally Hoffman with certainty. "They's jist goin' to walk right over it." The cold breeze whipped his earflaps, as he eyed the roll of #22 electric fence wire, then shook his head. The fragile wire seemed no match for a half-ton cow.

"It's the fence charger that keeps the cows in," Wally said. "Electricity from the charger goes through the wire." He pointed toward the metal box lying on the ground. It was about the size of a lunch bucket—small compared to a cow.

"Here, help me clip the wire on these fence stakes."

The two began screwing porcelain standoffs into 4-foot wooden stakes they'd hammered into the rain-softened ground. The stakes, about 15 feet apart, resembled tiny, stick-figure sailors standing at attention, and circled a 20-acre patch of just emerging hard winter wheat. Wally would harvest it early next summer, but for now, it would be cow pasture.

"That 'lectricity is goin' kill 'em, sure," Shorty said, frowning at the fence. He still had his doubts.

"It won't hurt 'em, it just pulses and gives them a little surprise," Wally said. "It's real low current, and it's not a steady burst—it just goes zap-a-zap-a-zap."

"Don't you mean somethin' like, kill-a-kill-a-kill-a-kill-a-killa?" Shorty was trying to be funny.

"You sure don't think this little battery is going to kill a cow, do you, Shorty?"

Shorty did not look convinced, so Wally said, "I tell you what, you can help me test it. That way you can see how harmless it is. Just grab a hold on the wire, I'll flip on the charger, and we can see if it's working."

"Not me, no sir-ree, I ain't touching that wire. I don't want to die!" Shorty said with a snort. "My mama didn't raise up no dummy!"

"Shorty, Shorty, Shorty. How could that little wire hurt you?" Wally asked, his face portraying an 'of course you can trust me' attitude.

"You know, Shorty, I would tell you a thing a thousand different ways...before I'd lie to you!

"Just grab that wire. You don't want to be a quitter, do you?"

Shorty stared at the wire, then at the charger, and then back to the wire, as the fall wind caressed the tops of the still young wheat. Rolling gray clouds scudded southward and a crow cawed in the cornfield. There would be frost tomorrow.

Whether from the cold or from dread, Shorty

shivered. Then he grabbed the wire, and Wally flipped the switch. The charger sent a brisk, pulsing current through the wire from the tiny stepped-up six-volt dry cell battery.

"Ouch, oops, ugh...dit, dit, ditttth," Shorty yelled, his teeth clicking together. He danced on one foot and then the other. "Aughhhhhh!"

Shorty, and anyone else who on purpose or by accident ever experienced the harmless electric shock, knows it comes in bursts. It is a quick zap, quick pause, quick zap—again and again—that jolts whomever touches it until contact is broken.

Shorty let go after the third pulse. However, each zap caused an unconscious muscular reaction—much more surprising than the zap. Not meaning to do so, he jumped hard, his spine undulating from top to bottom like an earthquake tremor. That smarted.

"You said that 'lectricity wouldn't hurt me," Shorty said, whining and glaring at Wally.

"It wasn't the juice that got you, it was probably the way you jumped," Wally said for clarification. "Maybe you didn't grab the wire right. Watch and I'll show you how to test it properly."

With that, Wally—not grounded in his rubber boots—grabbed the pulsing wire with both hands and then stood there for several seconds, grinning from ear to ear.

"See, it doesn't bother me. You just have to grab it right, is all. And don't jump."

That day, Shorty Brockman had a learning experience, and was literally shocked into gaining a new respect for Wally Hoffman—and electric fences. Wally seemed to have special powers, and although Shorty never tested an electric fence again, he felt honored to work with this amazing man.

Amazing or not, farmers and their helpers needed understanding and experience about a lot of things. Farm boys, like Freddy and George, did too, and when electricity came to the farm in 1946, they began the move to modern times.

§

<u>MOVING INTO MODERN TIMES</u>

In some ways, modernizing brought unwanted change, though some things were long desired. When the REA (Rural Electrification Association) set a mile of newly installed electric poles across the pasture to the house, we had light other than lamp light for the first time. Bare electric lights hung in every room and the old lamps were stored away for emergencies.

Dad installed a motor to replace the foot-spin pedal on the washing machine, and we got a used electric radio that worked great, though we had to wait for it to warm up each time. Soon, we even had an electric milking machine. That was a relief.

And, though the coal-fired kitchen stove served us well, it gave way to an electric range. Gone, too, was the coal-oil icebox, and in its place, Dad came home with an electric refrigerator. We were moving into the modern world.

For the first time, we experienced many things our ancestors never dreamed about. Still, modern or old-fashioned, it was family that glued us together. And we liked being with each other—most of the time

FIFTEEN

RABBITS WOULDN'T CROSS IT, IT MUST HAVE BEEN AN ENGLISHMAN, AND DIURNAL SPACE

[*Wamego Reporter* – October 6, 1946] ~ **HOME BEAUTY SHOPPE** (Advertisement) – New Nestle La Mur Machine - Plenty of Time and Careful Attention. The best of Supplies—Every permanent is guaranteed to be satisfactory. PRICE $3.00 FOR EITHER CROQUIGNOLE – SPIRAL OR COMBINATION. Other prices—Shampoo – Marcel 50c. Shampoo – Finger wave 50c, Finger wave or Push wave 25c, Marcel 35c. MRS. PEARL FLENTHROPE, Phone 369, 511 Elm St. I will work Sundays and evenings if necessary. Phone appointment or call at Home Beauty Shoppe, 2nd house south of Presbyterian Church.

RABBITS WOULDN'T CROSS IT

"It was absolutely the poorest 80 acres in Pottawatomie County. It couldn't have been worse," Great-Uncle Tom said, shaking his full head of graying black hair. "Yep, your Great-Grandfather, old John I., sure homesteaded a bum place. To tell the truth, almost nothin' would grow on my folks' first farm."

"It was so bad you couldn't raise a ruckus on it with two Irishmen and a jug of whiskey!"

His audience roared—Freddy and George and the 4D cousins—charmed again by the family's best story teller, who leaned against his brown Ford, and performed his craft in front of a backdrop of rolling hills framed by leafless cottonwoods, standing tall against a soft blue sky. Good humor filled his angular face, and with practiced ease, he paused and in a hush said, "It was so poor the rabbits wouldn't cross it!"

§

Our laughter came again. We made the connection for we passed that old farmstead every time we traveled the Wheaton Road north of Louisville. We knew it had plenty of hills and rocks with little good cropland. But, a rabbit wouldn't cross it?

In his early 60s, Uncle Tom captivated us with stories about our great-grandparents, John Irving and Margaret Wilson Burgess. He told us how in 1868, his parents overcame the arduous trip from Ireland to Kansas, filed a homestead claim, and began building a hand-hewn log cabin.

Uncle Tom—the 4Ds' grandpa—said John I., as everyone called him, had the reputation of being a driven man who did his utmost to be a successful farmer. He worked several hard years to make a go of it on the place that 'rabbits wouldn't cross,' then sold it, and in 1877 moved about four miles to the place on Adams Creek where he raised seven children, including Uncle Tom, his youngest child, and our Grandpa David.

That October day, the six of us soaked up the family's oral tradition—Uncle Tom's version of it—while a redtail hawk circled high above the timber calling its high-pitched whistle. To the east, had we noticed, a 'V' of late migrating geese headed south.

§

"So, Uncle Tom, what was John I. like? Do you look like him?" George asked.

"I guess I'm slimmer like my mom's side of the family. Pop was stocky and strong, and he worked everyone hard, including himself. He was a taskmaster, but a great farmer. Everything he built was solid. His stone barn was as strong as a mountain and the three strands of 'bobwire' fence he put around his place were tight enough to keep out the wind. He even had Adams Creek run just three days a week to save water."

Uncle Tom after church

George gulped. Was this possible? Before he could ask, Uncle Tom continued.

"Maybe it is true, as some say, the best people migrated from the old country, and that is why America is so great. Anyway, Pop had trader skills, and one time even swapped cattle for land. He also imported a Percheron stallion from Ireland. Of course, his was a terrible Irish temper that made us all afraid of him, 'cause his bark would peel paint."

Peel paint? When George started to speak again, the storyteller intervened.

"And, the good Irishman that he was, he did have a meeting with John Barleycorn from time to time, and would come home roaring drunk. One time, when he had too much whiskey, he rode sound asleep in his buggy behind his favorite driving horse, up what we now call Adams Creek Road.

"Guess the horse got tired, too, and pulled into Mom's cousin's farmyard, walked up to the water trough for a drink I suppose, and then went to sleep. Come daylight, Pop woke up and trotted the horse on home!"

§

While we wanted to believe everything, we had to laugh at some of the doubtful images Uncle Tom painted. How could a creek run three days a week? Or 'bobwire' keep out the wind? Yet, we knew about the drunken buggy ride and the imported stallion. We'd look at each other, then at Uncle Tom's mirth-filled face, and roared again.

Ole John I., the kingpin of family history, had been a bigger-than-life ancestor whose legend brought great pride to the Burgess name. He indeed provided us with solid roots.

OUR IRISH ROOTS

Those Burgess roots extended from County

Fermanagh, in what is now Northern Ireland, where John I. and Margaret married in a small country church near the city of Enniskillen on February 21, 1868. A month later, they said goodbye to family and friends and started for Pottawatomie County, Kansas.[1]

"Grandpa," Denny asked, "how did your parents travel so far? Did they come on the Mayflower or something?"

"They did come by boat, but not the Mayflower. Crossing the Atlantic took a lot of extra days because their steamship ran into bad weather and got blown 500 miles off course. Once they got to New York, they took a train to Buffalo, and then headed on to Louisville. There, they had more trouble."

"What happened?" Denny asked. "Did they get robbed?"

"They did get robbed in a way, for they were in Louisville, Kentucky, instead of Louisville, Kansas. And, no relatives came to meet them as promised. They still had to go west about another 600 miles."

A couple of the boys started to ask why they went to the wrong place, when Uncle Tom grinned, and said, "Bet you want to know what happened, don't you? Well, I think the clerk that sold them the ship and train tickets back in Ireland must have been an Englishman. And, that man did them a great wrong...just like the English have been doing to the Irish for centuries."

When Uncle Tom paused, Freddy asked, "How did they get to Kansas then?"

"Well, the station agent told them Kentucky was about as far away from Kansas as New York, and that

---

[1] Mary Elzine (Mollie) Burgess recorded a good deal about the life and times of her parents, John Irving Burgess and his wife, Margaret Wilson Burgess, by periodically writing in pencil on several simple grade school tablets. Following Mollie's death, her grand-niece-in-law, Dr. Barbara Burgess, collected the writings and self-published it as *Mollie's Heritage* in 1972. The booklet contains interesting stories, along with historical family pictures and sample letters written in the late 1800s.

their tickets were used up. They stewed a while until, at last, the agent took all of their remaining money—John I. wisely held back $15 he'd need for the homestead fee—and gave them two tickets to Kansas. They went down the Ohio River to the Mississippi and up to St. Louis, then up the Missouri River to Leavenworth, Kansas, all by riverboat. There, my mom's relatives, Uncle William and Aunt Rebecca Burgess, met them."

"Wait a minute," Freddy said, "how could your mom's relatives have the same last name? Was there something funny going on?"

"Oh, there might have been an Englishman in the woodpile, but not as far as we know, for they were from separate branches of the Burgess family. It's like all people named Jones aren't related, are they?"

"Anyway, they were glad to see relatives at last, even though they had to travel, I'd guess, about four more days in Uncle William's covered wagon to get to Louisville. When they got there, Mom, who had expected her rich American relatives to be living in a huge manor, was surprised to find their home was a simple little log cabin. However, Uncle William's 160-acre place with lots of cattle amazed her. In Ireland, families lived pretty well on small farms of 10 acres or so."

"Grandpa," Danny asked, "where did John I. pay the homestead filing fee? Could he do it at Westmoreland or some other county seat?"

"Your great-grandfather had to walk all the way to Topeka and back—about 70 miles each way—to pay the $15 for the homestead. And, at that point, only 80 acres could be claimed, and only the poorest farms were left. Of course, once they got the land, they had to prove up by building a cabin and farming it for five years before it was officially theirs. Some people say they got the land for free. But, did they really?"

§

*T*he story continued, and we sat wrapped up in it. Uncle Tom told how his mother took a job in Louisville at the Harrison store, and earned enough money to buy clapboards for the cabin roof. The problem was that when they awoke a few weeks later, the boards had let snow in, and it covered most everything inside of the cabin. To solve the problem, they ended up cutting slough grass and thatching the roof, the way people did in Ireland.

They used grass and straw for their mattress, too, to make a tick to lie over ropes stretched from the cabin wall. Another unbleached feather tick covered the bed. A wedding present from Mary Wilson, Margaret's mother, it was made from homegrown Irish flax.

Uncle Tom told us a small group of Indians lived not far from the homestead in the early days and gave Indian Creek its name. Other Indians had lived near Louisville, and another group camped some 10 miles away on the Vermillion River near the Oregon Trail.

We boys wondered what it would have been like to have a band of Indians living nearby. Were they ever mean, or did they steal from folks? Did real Indians steal kids the way movie Indians did?

We also wondered about the Oregon Trail that crossed the Vermillion not far away. Thousands of settlers—most in the 1840s and '50s—had passed within about four miles of John I.'s homestead while heading for the frontier. Did he ever meet any of the Oregon-bound wagons? Did he ever travel a part of that deep-rutted trail across the prairie?

One of the well-known stops on the Kansas part of the Trail had been Scott Springs, a few miles to the north and west of the homestead. Maybe its name came from the Scott side of our family. This history was good stuff.

§

In 1877, when John I. sold the original homestead for $900, he bought the 80 acres on Adams Creek, where it ran parallel to Indian Creek. Soon after, he traded eight calves and $20 for another 80 acres. Then he bought parcels of 120 acres, of 40 acres, and, finally, 80 acres of former railroad property.

"Pop loved horses, and that's why he imported the stallion for the old country. The horse barn had stalls for twenty-four with trapdoors upstairs to let hay and oats fall down into feeders in each stall. You could even drive a team and wagon right through the barn," Uncle Tom said. "He built the barn—the two-story house, too—with native limestone blocks and oak timbers."

§

***W**e had been in those buildings, for we visited Uncle Tom and Aunt Mabel there when they owned the farm…and later went by many times when the 4Ds' family farmed it. It would have taken a severe earthquake to make those buildings budge. They were strong and so—we concluded—were our ancestors who built them.

They needed to be strong, for our Great-Grandfather and Great-Grandmother Burgess overcame many hardships. What was it like to fight prairie fires, winter's cold and summer's heat, grasshoppers, tornadoes, and drought…at a time in history with no vehicles or tractors or electricity? We marveled how they persevered and raised a family.

John I. and Margaret's eldest, called Evan—really Irving pronounced with an Irish brogue—left home after a disagreement with his father and did not contact the family for years. He lived as a bachelor. We were about ages 8 and 10, the only time we ever saw him.

One son, Alexander, died of a burst appendix at age 28, and another named John, never fully recovered all of his mental abilities after being kicked in the head by a horse. Neither of them married. The youngest daughter, Mollie, cared for her parents in later life and never married either.

Of the seven children, only three married and only two had children of their own. Aunt Maggie married Dr. Ewing, and she had only a stepdaughter. Only Uncle Tom and Grandpa David had natural children, which seemed curious to us.

GRANDPA DAVID

Our grandpa, David Samuel Burgess, born January 14, 1876, was the third son of John I. and Margaret. In his mid-20s, he purchased a 160-acre farm, just two miles south of his folks and later married.

Dave, as he was known, might not have been as driven as his father, or at least not as aggressive, but he worked hard and was well organized, including how he cooked his meals. When he lived alone, he often put a pot of potatoes on the wood stove to simmer—so we heard the story—before he went to the field in the morning. At noontime, he stopped, fed and watered his team, and then ate a meal of cooked potatoes—after mixing in 3-4 raw eggs.

Ugh. Would the eggs cook in the hot potatoes and did they taste okay? After considerable discussion, we concluded, people with Irish roots could eat potatoes any way they wanted, though the dish didn't appeal to us. In fact, we never did try it.

§

In 1903, at age 27, Grandpa Dave brought his new bride, Mary Anna Shea Burgess, to the farm where they would live out their lives. They had four children: Alfred, Helen, Dorothy, and, of course, the boys' dad, John. Many said Dave Burgess had above-normal wittiness and that he also had the Irish gift of gab. He could make people laugh, and the family home bubbled with fun and humor.

Most folks agreed that the boys' grandpa out-farmed Uncle Tom, although Uncle Tom verbally controlled the audience, if he was around. However, they both had to deal with John I.'s forcefulness, and at least one time, Grandpa Dave experienced the brunt of his father's ire.

Though John I. retired to Wamego in 1915, he routinely went back to his big farm that Tom now operated to help with the harvest. He drove a team and wagon more than 12 miles each way each day—at a trot. Not only did he make the drive, but he'd arrive just after sun-up.

On one trip, John I. rolled past Dave's farm just at dawn. He noticed his son's horses still in the pasture, meaning he wasn't up and moving yet. The story was that John I. grumbled loud enough for all to hear; saying something about it must be a lazy man who would have unharnessed horses that late in the day.

Though his father might have questioned it, Dave Burgess was a dedicated farmer and accumulated considerable land. No one else doubted his farming ways, although some puzzled over how he cooked potatoes and eggs—and how he demanded to be baptized.

Grandpa Dave married Mary Shea at St. Luke's Episcopal Church in Wamego where her family attended. [2] After their marriage, the newlyweds also attended St. Luke's some, and Alfred, their eldest son, was baptized there shortly after birth in 1905. The distance from the

---

[2] Littrell, Dr, J. Harvey, *Kansas Churchman,* Topeka, Kansas, May 1985 issue, pages 8-9.

farm to Wamego, at that time over unsanded roads, made attendance a problem. As a result, the nearby Laclede Baptist Church became the family's temporary church home.

In 1920, when the boys' dad was eleven, his folks bought a car and started attending St. Luke's when they could. In the process of getting the three younger children baptized, it was somehow discovered that Dave had not been baptized either. He should receive the sacrament—his wife insisted—at the same time as the children.

§

***G**randpa refused the Episcopal baptism because of its sprinkling practice. That, he maintained, was not for him. He preferred, he said, baptism by immersion. After several years of disagreement—perhaps stalling on Grandpa's part—the St. Luke's rector consented to immerse him.

To everyone's amazement, once he got his way on this, Grandpa changed his mind about immersion. Maybe it was the Irish coming out in him, for he soon received Baptism by sprinkling, along with his three youngest children.

Through it all, the family was active at St. Luke's, and Grandpa Dave served as Senior Warden for many years. At one time or another through the years, his two sons, Uncle Alfred and our dad, also served as the Senior Warden at that church. And the tradition has continued. His granddaughter, our sister, Joyce, and her husband, Doug Elcock, have both been Senior Wardens at St. Luke's, in recent times.

Although our side of the family worshipped in the Episcopal Church, most of the other Burgesses were Baptists. This included our favorite Great-Aunt Mollie, who walked with the

Lord each day. Her faith and the way she lived inspired us all.

§

AUNT MOLLIE'S PLACE

Mary Elzine Burgess, nicknamed Mollie, moved with John I. and Margaret when they retired from the farm. The three lived on a small place, about 3 acres, at the north edge of Wamego. In their later years, Mollie looked after her parents and cared for them until they passed on, both in the early 1920s.

With the old folks gone, Aunt Mollie lived alone there for the rest of her life with no car, as far as can be remembered. She had plenty of company though, for Aunt Mollie's place was a regular stopover for every family member in the area.

None of her eleven nieces and nephews would drive to town without a stop to see if Aunt Mollie wanted anything and to drop off the kids—great nieces and nephews—of the boys' generation. They were the kids she never had…all 35 or so of them.

The white-frame house, with its big, screened-in front porch and sweet smelling lilac bushes, seemed to welcome young and old alike. The other buildings also reached out to the younger folk, almost begging exploration.

§

With various cousins, we gathered eggs from the handful of leghorns at the chicken coop, dared each other to jump out of the barn's hayloft, picked fresh vegetables from her garden, stirred up bumble bees, chased pigeons, threw rocks at empty bean cans perched on fence posts, played hide and seek, played with the old dusty leather harnesses hanging from nails on the barn walls, looked for evidence of snakes, rabbits, and mice…and found a host of other things to do outside.

The most intriguing outdoor structure, Aunt Mollie called the 'gare-ridge'…the word garage, pronounced with a bit of the Irish. It still housed an antique buggy, with red-spoked wheels, and had a cracking leather seat and top, covered with dust from years of idleness.

What was it like to ride, shaded by the high canopy, in that stately vehicle, we wondered? How did it feel to be dressed in your Sunday best, sitting behind a single horse that clip-clopped between the wooden shafts? Had Great-Grandfather John I. paraded into Wamego, sitting straight and tall with his full beard flowing in the wind? Did he have the air of a proud man? We were intrigued with our history and Aunt Mollie's place.

§

Attached to that house—another wonder—was Aunt Mollie's pump room. It had a grimy, oily wooden floor because of the leaky, one cylinder, donkey engine—probably a Fairbanks Morse Model Z from about 1910. It pumped well water into the large, black storage tank in the corner.

Running barefoot through that room turned kids' soles and toenails as black as a Model T Ford. This was a small price to pay for being able to examine the fascinating old-time tools and pieces of equipment—or to just use the room as a shortcut.

"What's this thing with the long handle?" George asked Aunt Mollie, one dark Saturday afternoon when steady rain and cool temperatures kept the boys inside.

"Is it some kind of hoe?" he asked, struggling to lift the heavy wide-bladed tool with a handle almost three inches thick.

“That’s a chopping hoe from the olden days,” Aunt Mollie said, her eyes radiating her special warmth. “The blade is extra wide and the handle is thick for chopping heavy weeds. After all, we did things by hand before tractors were invented.”

“No tractors? How could people farm with just their hands?” George asked.

“Well, we did have horses, but I still remember as a young girl doing a lot of the work by hand.”

George pondered. The idea of farming a hundred acres without a tractor was shocking. Wouldn’t it take a long time? How could it be? He just had to ask.

“Aunt Mollie, didn’t people get tired, in the olden days?”

§

Tiny Aunt Mollie, probably about five-feet tall, smiled and then nodded with warmth that conveyed patience and love. Her twinkling blues eyes reached out and her somewhat raspy deep voice—it seemed to us—had a soothing quality.

For all her diminished size and calm voice, she seemed large when it came to character and authority. Though seldom stern, young people visiting her home knew her rules and obeyed them, and in return, received love and her perpetual, upturned smile. We knew how we stood with her.

No doubt about it, Aunt Mollie was special, but she did have one strange eating ritual. She always seemed to eat Wheaties cereal—nothing but Wheaties—every morning and some other meals as well. She ate them, however, only after soaking them in milk for about 15 minutes!

She’d pour on the milk…sometimes from her own cow…into a large bowl of the cereal. Next, she’d go about her housework or kid tending for a time, to later return to consume the soggy food—

standing up! Is that strange?

DIURNAL SPACE

Strange or not, we loved Aunt Mollie as if we were her children and her house was our house. She made us feel at home, and she cared for us deeply—we just knew it.

Uncle Tom's and Aunt Mabel's eldest daughters, Margaret and Mildred, and son, Bob, lived with Aunt Mollie all four years they each attended Wamego High School. The youngest son, Charles, lived there one year, before transferring from the big Wamego School to Westmoreland with maybe 25 students.

In hindsight, we think it took true devotion to parent someone else's kids through high school. Aunt Mollie housed them and, in the case of Bob, provided lunch at her house daily.

§

"Every day during high school, I walked to Aunt Mollie's for lunch," Bob said, his proud blue eyes flashing. "It was six-tenths of a mile each way. I know, since I had a Jack Armstrong Walk-O-Meter and clocked it." It seems that Bob was another cereal box-top coupon customer.

"You know, high school wasn't much fun for me, 'cause I was purdy darn young when I started. My folks musta thought I was smart or something 'cause I went to the one-room Star Union School at age four and was the only student in my class."

He went on to tell how, for some reason, he completed the second and third grades together the next year. He was not quite seven when he started the fourth grade.

"That meant I got to high school at age twelve and graduated at age sixteen. Since I was young and from the country, I was pretty shy. It was hard for me to participate in things or to talk to my classmates, especially the girls," he said. "That was a real problem.

"One day on the way to Aunt Mollie's for lunch, Uncle Dave, your grandfather, drove by in his Buick and gave me a lift. When I told him about my problems with the ladies, he gave me some interesting advice. I guess it's something I will never forget."

It seems, Grandpa Dave told Bob how to ask for a date. He recommended asking the intended lady a simple, though complex question, using a combination of words that were supposed to work every time.

"Just ask this question: 'May I have the exquisite pleasure of escorting your eternal being...over the diurnal space...intervening between the edifice erected for divine worship...and your humble place of abode?'"

"That means, Bob, you just asked to take a girl home from church," Grandpa Dave said, then grinned with good reason.

Good gosh, the boys' thought! Grandpa Dave did have a way with words. Maybe he had kissed the blarney stone. As for Bob, they wondered if the advice helped. Either way, it truly made a good story; similar to the many tales they heard sitting around at Aunt Mollie's place.

SIXTEEN

MOLLIE'S HERITAGE, A LILY-LIVERED PUFF, AND GHOSTY PICTURES

[*Wamego Times* – November 23, 1944] ~ **WANT A DOG?** ~ As I am leaving for the winter, I will give away a 2-year–old pure bred Collie dog. Phone 1504. First caller gets him. T. J. Dronberger.

MOLLIE'S HERITAGE

"Aunt Mollie," eleven-year-old Beverly asked, "will you tell us some more about Ireland, and about how your mother grew up? What was her family like?"

While the late March wind gusted and roared outside, Aunt Mollie nodded to the small group of great nieces and nephews seated around the oil stove in her living room on that late Saturday afternoon. Beverly's folks, Uncle Alfred and Aunt Dot, plus Aunt Helen and the boys' folks, shopped in Wamego, while their children 'visited' their favorite aunt.

"My mother's grandparents were the Macklims and they owned a lot of land until the Irish Revolution of 1791. They must have been on the wrong side, for the government took what they had and forced them to farm it as tenants.

"However, before they lost the land, they were said to have done something exciting. What do you think it was?"

"Maybe they came to America," Beverly said. "Or maybe the king gave the land back."

"Or maybe they got beheaded," Ben Gordon said. "Yeah, they might have had their heads chopped off."

"Benjamin, you just hush. There hadn't been kings in Ireland for hundreds of years. What happened was that before they had to give up their land, they were said to have buried a pot of gold somewhere under a lonely bush. To this day, no one has ever found it."

Freddy's eyes lit up! Wow, he thought! Some

relatives buried a treasure. Maybe someone should go to Ireland to look for it.

Sensing the excitement, Aunt Mollie's blue eyes flashed and her tiny hands gestured to add drama. She nodded, as always, and that encouraged her audience to nod as well, to signal they were listening.

"The Macklims' granddaughter, Mary, became my grandmother after she married Alexander Wilson. They lived on only 10 acres leased from a large manor. With that lease came the right to cut peat from the bog. They raised potatoes, oats, kale, and peas. They also grew flax to make into linen and had cows, pigs, chickens, and geese," Aunt Mollie said, sipping her favorite orange pekoe tea.

"Aunt Mollie, how could a person grow enough food on 10 acres to feed themselves?" Freddy asked. "Most farms around here have more than 160 acres."

"Well, sometimes it was a struggle, but if they had lots of rain and put on lots of manure, they could do it," she said.

"Aunt Mollie, can I ask you a question?" George said, asking if he could ask. She nodded.

"Why did they leave the old country? Did they get in trouble with the law? Or...maybe...did they run out of manure?" he asked with a crooked smile. In typical fashion, Aunt Mollie smiled back and gave him a loving pat on the shoulder.

"Maybe so, George," she said, "maybe so. Or maybe they saw some signs or something. My parents and most other Irish folks of that day had lots of superstitions and even believed in fortune-telling. That happened to Grandpa Alexander's sister. She lived with the family and one day opened the door at a stranger's knock. There stood a man who seemed deaf and dumb, yet somehow communicated that he could tell her fortune."

"She said she didn't have money to pay a fortune-teller, but the silent man somehow conveyed she had four pence—about eight cents—hidden away. That was the truth, so she paid him to tell her fortune. He said she would go to America one day and marry a man named Nixon. Indeed, that was just what she did."

"Another story happened at a place called Canter Hill. While the Episcopal minister was away, his servants got drunk. His cook started chasing the other servants with a broom, then tripped and broke her neck falling down the stairs. After her death," Aunt Mollie said in a whisper, "people heard what sounded like someone running down the stairs, with chains rattling, and lots of moaning."

"Who did the moaning? Was it some kind of a spirit?" George asked, staring into the adjacent parlor with giant photographs of long dead relatives on the walls.

"BOOOOooooo!" Ben screamed in his ear.

"WOOOOoooooo!" George lost his breath and turned pale.

Ben, Rollie, and Freddy laughed and the girls snickered. George's neck began to turn red. He'd been tricked...again. Darn it, darn it.

"Benjamin, you just stop that," Aunt Mollie said. "It's not nice to shout in someone's ear. I won't have any more of that. You want to hear the rest of the story, don't you?"

When Ben—and everyone else—nodded yes, she continued. "The cook," she explained, "had been a Catholic, so they called a Catholic priest to come deal with the spirit. Among other things, the priest sealed the door to the cook's room.

"Later, Grandfather Alexander did some carpentry work at the manor, and reopened the door. After that, he had bad luck. He lost a horse, his cows became sick, and some of his pigs died. The Catholics said he should have left the room sealed."

The boys and their cousins sat in silence. How could that have happened? Aunt Mollie told the best stories. What a place to visit, while their parents shopped in Wamego.

COUSINS GALORE

Each week, the relatives, including the boys' parents, came to town for two reasons. The first was to grocery shop and the second was to jaw. They visited and visited—somewhere along Main Street—with the men leaning against a parked car and the women sitting in another car, with at least one door open. While the parents enjoyed a social hour, the young people socialized, too, at Aunt Mollie's.

Isolated all week at the farm, where the closest neighbor might be a half mile away, they now had instant companionship and reveled in it. And, on most Saturday nights, there were cousins—no warm-up time needed—galore.

Boys were everywhere…Freddy and George…Jim, Ben, and Roland Gordon…the 4Ds—Danny, Denny, Dean, and Dwight Burgess…and later, even the brothers Tom, Norman, Oren, and Richard Beach.

In reality, girl cousins, Beverly and Ruth Elaine Burgess, Mary Helen and Becky Gordon, and occasionally, Kathleen Wilson, could have been there as well. However, the boy cousins, being boys, tended to ignore them. They did make some effort to be nice to the girls, but….

How Aunt Mollie coped is a wonder, but she did and the young people loved it. They never wanted to leave and couldn't wait until the next weekend.

§

RAINY DAY STORE KEEPERS

The next Saturday, it rained hard, and though the road to Wamego was passable, our car did a lot of spinning and rut riding. By the time we reached Aunt Mollie's, the old gray Chevy was tiger-striped tan and brown from muddy water.

Though we made it, the rain meant we stayed

indoors to have our fun. The first event was a game of hide-and-seek—enhanced by lightning dancing across the dark sky outside and thunder rattling the windows. We had the run of the first floor, although we weren't allowed to hide in the closets. We could slide under the beds in the two bedrooms, or squeeze out of sight behind the bathroom door or a piece of furniture.

Smaller folk, like the Beach cousins or Dwight, could even curl up under the settee, below a huge painting where layers of oil paint formed mountains and trees. The kitchen had hiding spots, too, but Aunt Mollie shooed us out so we didn't interfere with her cooking. There came a time, however, when the game lost its appeal and she suggested another way to keep us occupied.

§

"Let's go have some fun in the store," she said, switching on the lights in the storm-darkened house.

As we followed Aunt Mollie, the northwest wind bent the elm trees along the drive, and we saw cars creeping along with huge sparkling raindrops flashing in the headlights. The wet pavement broadcast an eerie, church-like mother's shushing. Just as they started up the stairs, lightning flashed behind the clouds and an earsplitting clap of thunder rocked the walls.

"Whoa!" Jim Gordon exclaimed. Everyone stood in startled silence with George covering his ears.

"Man, am I glad I'm inside."

Ignoring the thunder, Aunt Mollie led the nieces and nephews into a room without furniture at the head of the stairs. The slanted ceiling made it seem cozy and provided just enough space for the boxes and benches of the grocery store.

"Who wants to be Mr. Kornemann?" she asked, as she sat down on an orange crate.

"I will," volunteered Freddy.

"Alright, the rest of you can be farmers coming to town for groceries."

Then looking at Danny, the smartest cousin of all, she said, "You can be Mr. Kornemann's helper. That means you make the change and help wrap each order."

Maybe she doesn't think Freddy can do that, George thought with a smile. He liked to see his brother challenged.

"You farmers need to make out shopping lists to give to Mr. Kornemann. He'll find each item for you and put it on the counter for wrapping."

A minute later, Rollie handed Freddy his list. He wanted a tin of Prince Albert tobacco and a box of Headstrike matches. Ben wanted three glass bottles of Coca-Cola and some Wheaties. George asked for a tiny bottle of Grapette Soda and some Van Camp Pork and Beans. Someone ordered a quart bottle of milk and a half-pint bottle of cream. Others ordered cartons of pretend eggs and tin cans labeled green beans, pineapple, peaches, and peas. Beverly wanted some Pillsbury flour, Calumet baking powder, and sugar so she could bake a cake.

As Freddy filled each order, Danny took the pretend money—bills cut from an old tablet—and used colored buttons to make pretend change. He and Freddy wrapped each order in newspaper and tied it with string. While the customers waited, Aunt Mollie wanted everyone to visit.

"How's your wheat crop?" Aunt Mollie asked Ben Gordon.

"It's not doing very well," Ben answered. "The field was too wet to get it planted on time and then the frost hit early. I didn't get a very good stand." He had pretty good farm lingo.

"My kids just won't behave," Beverly said with a customary grin. "I may have to send my youngest through the second grade again…just like you, Denny."

Of course, Denny, accused of flunking a grade, was

mortified. He protested that he didn't go through the second grade twice…at least he didn't think so.

This started the teasing. Dean, under his breath and without much tact, commented that Beverly needed to be a better mother. Mary Helen defended her cousin, saying Beverly's pretend husband was the reason the kids were bad.

And so, the banter continued until Aunt Mollie pulled in the reins. With that, everyone went back to playing store, ignoring the wind and noise, and enjoying each other…boys and girls.

§

BOYS WILL BE BOYS

> ***A***lthough Aunt Mollie managed us well, she could not be everywhere all the time. As a result, uncommon things happened every now and then. Though we were all related, some of us had different ways of doing things. And, some events were real antics, though some were just simple mistakes.
>
> One Saturday afternoon, we stood in amazement when Tom Beach, about 4-years old, stood in the front yard just outside Aunt Mollie's house and took a pee—with cars driving by. We did that every day out on the farm, but away from people…and certainly not next to the road in sight of passing cars.
>
> We quickly rescued Tom. He would have been in deep trouble if Aunt Mollie had witnessed the event. Tom was just a kid—a happy, pleasant guy and he made a simple mistake. Later—this has no connection—he became a fine Methodist Minister.

§

Other cousins also did some daring things. One such event left a burning impression on Freddy.

"Do you guys want to have a cigarette?" Rollie asked.

"Not me," said George, "I don't want to stunt my growth."

Not discouraged, Rollie walked into Aunt Mollie's garden, chasing away a chicken pecking at a ripe tomato, and harvested some dry corn silks. From his pocket, he produced two sheets of toilet paper and rolled a single cigarette.

While white and gray pigeons flew past toward the barn's open hayloft door, Rollie lit a match and puffed twice. Then he passed the glowing 'cig' to his brother Ben.

Next in line, Freddy went into the project full steam ahead. With the cigarette between his lips, he sucked with all his might. His tendency to overdo raised its ugly head, and enough wind whished through the rapidly burning toilet paper and corn silks for him to sing the *Star Spangled Banner*.

Freddy gasped. He had no breath. He began to cough and choke with smoke exploding from his mouth, both nostrils, and maybe even his ears. His eyes watered, and he began to sneeze. George's face showed concern, but in a second or two, he decided it was funny.

At last, Freddy controlled his breathing. Then, in customary fashion, he cocked his head and said, "Well, that was pretty good. I may have another one after while." He seemed a bit pale.

While the slight breeze rippled the browning grass of August and Saturday's setting sun dropped across the road, the drama continued, with George making sure he was last in line.

Why am I doing this?, he kept thinking. Sweat glistened on his forehead as his turn got closer, and soon he could be cautious no longer. He placed the smoldering cigarette between his lips and proceeded with a most timid draw.

Rollie shook his head and said, "George, that was sure a lily-livered puff." Lily-livered or not, George decided smoking was disgusting! Would that be enough to stunt his growth?

Inside, a few minutes later, Aunt Mollie looked at the boys and asked if they were feeling alright. She was assured everything was fine, though Rollie did have a comment.

"I think we have just been having too much fun, or at least Freddy has," Rollie said with a self-satisfied smile, and no doubt with a bit of questionable truth.

No doubt, Aunt Mollie grinned in secret about the corn silk cigarette and sickly looking boys, for she had a great sense of humor, and of course, she needed one with all of those boys around...and the girls, too.

§

GIRLS WILL BE GIRLS

In our early years, we tended to be indifferent to our female cousins; so most of the time, they went their way and we went ours. We weren't sure what they did, but we knew they played house and liked dolls and such—yuck! We figured the girls weren't up to the task of smoking, and besides, we didn't need any tattle-tales.

Mostly, we decided, the girls played at motherhood and that included caring for the family's health. We discovered evidence to support this.

One sunny Saturday afternoon, we raced around the corner of the house to find Ruth Elaine Burgess and Becky Gordon struggling with Aunt Mollie's squirming gray cat. For some reason, the girls had decided the cat suffered from constipation. It needed an enema. The cat—completely terrorized—gave evidence of wanting to be somewhere else.

Disregarding the cat's feelings, the two girls proceeded to solve this emergency. Their medical equipment included a green onion top—open at both ends—and a half-glass of milk. As the girls poked, prodded, and poured, the poor cat pawed and clawed to get free. At last—hissing and scratching—Pussy escaped, splattering milk all over the girls, herself, and a few curious houseflies.

At least that is the way we remember the event…though there may be denials about the accuracy of this story from some quarters. We have had no reports from the cat.

§

AUNT MOLLIE'S GREEN THUMB

Aunt Mollie had a green thumb and could grow things—including the corn silks used for questionable purposes. Her vegetable garden was large and bountiful, and along the driveway fence, she grew some succulents called chicken and eggs that flowered red, yellow, and white. Her only crop failure seemed to be the rather spindly roses in the yard along the road.

Inside the house, in the living room's oval window-seat, sat her pride and joy. This marvel—a huge sword fern—was bigger than a five-gallon bucket and had dozens of long, tapering green, zipper-like fronds.

"Don't touch that fern in any place," she said, again and again. "If you even brush the end of a leaf, it will die and fall off."

Of course, someone had to investigate the accuracy of that statement. However, with eyes in the back of her head, Aunt Mollie always detected when trouble threatened, and she'd say, "John Frederick Burgess, don't you dare touch that fern." She meant business.

§

The window seat also housed a large Christmas cactus that flowered with masses of long, double-fluted, fuchsia-colored blossoms at Christmas and again about Easter. Its beauty was stunning, but its timing was amazing. We couldn't figure out how it knew when to bloom.

Today, shoots from that same cactus are thriving houseplants in several of the cousins' homes. Those cactus shoots were just one of many gifts Aunt Mollie gave us all.

PINK FOR GIRLS AND BLUE FOR BOYS

Which of Aunt Mollie's gifts did we relish most of all? That was a most difficult question, but there were few things that could match the luscious angel food cake each of us received each birthday. Frosted blue for boys and pink for girls, the cakes put this wonderful relative on an almost angelic pedestal. Just before a birthday, the phone would ring.

"Are you coming by on Saturday?" Aunt Mollie asked early in March. "George's cake will be ready and I know he's anxious to get it."

Indeed, we were anxious, expectant, eager, and excited. We anticipated each bite of the most mouthwatering dessert imaginable. To us, no dessert or candy beat angel food cake.

As far as we can remember, a birthday cake seldom survived the day it went home. No need for it to get stale, we thought. Sometimes we might get a candle or two, but they were unimportant compared to a slab of that soft, white, blue-iced cake. Ahhhhhh.

"It's all in how you treat the eggs," Aunt Mollie said, anytime someone raved about her cakes, which of course happened every time someone tasted one.

"The secret is to use only the whites from thirteen—no more, no less—home-grown leghorn eggs, beat them just right, mix them in good ingredients, and bake the cake in the oven of a wood stove."

Her baking routine never varied, for she had a method for everything. Even the selection of Christmas gifts for each member of the family involved a system. Everyone got a book *that she had read* before she wrapped it. She wanted to make sure it was suitable for the intended recipient.

It is obvious; Aunt Mollie put a lot of effort into being our loving and caring aunt. From the birthday cakes, choice of books, to her play store, we loved her for her generosity. Her home welcomed all, and to some of us, her house was amazing.

§

WHEN IS A HOUSE A MUSEUM?

Aunt Mollie's parlor was a place of wonder that children visited only with supervision or by permission. It contained a tall china closet with real chinaware behind closed and locked glass doors. A couple of Queen Anne chairs with fancy, embroidered backs and seats sat on either side of a mammoth walnut rocking chair.

The room had the first settee Freddy and George ever saw. Red and yellow designs festooned its black fabric and the room smelled wonderfully of furniture wax and musty velvet. It was a museum of sorts the boys guessed, though they'd never seen a real one.

§

*T*he parlor walls held two huge gold-framed pictures taken by a professional photographer. We looked at them in awe—our farmhouse had only a single feedstore calendar or a pinned up dress pattern—yet, in Aunt Mollie's home, there were these and other works of art.

Each time we entered the room, we stared at the black and white photos, each about half the size of our kitchen table, of our unsmiling great-grandparents. Great-Grandmother Margaret Wilson Burgess stared back with a very stern and exhausted look. Great-Grandfather John I. Burgess seemed severe as well, though a large beard and mustache hid much of his face.

Ghosty Picture of John I.

How could they, no matter where we stood, keep looking at us? These were ghosty pictures! Were they mad at some-thing? Had the professional photographer done something to irk them? Or, had we? Oh, boy!

Stern or not, they were our ancestors, and we studied them in detail. Could we see ourselves in them? Did we have Margaret's eyes or John I.'s nose?

John I. was a legend to us. Would we grow up to be like him? We sensed that he had been both saint and sinner, and in his picture, he had the air of a true patriarch. His stern countenance and hard eyes seemed intimidating to us...always following us. Why did we feel he disapproved?

Perhaps, John I. and Margaret deserved to look severe. They left Ireland and their families as newlyweds and never returned, plus they homesteaded in a new land and farmed it at first with nothing but their bare hands. Though they lived productive lives, the effort had been strenuous. No wonder they looked tired.

§

What was it like in the old country?, George thought. He almost asked his great-grandfather that question. Are we like the people there? What were you like?, he wanted to say out loud. But what if the pictures spoke back!?!? Oh, man.

HOW MUCH LOVE MAKES A FAMILY?

Every visit to God-fearing Aunt Mollie's home was worth it. She typified the loving and caring Burgess family, always willing to help people at a moment's notice. When Aunt Mollie or others of the family helped out, they felt no imposition. Rather, helping others was a joy, not a duty.

Perhaps some of the problems of modern society would no longer be problems if family members genuinely cared for each other—and demonstrated it—the way Aunt Mollie did.

Her life was serving others, and while she never married or raised her own children, she was a loving mother or grandmother figure to all. Being of service to others came before self. She indeed cared.

Where are the Aunt Mollies of today? Of course, there are many around, but too often families get lost in the hustle and bustle of busy lives or are drowned in the drone of the television.

Are people willing to put the needs of their children before their own wants? How can families interact and demonstrate love if they are constantly on the move or can only discuss the latest sitcom?

§

Looking back, we were blessed to have an Aunt Mollie and a family that shared and cared. Sure there were disagreements, but there were never battles. We loved one another, as the Good Book requires. On top of that, we even liked each other, because that was what was expected, and we all made it work.

How did this affect our lives? Where did it take us? Those are grand questions.

SEVENTEEN

IS THAT YOUR TOE, COW-TAIL SKIING, AND GOOD ENOUGH FOR COLUMBUS

[*Wamego Times* – June 6, 1944] **THE INVASION** ~ Tuesday morning we awoke to hear from our radios and newspapers that the D Day had arrived. The invasion had started and our troops had crossed the channel and landed in France. This does not mean the war is over or that there will not be more severe fighting, so as you read these lines, stop a moment and say a silent prayer....

IS THAT YOUR TOE?

Thunk! The old, under-inflated football squirted far right, across the lane, just cleared the calf pasture fence, and plopped between a pair of Holstein-Hereford cross steers. They fled—tails flying—to hide in the far corner amid the fiery red sumac of late August.

"You dumb cluck. Why can't you punt right?" Freddy asked, jumping the fence to pick up the ball. From there, he sent a wobbly, but accurate, kick back toward his brother. "For crying out loud, you ought to be able to kick good with feet like yours."

Why can't I kick that ball right? George thought. He stared at his big right foot encased in a brand new, extra roomy, size-10 shoe. Wouldn't such a big foot make him a good kicker?

He stared at the ball, and then with a mighty grunt, kicked his foot upward, just nicking the back of the ball. It fluttered end-over-end for a few feet, bounced twice, and landed spinning in the dust of the lane.

What's wrong?, he wondered. Are my feet too big? Why do they grow so fast that everybody has something to say about them?

Just that morning, his dad had grumbled about spending money to buy him more shoes. "Darn it, George, getting you those shoes was just plain expensive. If you don't stop growing so fast, we'll all end up on the Poor Farm."

Rats! Not the county Poor Farm business again, George thought. Man, I have to do something.

All day he had pondered his problem. Now, as he sent his third poor kick of the evening toward Freddy, a thought flashed into his mind. Maybe he could train his feet to stop growing so fast.

Well, we can train cows to walk right to their stanchions, and we trained Pep to lie down and roll over. I'll bet I can train my feet to slow down.

Freddy kicked the ball back, and it sailed far over the daydreaming head of his brother. "What the crap are you doing?" asked Freddy. "You didn't even try for it."

George wasn't listening. Clearing his throat, he looked down and whispered, "Don't grow, don't grow!" He could feel the message going straight to his feet.

With more force, he repeated, "Don't grow, don't grow."

"Who you talking to? What's going on?"

"I'm trying to train my feet to stop growing."

"You dodo, your body's not a dog. Man, you do take the cake sometimes. That'll never work."

Undaunted, George continued his commands for weeks. But to his regret, he found that Freddy had been right. The feet just kept right on growing, adding the unpleasantness of shoe buying to his long list of ordeals, like upchucking at the S-curves, his first day at milking school, and agonizing over what to buy Rita Straub at the Christmas gift exchange...just to name a few.

§

Our Saturday night trips to Wamego for shoes always made us jumpy. Owning new school shoes was great, but the buying ritual was a fretful moment for all concerned. The game was simple, however.

The folks wanted the best buy—basic brown or basic black—and each pair had to last all year. Whether shopping at Knostman's or Larson's clothing stores, each owned and operated by a pair of brothers, the process began with a measurement.

§

"Put your right foot in here, George," Bill Knostman said, pointing to the mechanical foot on the floor. With practiced effectiveness, he moved the little slides—side and front—and smiled.

"You're a good nine and a half or ten," he said, speaking to the foot. Then to George's mom, he said, "Your son has substantial feet for his age."

"Yes, and they just keep growing. It's so hard to buy shoes that will fit the whole year. Please try on sizes that have a lot of room to grow."

As directed, Bill soon carried an armload of boxes from the back room, each holding a new pair, at least two sizes too big. With the intoxicating smell of new leather, came anxiety for George and his parents. The adults worried about the expense, while the boys feared the sizing struggle to follow.

"Just slip this on," Bill said, setting a brown high-top on the slanted-nose fitting bench. "Isn't this a good looking shoe, George?" he asked, while shoehorning the right foot into the stiff cowhide.

"Now, let's test it for fit," Bill said, pushing down on the end of the shoe. "Is that your toe?"

George looked up and to the right and then rolled his eyes to the left. He couldn't be sure. The stiff leather had no give. Could he feel Mr. Knostman's finger pushing on his toe, swimming in there?

"Yeah, maybe it is," George said, at last, and without confidence. "Well…I think so…maybe…"

"I guess…"

"What do you mean, you guess?" his mom asked. "You should know if it's your toe he's pushing on. What's the matter with you?"

"Yeah, that's it," George said with a thin, squeaky voice. "Maybe."

"Honest to goodness, George David, you amaze me sometimes," she said, raising her voice. She had little tolerance for her son not knowing his own toe.

"There," George whispered, "You touched it that time. I'm pretty sure."

His mother could stand on the sidelines no longer. "Here, let me see."

With that, she jammed her thumb down so hard, if it had touched George's toe, he might have lost a nail. "Why that's not your toe! These are way too big."

So, off came that shoe, out came another, and down went her thumb again. The process went on shoe after shoe, until at last George winced. This was the right shoe, his mom decided—and it was no doubt the size Bill had suggested in the first place.

"Now we need to see how they are when you walk in them, George," Bill said. "Take a little trip around the store to see if they feel okay."

After a few paces, George said, "I guess," while he stopped to admire his feet in the slanty floor mirror. "Yeah, I guess."

"George David Burgess, what do you mean you guess? You have to know. Those shoes will be on your feet all year. Maybe you'd better walk some more so you are sure."

George went on down the aisle toward the front door, and then looped back through several aisles. What did he feel? In truth, he couldn't really tell. However, he wisely used the time to think up a more convincing explanation.

"You know, I kinda like these shoes. I think I'll get a lot of good wear out of them. And Mom, don't you like the shiny brown? Maybe Freddy can get a pair like them, too."

There it was. George was off the hook and Freddy—convinced he had no say in the matter—got his brown high-tops without too much pain or enthusiasm.

The buying decisions made at last, Mr. Knostman went to the push-button cash register and rang up the sale. The boys' dad paid with cash from the wallet in his clean overalls' bib pocket.

Brown butcher paper, tied with cord, soon wrapped each box and the family headed home. For now, the ordeal was over, and George and Freddy had new shoes to wear—rather to swim in—for a while. All went well for a few months—except maybe for inaccurate punting and George's self-consciousness—and then new trials arose.

DOWN IN THE HEEL AND HOLEY SOLES

In April, a Friday night shower left the outside world glowing clean and fresh, while the scene inside seemed cloudy and troublesome. "Will you learn to walk straight?" Freddy's mom said. "You're running your shoes over in the heels. And look at that sole. Those shoes have to last 'til the weather gets warm."

Well, Freddy thought, I have to walk, don't I? How am I supposed to save my heels or my soles? What does she want me to do?

His shoes did show the results of constant wear, mistreatment, and inexpensive quality. The heels were well rounded and the tape job on the right sole hadn't stopped all the flapping. It seemed some home remedies made the problem worse. It was time to seek professional help.

So that Saturday morning, the family headed to see one of the nicest men in Wamego. Adam Bellinder was the owner, manager, and the only full-time employee of *Bellinder's Shoe Repair Shop,* although his older sons, Francis and Eugene, helped out some.

Adam's shop smelled of leather, linseed oil, and shoe polish. Rows of different kinds of shoes filled the back wall, and Adam worked right at the counter where all could see their shoe problems solved.

"It looks like a couple of half-soles and some new heels should do it. Then these shoes will be good for a lot more miles," Adam said with a grin. "Do you want leather or composition soles?"

"What's the difference in price?"

"Well, leather is cheaper, but composition will last longer and isn't so slick."

§

You guessed it. We got leather. We really wanted the better traction of composition, for leather slicked up in the blink of an eye. At school, we didn't want to be spinning when we needed to be going. But, Dad made the frugal choice, and we made do, though it meant the girls caught us easier.

Dad also ordered our shoes reheeled with leather. To our relief, he made another frugal choice and omitted metal taps on each heel. These helped keep the heels from running over, but they made embarrassing noises on the wooden school floor and hung up in the grass.

Our shoes, too big at first and just right six months later, were far too tight by the end of the school year. As summer approached, they were at least a size too small. Kindly Adam could work magic with soles and heels, but he couldn't make a shoe bigger. Only extra special attention could do that.

§

TOELESS SHOES

George's oversized feet forced his dad to take up the art of shoe whittling. Using a technique common in farm country—brute strength before artistic skill—he cut out the toes. This surgery extended the life of the slick-soled shoes through the summer.

And, a summer with slick soles could work to farm kids' advantage, the boys discovered. With their leather soles buffing up like grease from trips across the pasture, stepping in spilled milk, manure plops, and mud, they discovered they could ski in them!

Ski?

COW-TAIL SKIING

"Hey George, look at this," Freddy said, demonstrating the proper technique of skiing behind Hazel, the biggest Holstein.

George watched his brother, then edged up behind another Holstein, flighty Louise, and reached for her tail. She eyed George, decided he was up to no good, and hurried down the well-worn path as if to say, "Oh, no you don't, you skinny kid."

"Maybe you should try Claudette. You can get closer to her," hollered Freddy as he slid around behind his cow.

George moved toward the big Guernsey and grabbed her tail. Nothing happened. She didn't move, just arched her back and stood there. She was a big flop as a ski tow.

"She won't move," George said. "She just stands here. I think I'll try Bubbles."

He crept into position and stopped behind this big, almost all white Holstein. She looked at him for a moment, and then went back to grazing. George sidled to within a step from her, grabbed her tail, and—whoosh—off they went on the ride of a lifetime. Bubbles bolted and headed across the pasture, pulling George's sixty-five pounds along as if he wasn't there.

"Hold on tight, and keep your feet rigid," instructed Freddy.

George slid along without a word, trying to keep his balance as he zigged and zagged behind the powerful, rump-bouncing cow. This is great, he thought.

At that moment, the long ride ended, as Bubbles plowed him into a clump of ironweed and he let the jerking tail go. The weeds grabbed and jabbed at his exposed toes.

"Ouch! Dang that hurts."

Meanwhile, Freddy grabbed Hazel's tail again and skied a good 15 yards before she zigged and whipped him into a gigantic, disgusting, and still steaming cow pattie. He released the cow's tail just as his toe-less shoes scooped up the messy goop. "Arrrrrrgggggg!"

By now the cows had scattered, so George joined his brother. "You gotta mess, don't you?"

Freddy's glance said it all. He just headed for the windmill to wash off. Then he grinned. He would ski another day.

§

Our cows had led us to invent a new sport—suitable we thought—for the next Olympics. The person with the longest slick sole shoe ride would win the gold medal as the Cow-Tail Skiing Champion.

The sport needed perfecting, and of course, lacked rules of procedure and should have regulations about the size, breed, and length of tail for all cow tow-mobiles. Would larger feet or slicker soles add style points? What about the toeless shoes? Didn't they add to the degree of difficulty?

Difficulty or not, it's easy to picture us, each dressed in toeless shoes, overalls, and a floppy hat. We were a picture of style—farmer's style—and that caused us some grief from time to time.

You see, there were times when we wanted to look cowboy, not farmer. We longed for bib-less attire.

GOOD ENOUGH FOR COLUMBUS

Certainly bib overhalls—as we called them—marked us as farmers. In the movies and comics, farmers were hicks, and called hayseeds or yokels.

Were we slow of wit like the hicky farmer, B. O. Plenty in the Dick Tracy comics?

We didn't feel dumb—our dad certainly wasn't—because of our denim-clothed overalls, but we sometimes thought other people thought we were. On the other hand, cowboy style jeans and belts could help us avoid the whole issue.

Our mom insisted, however, overalls were practical and that everybody else wore them. And, she said, they were normal farm attire for very good reasons, though in our opinion, style was not one of them.

§

"Now, you listen here, young man, if overhalls are good enough for your father, they are good enough for you!" Freddy's mom said. "They even say the sails on Columbus' ships were made of denim cloth."

It followed—at least to her—that if the cloth was good enough for the Nina, the Pinta, and the Santa Maria, it was sturdy enough for her son to wear for school and for farm work. What could be better than a good pair of denim overhalls?

§

For one thing, overhalls eliminated our need for belts, and had lots of pockets—four below the waist, and two pockets and a pencil slot on the bib. A hammer-hanging loop attached to the left leg and there was a narrow tool pocket on the right.

Since the simple machinery and engines of the day required constant tinkering, farmers needed pockets for wrenches or pliers. Lots of pockets provided places for nuts and bolts, pocketknives, and the ever-present billfold in the bib. Our pockets sometimes also held a frog, eggs from a newly discovered chicken nest, and even fish worms. Indeed, overhalls were just plain handy.

But, handy or not, we longed for Levi's. Can you imagine your favorite movie cowboy riding his big black stallion in bib overhalls? No! They wore jeans and so should we.

We tried to convince the folks to buy us jeans, but Mom was dead set against them. Dad didn't take as hard a line, but he did support the practical, down-to-earth side of wearing overhalls—though he recognized jeans were also made of Columbus' denim.

The overhalls versus blue jeans issue came to a head just before school started, when we headed to Wamego on a late August evening for a back-to-school shopping trip.

Had we paid attention, we'd have seen the landscape flooded by a giant harvest moon and nighthawks swooping in the warm air above the road. However, we fidgeted in the backseat, hoping against hope we could somehow talk our folks into some brand of jeans, and move forever from the disgrace of overhalls.

§

AN ARMISTICE IN THE NICK OF TIME

When the car stopped in front of O.B. Larson & Son's, Freddy hurried inside to the blue jeans display. While his mom stopped at the table with overhalls, he eyed a pair of very blue Lee's *Can't Bust 'Em Dungarees*. How could he convince the folks he needed these jeans? Seventh graders just didn't wear clothes with bibs in the modern world.

"Now, young man, you know we are here to buy overhalls," his mom said. "We talked about that at home."

Outside, dozens of moths flitted around the

streetlights along Lincoln Avenue. Over the grass in the City Park, lightning bugs flashed on and off like beacons. The park's famous Dutch Windmill looked down on the unhurried activity below, its blocks of cream limestone brightening in the light of passing cars. It was a tranquil scene—that evening of August 26, 1946—except in Larson's store.

Freddy sensed the need for persuasion, for the battle-lines were drawn. Both he and his mom possessed redheaded tempers, and confrontation was the rule. When frustrated, most of his 'comebacks' came back long after he needed them. Still, he had to try.

"Ah, Mom, a seventh-grader can't dress like a hick. I need some Levi's. The kids don't wear overhalls today. Don't you love me anymore?"

"Anyway, Jim Scully and Barney Gava both had Levi's by the sixth grade, and the cousins, too. Please."

"Now you listen here, young man. These overhalls are just fine. Because some people wear jeans, that doesn't mean everybody should. After all, what other people do is their business, not yours."

Freddy felt defeat. He had no more arguments, and he knew he faced another year playing the hick. No seventh grader would be caught dead in overhalls. Some of the four girls in his class—he was pretty sure—wore bras. How could any self-respecting male, wearing overhalls, possibly interact with lipstick-painted, bra-wearing females?

Just when all seemed lost, Neville Larson came to Freddy's rescue. "You know, Freddy might be right. We sell jeans, almost exclusively, to kids his age. And, they are cheaper than overhalls, if that is of interest."

"If you want, Veda, your boy could try on this pair. That way we can see if they fit. Will you want to have enough room for him to grow? He'd have to wear them all year, wouldn't he?"

That Neville sure can ask good questions, Freddy thought. The folks can't say no to any of them.

"You'll want him to look good in them, too, won't

you?"

Freddy's mom shrugged and looked away. After a time, his dad gave a silent nod. Neville had gotten another yes!

Two minutes later, Freddy came from the dressing room and walked to the long wall mirror. He was stunned. He wasn't a hick anymore. Wow!

In the end, Freddy had achieved an armistice. This would be the year of the boys' apparel breakthrough.

At last they shed their B. O. Plenty label, and looked like real cowboys. They were no longer country bumpkins, and felt grown up and ready for high school.

Still, the farm work had to be done, no matter what the boys or their dad wore. While Freddy was relieved that his folks had avoided a serious mistake—thank you Mr. Larson—and let him wear jeans, there would be many other opportunities to make mistakes. And, not all would be the boys' doing. How about inept tractor driving?

EIGHTEEN

PAINTING LIKE P. KOSSO, DAD GUM THAT SHORTY BROCKMAN, AND GOING, GOING, GONE

[*Wamego Times* – July 5, 1945] ~ **PRAIRIE VIEW** – Miss Rita Straub spent a few days last week with Miss Iona Graf. She is spending a few days this week with her aunt, Mrs. Joe Daylor and family. Bob Scully of the Navy who is stationed at Olathe Naval Base spent Sunday with his parents.

PAINTING LIKE P. KOSSO

"It's all over the car! What in the world happened, John? How will we ever clean up this mess? Oh, how did this happen?"

§

Dad shook his head three times and eyed the glossy—and well-dried—orange paint and the broken glass that speckled the '36 Chevy's backseat. After a moment, he pulled his lips together, clinched his jaws to form bulges like walnuts and sucked in air through his teeth. As he shook his head again, a crow, high on the barn roof, uttered a belittling caw.

Like the crow, we felt Dad's self-disgust. He hadn't considered the hot July sun, the closed car, and the glass jar full of paint, had he? The heat did its job, and now the car had a special paint job—inside! It would never clean up.

Mom, sick to her stomach, began walking toward the house just as Wally Hoffman drove up the lane with Bill Mansfield in tow. Wally closed his car's door, took two steps, and peered into our backseat. A wide grin spread over his face.

We sensed the wheels turning in his head, while he devised ways to make the best of the situation. At last, he rolled the toothpick between his teeth—grinning ear to ear—and cleared his throat. He looked in the car, then at Dad, and then back at the car.

§

"So, John, I never knew you were an artist." Eyeing the backseat again, he said, "That is a darn good use of color, although it maybe has a little too much orange for me."

"So, just what style is this? Is it one of those depressionist things? You know; color every which way like that guy P. Kosso paints."

"I think that's it, Wally. This looks like that guy's stuff. See over there on the seat is one orange eye and there's another on the back window, ain't that so?" Bill Mansfield asked, grinning at his own joke.

Then he added, "Of course, they say you can train a monkey to throw paint to make a picture, so why not John? This has to be that good, doesn't it?"

"I don't rightly know," Wally said, "but I sure do like how that orange is kinda exploded here and there. Maybe it's how the monkey would do it!"

"Have you given any thought about selling this masterpiece, John? I've got me a big old boar pig I might be willing to trade for it."

§

Wally and Bill laughed—to the point of tears—and, so did we in spite of ourselves. Bit by bit we watched fun creep into Dad's eyes, until he joined in. What else could he do? What was done was done. Thank God, no one got hurt, unless you counted the car and a bit of Dad's pride.

The whole thing started when Dad—rushing to finish cultivating before it rained—cracked the AC's front steering housing crossing a ditch in the south field. That meant he had to order a special factory part—it cost $22.75—and lost two days of field time waiting for it.

When the unpainted housing arrived, Dad said to the AC dealer, "I don't want to wait until you paint it Abe, 'cause I need to get back to the field. Sell me a quart of orange paint, and I'll paint it myself when I get the time."

Later that day, the jar exploded. That, as Wally Hoffman said later, moved John Burgess from the cornfield to the field of modern art.

§

Some days, no matter what people did, things just went to heck in a hand basket and this was that kind of day for the boys' dad. And while some farmers would only cuss their luck, he took things in stride.

"Boys," he said, again and again, "the good days outweigh the bad because God cares about us. Look for good in everything."

"And get along with everybody, even if they tease you. Pay attention to how you treat others, and always keep your fences mended. That makes for good neighbors."

DAD GUM THAT SHORTY BROCKMAN

In farm country, shared fences were property lines and good neighbors worked together to keep them in repair. An unwritten rule said farmers should meet at the middle of the fence, shake right hands, and point to their half of the fence with left hands.

That rule worked when both neighbors remembered it and didn't mix up their right and left hands. Trouble started if a neighbor fell down on the job and let his half fall apart.

"Dad gum that Shorty Brockman, he never gets around to fixing his share of the fence. Now, his cows are all over Wally's wheat. We better put 'em back boys."

"I'll leave the car here in the road, and George, you stay with it to turn them back if they head this way. Freddy, you circle around to the north and force them back toward their pasture. See the hole in the fence?"

Stopped on the way to Wamego, the three herded the mixed bunch of cows where, at the fence hole, an old brindle cow eyed the barbed wire and then stepped through. One at a time, the others followed, as if it was a routine, and no doubt it was.

"Let's pull up these wires, and then Freddy, you splice that broken one with the baling wire hanging on the fence. George and I will tie everything to the posts. It won't be a first-rate repair job, but it will have to do until Shorty gets to it—if he ever does."

In Shorty's defense, all fences needed repairs from time to time, for livestock caused damage and severe weather could produce washouts or down wires with fallen trees or big limbs. And, after several years, all fences had some rotted, wobbly posts and sagging wire. Many a Saturday morning was spent working on a fence.

"Boys, this is a good day to fix the fence along the east side of the meadow. We'll get started right after breakfast. We can be done by noon, if we all work at it."

Darn, thought Freddy, we wanted to go BB gun hunting this morning. Oh, well, maybe we can do it this afternoon if we hurry up with the fence.

So with urgency, he bolted down his food and headed outside. There he hooked the AC to the trailer and helped load a dozen knobby hedge posts, the auger-style post-hole digger, hammers, staples, wire cutters, the rope and pulley wire stretcher, some new barbwire—everybody called it bobwire—and of course, baling wire.

Freddy drove down the hill at the end of the brown meadow, while overhead high October clouds scudded northeast and a slight, warming breeze moved in from the southwest. The sun filtered through hazy clouds, giving the landscape a soft, contented feel, in spite of the labor ahead.

As Freddy drove, his dad surveyed the quarter mile of fence and said, "You know, a lot of these old posts look good and solid, but about a dozen need replacing. There is some sagging wire to mend or replace, too."

When the tractor stopped he said, "George, you take a hammer and a screwdriver to pry out the staples from those first few posts. We'll have to stretch and restaple each wire. Freddy, you can help me dig out the old corner post."

Within minutes, the corner post—the fence line turned around it—was out and the hole augered clean. Then they moved the biggest and straightest replacement post into place.

"Shovel in some dirt and I'll tamp it down to set the post tight. That way the wires will stay stretched. We can cross brace it with diagonal posts and bobwire. With luck, we'll be done here in a couple of hours."

Not long before noon, a line of posts, some new and some old, marched up the hill. These plentiful Osage Orange posts were split from the rough, mature rows of the thorny trees that kept cattle in before the invention of bobwire. Now, they became posts with lots of unorganized knobs.

Most farmers swore by the hedge posts' iron-like quality—they resisted the ax when dry—and some lasted for fifty years or more. They might even outlast the three or four bobwire strands of most fences. However, producing a straight line of knobby marching posts took skill. The joke was to point the knobs and curves north and south and the fencing east and west—or vice versa.

In the end, a good three-wire fence kept non-mistreated livestock in the right pasture and made for good neighborhood relationships. And, these turned into trusting friendships.

§

KNOWING THE NEIGHBORS

*I*n the '40s and '50s, our straightforward neighbors were easy to like. They looked out for us as we did for them and handshakes sealed agreements. Farmers swapped labor, loaned equipment, and trusted each other to protect a neighbor's property, livestock, and even the family honor. No one bothered to lock the house and most would offer to help out in any way they could.

We did have a loner-type neighbor called Strawberry Sam. Only a mile away, we seldom saw him coming or going from his small farmstead back in the cottonwoods at the end of a long pasture lane. A wire gate across the lane seemed to say, "Don't enter this place."

Because of his hidden existence, we wondered if Strawberry Sam had something to hide. His name was a puzzle, too; who knows where it came from?

We met our first neighbors—the Heigers and Riats—on that rainy day in March in 1944 when we moved to the farm, and thank God, they were there. They became special friends, and there were more just like them.

Although some people moved in and out, over the years, we met the Picolets, the Grafs, the Pittengers, and the Mansfields. The Otto and Ted Straubs had nine kids between them, all who attended our one-room school.

We knew the Hoffmans, the Randalls, the Hableutzels, the Waggoners, the Hupes, and the Scullys, and later Herman and Onie Elder. On the place just south of us, Frank Cotton moved in after the Grafs left, and then the Kensings and finally Joe and Dorothy Straub. The Rinikers moved in further south of us a little later.

Each neighbor influenced us in one way or

another. One who had special impact was Leo Scully.

WHAT AM I BID?

"Why don't we meet at Leo Scully's sale tomorrow and see if we can buy his fertilizer spreader?" the boys' dad said to Wally Hoffman. "It would be handy for some of the rented ground we farm together, and we could each use it at home when we need it."

"Okay," Wally said. "The way it's raining this evening, we won't be able to get in the field anyway. Besides, I'd like to go just to help Leo."

"We'll miss him and his family. He told me that with all of his boys coming home from the Navy, the farm wouldn't be big enough. So, Leo and Marie reckoned it was time to sell out and move to town."

"Yep, I guess it is. Well, we'll see you tomorrow."

§

The next morning, Dad drove the old International truck through a crystal clear, rain-cleansed countryside to Scully's place. A sparkling sun highlighted the trees, grass, and muddy fields of young corn, refreshed by the air-born nitrogen from the storm's lightning. Farmers—they came to the sale by the dozens—seemed refreshed, too.

The big crowd meant a good sale. Scully's public auction—we sensed it was difficult for them—would be successful. And, that helped remove some of the pain of selling their livestock, machinery, and a lot of household goods.

Sale goers came for many reasons. We saw most were farmers and knew some of them came looking for bargain livestock or machinery. Others, like Dad and Wally, came because they wanted a certain item or piece of equipment. Still others, released from their fields by the rain, came to look around and enjoy this unique kind of social event.

Sales were exciting, and sale goers, including us, were talkative. In the warm and humid air, they greeted each other, and the joshing began, as small groups of men examined the machinery or leaned on the corral fence to inspect the livestock.

The smell of boiled coffee, served by the Louisville Rebekah Lodge, drifted on the soft breeze. Homemade donuts tempted us, but with only a dollar each in our cardboard wallets, we decided to wait.

§

The day Scullys sold out—people called it that—was in early June. Mr. Lawrence Welter was auctioneer and manager of the sale. He organized a good sale people said, by printing and distributing descriptive handbills and running ads in several weekly papers.

Welter, expert at getting bidders to pay good value, had a rapid-fire, sing-song auctioneering banter. This style also helped swell the crowd.

Promptly at 9:00, while sparrows twittered around the barn and a cardinal sang high up in a hackberry tree, auctioneer Welter called for quiet.

"You all know the Scullys are retiring from farming and at this sale, they'll sell everything listed on the handbill. I'll be the auctioneer, and Harold Carlson over there is clerk of the sale. Be sure to pay him in check or cash for any items you buy before you leave today."

"Everything is sold in an 'as is' condition, so look things over good before you bid. As usual, at this type of auction, all sales are final. The Scullys are moving out so nothing can come back if it isn't right."

"Okay, let's get started with this machinery. How much am I bid for this McCormack-Deering mower? It's fixed to pull behind a tractor, so let's start the bidding at...ah...forty ah dollars...do I hear forty...a forty...a forty…let's have a forty dollar bid."

While dozens of people braved the muddy footing, Welter auctioned all of Scully's old tractors and implements. The fertilizer spreader—the last item—went to the boys' dad and Wally for $18. Next Welter sold the cattle, other livestock, and the poultry, with the crowd following from one spot to another to bid or to gawk.

§

Just before noon, Welter, needing a rest, stopped and suggested it was time for everyone to have lunch. He'd start again, he said, about 12:30.

In a hurry, we joined Dad and headed for the big tables filled with fried chicken, pork and beans, scalloped potatoes with ham, chicken stew, and ham sandwiches on homemade bread with dill pickles and mustard.

Everything was mouth-watering, though the prices seemed high. After looking things over, we ordered ham sandwiches—fifteen cents each—and scoops of pork and beans for a dime apiece. We paid the Lodge lady from our wallets.

Dad bought a sandwich, too, and then began examining the pies. He seemed willing to spend more, so we let him. He bought slices of pie for us—one apple and one custard—for ten cents apiece. Wow! Were we glad he had that sweet tooth!

We had just finished eating—devouring, in the case of the pie—when the sale started again. Now Mr. Welter moved between the smaller household and appliance items at a rapid pace, rat-a-tat-tating out the bids, seeming to always know the price to start each item. He seldom missed a bid—slight nods or simple hand flicks—as his eyes flashed from person to person.

By now, we understood his auctioneer's lingo and sing-song chatter when he said, "What am I bid for this fine icebox? Let's start the bidding at $10...a-ten-a-ten-a-ten-a...eleven-e-leven...e-leven fifty...e-leven fifty...twelve-a-twelve-a-twelve...and-a...sold for twelve dollars!"

§

GOING, GOING, GONE

Welter moved to sell a kitchen table, and the boys shifted, too, stopping beside an old music box. Curious, Freddy lifted the lid and eyed the turntable and playing arm. Hey, he thought, this could play some good music like we heard at Grandpa and Grandma Scott's when we were in Michigan. Then he opened the cabinet doors. Inside, a dozen black records stood in narrow slots. Wow, wouldn't this be great?

"Look at this Victorola," Freddy whispered to his brother. "Let's see if we can buy it. It even has some records here behind this door."

Frowning, George said, "We don't have much money, and I may need something else to eat. Anyway, we'd better ask Dad."

"Some of these old things are selling cheap. And, we can't ask Dad, he's way over there. We have to decide in a hurry," Freddy said. When his brother was non-committal, Freddy assumed they agreed.

Welter moved to the Victorola, opened the lid, and after a couple of seconds said, "What am I bid for this fine music box? Let's start the bidding at $1.50."

Freddy's eyes popped. He stepped out so Welter could see him and began nodding his head like a bobble-doll. The auctioneer nodded back, and kept his lingo going. Few in the crowd moved a muscle, though some did look away while others eyed the boys with knowing smiles. After long seconds—at least to Freddy—Welter said the magic words: "Going, going, gone!"

§

When Mr. Carlson moved over to take seventy-five cents from each of us, the realization hit. We had done it and now owned one genuine, hand cranked Victorola. And, we'd been lucky to get it so cheap!

Feeling excited and a bit nervous, we never once considered why no one else had bid. Perhaps, we should have suspected something was wrong, but we didn't. We just stared at our heavy old antique, and even admired the extra parts inside the hinged hood.

Later, Dad just shook his head, and then helped us load the old machine onto our truck to haul it home. There, he suggested—we didn't question it—we place the Victorola in the unused smokehouse. We couldn't wait to play the large, round 78 r.p.m. records, and hear the magical sounds of music—scratchiness and all—like we had enjoyed at Grandpa and Grandma's.

§

"You wind it up," Freddy said, "And I'll pick out a good record."

George cranked the handle a few turns and Freddy thumbed the titles and then placed a big black disk—*The Waters of the Minnetonka*—on the turntable. He dropped the needle arm onto the record and said, "Ok, turn it on."

The click of the 'on' switch was the only sound. Nothing moved. The turntable sat frozen in place.

"Ok, try it again. Maybe the switch is loose," Freddy said as his stomach began to feel queasy. Again, a flip of the switch and nothing happened. Oh, no, he thought, this thing must be busted. Maybe that explains all those extra parts. Drat, drat, drat.

§

The Victorola was never going to play music again in its 'as is' condition. We felt crushed and spent a good deal of time blaming each other, though we had no one to blame but ourselves.

Finally, we left the smokehouse to let the Victorola rest in peace. As weeks passed, we forgot the setback and moved on to other pursuits. Somehow, by shutting the smokehouse door, our mistake just went away.

A couple of months later, however, we got a grand surprise when Mr. Scully—he now lived in town—showed up with a workable Victorola for us. He'd found out about our disappointment and decided to do something.

At another farm sale more than 50 miles away, he purchased a player for more than it was worth, just so he could replace the one that we—his young friends—had bought.

Although we still had a lot to learn about auctions, Victorolas, and life in general, we did understand what this man had done for us. We learned a lot from this incident about personal character...and in particular...that Mr. Scully was a special kind of neighbor.

FUNERALS AND DECORATON DAY

Strange as it may seem, we learned a great deal about our neighbors and our community at funerals. We noted that the immediate family sat in tearful sorrow throughout the memorial ceremony, while friends participated with a tender solemnness.

Whether at a church or a funeral home, we saw the constant fluttering of free cardboard funeral home fans. People fanned, perhaps because the room was warm, or because they were farmers wearing suits and ties, or maybe they were a bit uncomfortable and just needed something to do.

§

Everyone sat with reverence while groups like the Baptist Quartet sang *Beyond the Sunset* or the organist played *In the Sweet Bye and Bye.* Someone always spoke kindly about the deceased, and the preacher led prayers commending the deceased to the Lord and requesting comfort for those left behind.

Next, it was time to view the open casket. With a sense of hurt and loss, people looked at their friend or loved one for the last time. How many years had they known each other? Uncle Bill, or Aunt Alice, or neighbor Howard would be missed.

Then the pallbearers loaded the shiny, expensive looking casket into the big, black hearse for the trip to a cemetery called Pleasant Hill, or Louisville, or Broderick, or Wamego, or Manhattan. With lights on, it led the procession of cars and trucks toward the graveyard. Cars coming from the other direction always stopped, out of respect, until the hearse-led procession passed.

At the cemetery, the green grass contrasted with the brown earth piled beside the open grave. The air smelled of fresh soil and mothballs from long-stored suits and Sunday dresses. Somewhere cottonwood leaves rattled in the soft breeze. Someone cried softly while people grouped around, heard the final words about 'ashes to ashes and dust to dust' and, then watched the casket being lowered into the ground.

As neighbors and friends left the graveside, they walked by the grieving family and extended their callused hands and said simple words like "sympathy" or "condolences" or "I'm so sorry." The farmers wore their only suit and tie and, with hats removed, showed white foreheads above the sun-wrinkled faces and tired eyes. Wives came forward in their best dresses, many fitting snuggly around aging bodies.

This was a genuine display of shared sorrow. Everyone knew what neighbors felt, for they conveyed the message that they cared in many ways. The community honored the dead at funerals and with later visits to the cemetery.

§

We always went together to make an annual cemetery visit each Decoration Day…now called Memorial Day. Usually, other family members joined us at the Pleasant Hill Cemetery where John I. and Margaret Burgess were buried. Many relatives rested there and at the Louisville Cemetery. Later, our own parents would be buried in the Manhattan Cemetery.

On Decoration Day, rural families like us often placed tinfoil-covered fruit jars with large bunches of red or white peonies or gold and brown iris alongside relatives' tombstones. Those colorful remembrances completed, we'd move into the shade of a majestic elm or sycamore, and for a long time, the adults would talk about 'Mom' or 'Dad' and many of the other people from a generation we did not get to know well.

Younger folks, including us, often darted among the gravestones to read names and dates, and to wonder who those people had been. What had they been like? Were we like them? Truly, we looked forward to these times together as a larger family. Thank God for families and neighbors.

§

Of course, not all encounters with neighbors were at funerals or when work was on the line. In fact, neighborly contact could happen over the fence, along the road, or in town. Men and women who worked alone day after day, found much pleasure—usually—in talking with each other.

Some neighbors met and talked at church. Our church friends were people who seemed to care about us a great deal—especially when we helped serve them pancakes.

NINETEEN

THE SEATING OF PEW NUMBER THREE, NOT ON MY COFFIN, AND THE BISHOP'S VISIT

[*Wamego Times* – November 15, 1945] ~ **ST. LUKE'S PARISH DINNER** – The annual Parish dinner of St. Luke's Episcopal Church was held in the Guild Hall last Thursday night with a good attendance. Special guests from out of town included Bishop and Mrs. Goodrich Fenner of Topeka, Rev. Charles R. Davies, Mr. and Mrs. W. L. Lindsey, and Mr. and Mrs. Wayne Sieh of Manhattan. A musical program was given by Mr. Ralph Flowers of the High School faculty, Bill and Ben Sessler, Misses Natalie and Gloria Hill, and Miss Connie Whitmyer.

WHERE'S THE SYRUP?

"They want more syrup at table number two," Hank Schroeder hollered to the kitchen crew through the serving window of St. Luke's Guild Hall. "They're sucking it down faster than quicksand."

"Some of those ole boys can really eat," the boys' dad said as he continued turning the 15 golden brown pancakes on the grill. "Looks to me some of 'em are eating syrup…with pancakes on the side…instead of the other way around."

§

Dad, Hank, and several others—including the two of us—belonged to the Brotherhood of St. Andrew, an Episcopal organization dedicated to sharing Christ with men and boys. This second Saturday in May was its annual Pancake Breakfast featuring pancakes, bacon, and eggs.

It looked like all of the church's men and boys were there, sitting on folding chairs at seven of the Guild Hall's long tables, eating this special breakfast. The Sessler twins, Ben and Bill, plus the two of us, served as waiters.

"Jim Boyce wants three eggs and four slices of bacon with his pancakes," Ben said through the serving window. Grinning about the big man's appetite, Uncle Alfred dished up the order and said, "We'll give 'em what they want, as long as the eggs hold out."

He handed Boyce's plate to Ben and other plates to us. The look and aroma of food made our stomachs rumble yet again. We were starved. We'd gotten up before six o'clock, done an hour's worth of chores, washed up, changed clothes, ridden to town, and helped set up chairs and tables—all without breakfast. Now as waiters, we could only stare at the luscious, mouth-watering meals—and watch others eat!

But, while we did feel tortured by hunger on the one hand, we were proud to work with Dad, Uncle Alfred, and the others for the Brotherhood. We respected its mission: 'To spread Christ's Kingdom throughout the world, especially to men and boys.' We just wished we didn't have to wait for breakfast.

If that Mr. Jay Hill, the Wamego Postmaster, would eat more and talk less, we could begin the clean-up...didn't he know it was after nine?

§

George, by this time, felt weak from the smell of frying bacon and maple syrup. To take his mind off his stomach, he thought of a quip from Bill Mansfield.

"Man, I'm so hungry I could eat the north end of a south bound horse!" he whispered, as he handed his pal, Don Tessendorf, a second serving. "If I don't eat soon, I'm gonna break down from the lack of groceries."

Don laughed and that alerted Uncle Alfred to the servers' problem. "Boys," he said from the kitchen, "why don't you come and get your plates? We can clean up the tables later."

In just seconds, the four waiters were digging into high stacks of pancakes, dripping with homemade butter, and the sweet liquid from the Log Cabin syrup can.

Ahhh, thought George, as he puffed-out his cheeks and his satisfied face told a story of contentment. I guess God's Kingdom was indeed worth the wait!

"Hey, Uncle Alfred, can we get seconds?"

§

THE SEATING OF PEW NUMBER THREE

God's Kingdom—with or without seconds—meant a great deal to us, and we expressed our relationship with the Almighty in many ways. We had family prayer, grace at meals, and went to church every Sunday, even when winter storms made driving difficult.

Much of our early lives we worshiped at quaint St. Luke's Episcopal Church in Wamego. Built of white, native-limestone blocks in 1894, it had two square Norman-style towers like those in England, and had bright red front doors with embossed brass handles and hinges.

Stained glass windows—Mom loved them—depicted scenes from the Bible, and filled the Gothic arches in the foot thick walls. At services, the sun's movement also moved the intense sunlit shapes of green, blue, yellow, and red that scattered across the red carpet and the white plastered walls.

Our church held about 40 worshipers, including the choir, organist, acolytes, and clergy. This became a very close-knit group when another 10 or more showed up at times like Christmas, Easter, or a well-attended funeral.

The church seemed holy. It produced a feeling of reverence for most people. Our mom, for example, took on a solemn look of piety upon entering. She pulled her lips against her teeth, formed her mouth into a straight line, and clasped her hands just so.

She is very pious, we thought, for she held that pose throughout the service—all from her favorite seat. That was pew number three on the left side—our family's if at all possible—every Sunday. We weren't sure why Number Three was different from pews one, two, four, five, or six—Uncle Alfred sat there—but somehow Mom felt very close to God in the third row.

If a visitor—by accident—beat her to that pew, Mom tried not to be put out. However, with a pitiable look, she'd make eye contact with them and present the narrowest of smiles, as if to say, "It's okay, you don't know any better. Normally that is our pew."

Our loving mom also directed our seating in pew three. She put us on her left—for control purposes—with Dad on the outside. This trapped us next to the wall with the only escape past her pious body. That was a road less traveled, unless very necessary.

During services, Mom seldom broke her character, except to smack a right thigh or to whisper a sharp, "Shsh!" She must have thought God wanted quiet, for we sat very still during worship.

We wanted to please Mom, but of course, some prayers went on and on. That did not disturb her, for she insisted her week was not complete without a long period of worship. Upon leaving church, her face took on a look of what we assumed was heavenly bliss. The look lasted quite a while—or until one of us messed up her tranquility on the way home.

Mom's piety also extended to her role as a member of the Altar Guild. This group of dedicated ladies cleaned up, set up, and organized the altar before and after each service. Members of the guild were happy to be of service and were convinced they did the Lord's work.

BRUSH ON THE ALTAR

And the most important Guild task—so we believed—was draping the Altar before each service with special linens the ladies had washed and ironed at home before each use. They also polished the candlesticks, the Chalice, and Paten, used during Eucharist, or Holy Communion as we called it.

The Chalice for the communion wine and the Paten for the bread belonged on a Holy Table beside the Altar. Because St. Luke's tiny Altar area had no space for a table, we used a broad, deep windowsill instead. We never called it the Holy Table, but then no one called it a Holy Sill either.

§

The Guild lady assigned for each Sunday or special day also placed vases of flowers on both sides of the Altar Cross. They used plants and flowers from their yards or what was seasonally available. Some women had great taste and arranged delicious sprays of lavender and white lilacs or a bouquet with yellow daffodils and bunches of yellow forsythia.

Some, however, used flower groups with a hurried, inexpensive look, or showed evidence that not much was blooming. Sometimes, vases contained no flowers at all—especially in fall or winter—but held small sumac limbs with red, brown, and gold leaves merged with buckbrush clusters containing small red berries.

§

We thought these woodsy bouquets looked fine, but Mom disagreed with force. We would like to tell you our sweet, caring mom had no quirks, but in truth, that was not the case—at least when it came to Altar flowers. Besides disliking vases of brush, she objected to the use of growing plants, potted in gardener's soil.

"Why would anyone put all that dirt on the Altar?" she asked no one in particular. "That is just not right!" Then, from the back of her throat, in a low, almost guttural tone, came her most famous statement, "Uahhhgh."

That meant strong disapproval, and she used it quite often. We considered the word to be an early form of 'yuck.'

NOT ON MY COFFIN

One last Altar flower really triggered Mom's passion, at that time in her life. For some reason, lost in the annals of history, Mom disliked calla lilies for years. For some reason, she was irritated by the tall green shoots that gracefully formed into fluted white trumpets. If, when she walked into church—lips pursed and hands folded—she spied calla lilies beside the Cross, out came an, "Uahhhgh."

"I just don't know why anyone would use smelly calla lilies. They look so awful." Turning to us she said, "When I die, don't you dare put calla lilies on my coffin! If you do, I'm going to sit right up and tell you about it!"

We got the message. There would be no calla lilies for Mom's funeral or any other time she was involved. Like when the Bishop visited.

"We'll have a great Easter service this morning. I'm so excited," Mom said on the way to church. As we drove past fresh green fields, alive with bright spring sunshine, she added, "It is a thrill to have Bishop Fenner come up from Topeka again this year. When we can get someone like him for supply clergy, maybe it's good not to have a full-time priest."

When Dad turned the Chevy on to Highway 99, she said, "Now you boys need to be on your best behavior. You're his acolytes, and you don't want to make any mistakes. He's a great man you know."

§

Wow, thought Freddy, I can't wait to see that ole bishop. He's huge—bigger than Jim Boyce. I wonder how come he can sing loud like that. He makes the whole church tremble. And, he's kinda funny, too.

A few minutes later, in the Sacristy vesting area at St. Luke's, the boys said hello to the big man. "It will be good to have the two of you as my acolytes this morning," the Bishop said. "We'll celebrate a great Easter together. You boys are lucky to be part of this fine congregation here at Wamego."

Then he looked at George and said, "And you, young man, you're going to light the candles on the Altar I hear. That will be fine. Just be sure to light the Epistle side first."

"Yes sir," the shy fourth-grader said, his hands tightening on the handle of the slow burning candle lighter. With not a hint of understanding, he headed out the door.

"Just a minute, young man," the Bishop said, gripping George by the shoulder. "You do know which is the Epistle side, don't you?"

"Well, sir…," George said, stalling to see if he could come up with an answer in his unsettled brain. The Altar had only two candles, but which was the Epistle? "Well, yes, maybe I do, but…I'm…not…so…sure. I guess it must be whichever side you say it is."

With a soft chuckle, the fine man of God explained the candle lighting process—yet again. "The candle to the right of the cross is on the Epistle side. In this Diocese, we light it first and the Gospel side second. And, be sure to bow when you move over in front of the cross."

George needed this important information, but instead, barely listened, as his eyes widened and his mind raced. For the first time, he noticed the Bishop's ears. They seemed too big for his head. The ponderous lobes almost touched his shoulders. Each ear seemed double-sized—like a saucer!

"And put them out in reverse order. That way the candle on the right burns longer," the Bishop said, bobbing his head for emphasis, while his lobes flapped in the process.

George stared, then nodded. Do you suppose all bishops have ears like that, he thought? And do you suppose Bishop Fenner's flutter in the wind? He grinned a nervous grin and wiped one sweaty palm and then the other against his white cotta. Still grinning, he walked to the Altar—his mom's eyes followed his every move—and lit the candles in proper order. Epistle side first.

Meanwhile, the Bishop put on his robes and symbolic attire. First, he placed the hooded amice on his head, then pulled it down to form a white collar, and tied it in front. Next came two shirt-like robes that reached his shoe tops; the white linen alb, and over it the long red cassock.

"What's that white lasso you're tying around your middle?" Freddy asked. "Does it tie you to God, or something?"

"In a way, it does," the Bishop said, "in a way it does. It's called a cincture, or girdle."

Freddy's eyes twinkled. Just think of that, he

thought, a man wearing a girdle! And, he's a bishop, too.

Bishop Fenner then kissed the four-inch wide white stole with red fringe ends, placed it around his neck and passed both ends through the girdle-rope. Over this went a long white rochet with puffy sleeves and ruffles at the wrists. The filigreed red and white chasuble slipped over his huge, graying head, past his ample waist, and extended to his knees.

A massive gold pectoral cross hung around his neck, the silver dollar-sized Episcopal ring adorned his right hand, and he gripped his tall wooden Crosier—like a sheep's crook—in the left. Now he was ready to celebrate the Eucharist.

HIS VOICE COULD PEEL PAINT

Bishop Fenner nodded to organist Virginia Boyce, and she began the processional hymn. Everyone rose and sang.

Jesus Christ is risen today~~,
Allll...le..luuuuuu....ya,
This triumphant, holy day~~,
Allll...leeeee...lu...ya!
Who did once upon the cross~~,
Allll...le..luuuuuu...ya,
Suffer to redeem our loss~~,
Allll...leeeee..lu...ya!

George—now in the role of crucifier—lifted high the polished Cross and led the procession of acolytes and choir, in black cassocks and white cottas, down the short aisle with the Bishop following. The glorious hymn resonated back from the pressed tin ceiling with the Bishop's strong voice above the rest. Even the rich wooden pews and the oak lectern vibrated, and the high stained-glass windows seemed to hum. The old limestone building had picked up the joy!

To the boys, the Bishop's robust baritone seemed

powerful enough to peel paint. Later, people joked that no one needed to dust after his visits. Oh, he could sing!

Freddy, his eyes watering and his voice cracking, marched beside Don Tessendorf, with his dad and Uncle Alfred behind. Though he told himself not to choke up, he always did when the congregation sang that wonderful hymn.

"It must be the pollen in the air," he said later. "My eyes seem to water every time."

The singing choir marched into the stalls on both sides of the aisle as the song ended with one final, Allll...leeeee..lu...ya! The Bishop then turned to face the congregation, and his voice boomed out, "Alleluia! Christ is risen!"

"The Lord is risen indeed," the congregation responded in one voice. "Alleluia!"

The most important celebration of the Christian calendar continued with great joy for the next hour, with more singing and prayers of adoration, repentance, and thanksgiving read in old style English from the 1928 Prayer Book.

With great enthusiasm, Bishop Fenner preached, proclaiming the Good News. He told of the first Easter when Jesus overcame death and the grave, took on the sins of the world, and provided humankind with the opportunity for life eternal. Next—Freddy and George were now his Altar boys—he consecrated the bread and wine of the Eucharist and dispensed it to the people.

§

With final prayers and another vigorous hymn, our service concluded. The great celebration was over. Indeed, our church was a glorious place—at least most of the time.

GOLDEN RULE #2, 'HOT DAY, SHORT SERMON'

Like Easter worship, most of St. Luke's other

services were lively. For one thing, singing in the compact church was somewhat like singing in the shower. And we knew the hymns, for it seemed organist Virginia Boyce preferred just a few songs, and we sang the same hymns over and over, most with great flair.

However, good singing could not always overcome the lack of full-time clergy. Bishop Fenner could only visit us a couple of times a year, and there were times when a supply priest could come only once a month from a nearby town. On other Sundays, a congregation member, like Mr. Hill, led the service called Morning Prayer and read a preprinted sermon from the Bishop's office.

To us, many of these sermons were uninspiring. No doubt our appreciation was affected by the humid summer's heat, entering through open windows, and by our stifling cassocks and cottas. The high ceiling fans didn't help much and slow sermon readers added to our discomfort.

Many sermons caused heavy eyelids and abundant perspiration. So, with a certain amount of inspiration, we devised Golden Rule #2, 'Hot Day, Short Sermon.' Still, when the heat reached the unbearable, we drowsed, and from time to time, fainted—on different days, of course.

§

On the first hot Sunday in June, George melted, with relaxed grace, down off the acolyte pew to thunk across the kneeler and sprawl onto the floor. The noise stopped Mr. Hill in mid-sentence. He stared down from the lectern at the crumpled pile of white robe over black.

"Looks like George has fainted. We need to get him up," Mr. Hill said.

The boys' folks and others rushed forward. "The poor darling," his mom said. "Is he going to be alright?"

"He'll be fine, Veda. Just stand back, and give him air," George's dad said. "I'll just take him to the parish hall and get rid of those hot robes. He just got too warm."

"We're so sorry he stopped the sermon," she said. "I know he didn't mean to."

"Everyone understands, Veda," Mr. Hill said. "We'll go ahead with the service while he rests."

Picking up his limp son, George's dad said, "I'll take him out and give him some water. He should be alright."

In a couple of minutes, George—a rumpled mess—sat on a table in the coolness of the Guild Hall, groggily sipping water from a coffee cup. Bit by bit, he realized what had happened. He rubbed a slight knot on his forehead and began to feel embarrassed. His going under had stopped the service—in front of family, friends, the congregation, and God! He felt terrible. He had to do something.

During the next few services, he struggled with the heat—and the long, boring sermons. In desperation, when he felt woozy, or his mind wandered, he'd count the tin squares in the ceiling or play 'I Spy' with himself using the colored glass window panels. He even tried to memorize each window's Bible message. Once he counted a spider's steps, as it crawled in the open window and moved down the wall.

One day, he compared the lay reader's ear lobes—not Mr. Hill—with the Bishop's. These diversions worked for a time, until one hot, sticky July Sunday, he passed out again.

It was his brother—he'd done some fainting, too—who came to George's rescue. "You know," Freddy said with a grin, "if you were asleep, you couldn't faint."

Brilliant. Brilliant.

And so, George mastered this perfect defense mechanism. He'd sleep through the sermon so that he wouldn't notice the heat. What a great idea! And it worked.

Sunday after Sunday, he'd doze behind his open hand and service bulletin until his brother awakened him with a nudge.

"It's time for the Recessional."

§

One thing about St. Luke's, in spite of the heat, long sermons, or fainting spells, we somehow came to know God there. In spite of ourselves, we grew spiritually through worship, song, and prayer. We had prayed the 'Now I lay me down to sleep' prayer at bedtime all of our lives, but St. Luke's allowed us to pray with a special church community as well.

Later, as high-schoolers, we would even lead the Morning Prayer service and deliver the preprinted sermons. We did wonder why the 'elders' seemed so pleased to let us do it. Perhaps they knew we wouldn't faint while reading out loud.

And please believe, it seemed very effortless for our adoring Mom and Dad to volunteer us. It is also easy to understand why Church activities became a bigger and bigger part of our lives.

TWENTY

MORE TO CHURCH THAN RELIGION, UNDERCOVER UNDRESSING, AND THE MANLY ART OF SELF-DEFENSE

[*Wamego Reporter* - July 5, 1946] ~ **SHOO THE RIVER BACK** ~ If Old Man River doesn't grow in height to over twenty feet, a number of the farmers southeast of Wamego feel he won't get wide enough to sneak into their back yard and muss things up so their crops won't grow.

MORE TO CHURCH THAN RELIGION

"Mom, I'm feeling sick. I don't think I can go to camp today." At that moment, the bawl of a confused baby calf interrupted the warm summer morning. Like the calf, George needed his mother. He didn't want to go all the way down to Iola and the church camp on the Neosho River after all. "Can't I just stay home with you?"

"You're just making yourself sick worrying about it. You will be just fine once you get there. There will be lots of other kids your own age." His mother's radiant, loving smile made leaving harder.

Freddy, Judy, & George in their Sunday best.

"Maybe by the time you get back, you'll have a new brother or sister. I'm due in a week or two, and I'll need you boys' help with the new baby. Just go on and have some fun. You'll just be gone a few days"

George sighed. I don't want to be gone any days, he thought. We've never been away all night, except for staying with the cousins. What if I don't know what to do? What if I look stupid?

"And remember, you'll get to sleep on your new

cot."

I don't like that cot, he thought. It's just a bundle of mumble-jumble. What if I can't stretch that thick canvas to lock down the legs, or put on the end pieces? What if I can't even undo the bundling straps?

And, how can I sleep out in the open?, he wondered. That picture in the brochure showed rows of cots—like in the army—in a big gym. How can I sleep with all those people? How can I undress in front of them? His face turned pale, as he wondered, what if people see me naked?

"Come on, George," Freddy said. "Don't be a fraidy cat. I'll be there, and we'll get to go swimming every day. Anyway, Dad said he'd come get you if you had problems. Besides, the pamphlet says they're supposed to have lots of great food."

The thought of food—mounds of it—led George to think about the good possibilities. Part of him really did want to go. And, he did want to swim in a real pool instead of the slough, creek, or pond. Maybe my stomach is getting better, he thought. Maybe I can go after all.

§

> ***L**ater, the curvy sand roads seemed long and slow, but at last, we saw a big red and blue Episcopal shield on a sign that read, 'Episcopal Church Camp.' Dad turned in and drove beneath a high, green arch formed over the lane by giant elm and pecan trees.*
>
> When the car passed out of the shade, it rolled to a stop in front of a building marked 'Registration.' The two of us jumped out and began unloading our cots and the battered, old brown suitcase we shared.
>
> Once inside, Dad signed us in and delivered final words of instruction. "Be nice to people, don't get in trouble, be sure to brush your teeth, and have a good time. They have a phone here, so

have them call us long distance if you need us." He said some other things—his mouth kept moving—that we didn't hear, for by this time, all our senses were surveying this wondrous place.

Hurriedly, we shook Dad's hand and mumbled our goodbyes. When he walked to the car, we felt great excitement. For the first time ever, we had no parents or other family to tell us what to do. We were on our own.

We turned to face the huge guy behind the registration desk. Gene—maybe in high school or something—said he'd be our camp counselor for the next five days. Then, to our amazement, he picked up both cots with one hand and led us toward the gym.

Had we looked back we would have seen Dad drive away smiling, but our eyes were on the buildings, the swimming pool, and the huge gymnasium. Several other counselors, some priests without turned-around collars, and even some women walked about and talked with groups of kids. Some boys and girls chased each other, shouted, and acted out of control. Was this allowed?

To this point in our lives, church activities always involved Mom standing by to 'shsh' us if we got overactive. Not sure how to act, we just followed Gene to gym-dormitory. It looked like the brochure's picture, but bigger. Near a door marked showers, about ten rows of cots—seven or eight per row—used up just a corner of the space. This building could hold our cattle, hogs, horses, and still have room for the tractor and some machinery.

§

The size of the room and the newness of the situation made both boys nervous. When Gene led them across the shiny floor, Freddy's palms began to sweat. If only I could laugh, he thought. A couple of steps later, he attacked his tension in the usual way, when he said, "Sure could put a lot of hay in this barn."

Gene's face barely changed expression. He'd heard that one before. George—totally unsettled—stared ahead with blank eyes. However, seconds later, the counselor redeemed himself when he said, "Let me help you set up your cots. We don't want to be late for dinner."

The boys looked at each other. They breathed sighs of relief and tried to look busy, while Gene put the cots together. So far I haven't embarrassed myself, George thought, but what is this dinner at suppertime business?

Freddy, now recovered, said, "Good location, Gene. Now I won't have far to go to the outhouse, er...bathroom." His new friend smiled, and Freddy's confidence rose. He was right too, for the cavernous toilet and shower facilities were just steps away.

On the other hand, George continued to be puzzled. At home we eat dinner at noon with lots of fried chicken and mashed potatoes, and have leftovers in the evening at supper. Wonder why they have the big meal at night?

Just then, a loud bell clanged and George jumped. "What's that?"

"That's means it's time for dinner," Gene said. "Hurry and wash up so we can go eat."

The boys walked through a high archway, and turned a corner to find rows of sinks, mirrors, toilet stalls, and urinals. This was the biggest toilet in the world, they thought, as they washed up and then followed Gene up the hill. The sign said 'Dining Hall.'

"Hey, look at all those rows of tables. They're like the ones in the Guild Hall, but there are a whole lot more," Freddy said. "It's like a big family reunion."

"In a way it is," Gene said, "because everyone here is a fellow Christian. So, just get yourselves one of those stainless steel trays and join the line. They serve you right on the tray."

George picked up a heavy tray and moved to follow

the boy in front of him. After a couple of steps, a huge lady slapped a slab of roast beef down in the center of his tray. With another splat, a double handful of mashed potatoes dumped almost in the tray's corner area. Sploosh—spotted, brownish gravy flooded the tray and a thick slice of bread plopped on top of it all.

The servers—also the cooks—wore lumpy dresses, full aprons, hairnets, and pinched faces. Maybe their feet hurt, for they had little patience with slow-moving and shy youngsters.

"Keep the line moving, keep the line moving," a gruff, scratchy voice said. The lady waved her arm and rolls of flabby skin waddled in rhythm, as she ladled on fruit salad and plunged a slice of watermelon on top of the mashed potatoes.

"Keep the line moving!"

George's heart skipped a beat, and he pushed forward. He had a mess on his tray, but his mouth watered from the smells. He was famished, and when Gene went to eat at the counselor's table, George followed Freddy to an empty table in the corner.

With deep concentration, he chowed down. After a good five minutes, out of the blue, he exclaimed, "I think I like camping, even if they don't know when to serve dinner."

UNDERCOVER UNDRESSING

Following the meal, a priest introduced himself as Fr. Bonham and welcomed everyone to camp. He went over the rules—mostly don'ts—said a couple of prayers and then told the group to go sit on the logs around the bonfire outside.

When everyone was quiet, Fr. Bonham and Gene began strumming guitars and led the singing of what they called campfire songs. This must be how angels sound Freddy thought when the voices of about 60 boys and 60 girls, plus priests, leaders, and counselors, blended together. He didn't know the words to *Kumbayah* at first, but he sang along after a few lines. This was better than Bishop Fenner on Easter.

The group sang verse after verse while the fire crackled and reflected in the upturned faces around the circle. George loved the smell of an open fire, and thought of roasting hotdogs and marshmallows. And, although few knew what *kumbayah* meant, everyone seemed moved by the singing.

After a while—George had begun dozing on and off—Fr. Bonham asked for quiet and prayed, "Heavenly Father, thank you for bringing us together here at this camp. Protect each of us as we go about the activities of the next few days. And, dear Lord, give us rest in your grace, this night and forever more. In Your name we pray. Amen." Then, in a soft voice, Gene began the singing of the last song.

Amazing Grace, how sweet the sound,
That saved a wretch like me,
I once was lost, but now am found,
Was blind, but now I see.
Through many dangers, toils and snares,
I have already come;
Tis grace that brought me safe thus far,
And grace will lead me home.

As the song ended, each person got up and walked to the gym or toward the girl's dorm across the way. What a comfortable way to end the day.

Everyone seemed at peace; that is until George, with a growing sense of anxiety, came fully alert. How could he get ready for bed? Did he have to undress in front of all those people? How could he stand there bare-naked? And, why were his pajamas—they no longer had feet—covered with teddy bears?

As he stalled, his panic grew, but at last a solution popped into his mind. Why couldn't he undress under his blanket? So, taking off his shoes, he crawled in bed fully clothed. One by one, he removed his pants, shirt, underwear, and socks, and slipped on his teddy bears. Ah, he thought with a smug grin, that worked out great. He relaxed at last.

In the next instant, however, a new terror gripped him. He needed to go to the bathroom and to brush his teeth. For several slow minutes, he eyed the other kids' pajamas, then at last, took a deep breath and tried to walk casually into the restroom.

"Hey, where did you get those pajamas?" asked Darrell Horton from Waterville. George's heart sank, and his face reddened. He was going to be tease-bait again. Then Darrell added, "They are kinda neat. Wish I had a pair."

George sighed and looked the other way. Whew. With purpose, he brushed his teeth and finished the other necessity. Back at the safety of his cot, he again felt good about camping. Within seconds, he fell asleep and started dreaming about breakfast.

AN INFESTATION OF GIRLS

Just a bit later, or so it seemed, Gene began banging a large wooden spoon against a metal pan. "Everybody up! You have 20 minutes to shower, get dressed, and get to the Dining Hall."

Shower? Freddy and George bolted upright. They always took baths in a galvanized washtub. Now they were supposed to take their first shower ever, in front of dozens of naked men and boys. What should they do with their eyes? Would others be looking at them?

With caution, they watched the kids climb out of their pajamas, wrap towels around their middles, and walk methodically toward the showers. Nodding to George, Freddy undressed, wrapped up in his towel, and soon found himself among a dozen unclad humans.

Uneasy here, he reverted to form and tried another joke. "This swimming pool sure does leak," he said. "It must have holes in the top." A couple of younger kids, also having their first community shower, laughed and the tension broke.

George hung back until most had finished, then slipped into the shower area, unwrapped his towel, and stood in a corner, facing the concrete wall. He dared not look around or make a sound, even though the cool water—the hotter water was long used up—made him shiver. In thirty seconds, he'd rinsed himself—his soap was back at his cot—and then wrapped up again and sped back to his clothes.

He sat on his cot, pulled his blanket and pillow up around him, and worked his way into his clothes. He didn't notice that the others were too busy to notice his oddball manners. Everyone had dressed when the Dining Hall bell clanged.

Soon the boys joined a long line of others with trays in hand. The first serving tub held lots of gooey, gooey scrambled eggs. George screwed up his nose, and the server lady sighed.

After what seemed like minutes his stomach groaned—or so it seemed—and an overwhelming aroma of bacon made his mouth water. The server lady's eyes questioned him. Maybe he'd just eat the meat, he thought, and maybe some toast with jelly...and maybe...even some of the eggs from off the top.

The server nodded, wiped her arm across her forehead, motioned for him to hold out his tray, and then scooped up an eggy glob. Before he could react to the watery mess, she laid down two thick slices of heavenly bacon, and the next lady scooped on fried potatoes, and the toasted store-bought bread with IGA grape jelly.

He then looked up to hear his brother say, "Let's go find a table somewhere."

George followed Freddy's eyes around the room. What's this?, he thought. Where did all these girls come from? *Girls were everywhere!* Why hadn't he noticed them last night? Short ones, tall ones, plump ones, and skinny ones infested every table. Avoiding them would be impossible.

In the lead, Freddy spotted Darrell Horton, who

liked teddy bear pajamas, and started toward him. That is good, thought Freddy. Darrell is a guy.

When they neared the table, however, they saw he was not alone. Four other chairs had occupants—all girls! What to do? He'd try a joke. "So, Darrell," he said, "was this the only table you could find?"

Blond-haired Bonnie Wigglesworth answered his question. She frowned at Freddy and responded with a semi-hostile blue-eyed glare. "You didn't have to come to this table. Besides, we were here first." And then for good measure, she added, "What's the matter, you scared of girls?"

Ah, a challenge. Freddy decided he'd show her.

And so for the next five days, he did a lot of dumb things to get Bonnie to like him. The two of them became an 'item' for much of the week. He teased her, sat beside her, told her disgusting stories, and in general, paid her considerable attention. Freddy even signed up to take boxing lessons to impress her.

THE MANLY ART OF SELF-DEFENSE

In truth, Freddy had little interest in boxing, but Bonnie said she liked men who could box. So when Fr. Bonham—a former amateur fighter—announced the boxing class, Freddy was stuck. He joined a dozen other boys to learn the manly art of self-defense. Bonnie watched.

"Be sure to pull the gloves all the way onto your hands when you lace up. And be sure to lace tightly. Otherwise you might break a knuckle."

The idea of getting hit, even with a gloved fist, didn't have much appeal, though punching someone might not be too bad, Freddy decided. He did wonder if he could see well enough without his glasses. And, did he want to risk a broken knuckle? I don't really need to box, do I? Maybe not, but by now it was too late, for there sat Bonnie batting her blue eyes at him.

Fr. Bonham demonstrated how a good boxer placed

his left foot and left arm forward and rocked on the balls of his feet. He showed how to block punches with the right hand, and how to deliver a jab, a cross, and an uppercut.

"The most important blow is the left jab," he said. "It is powerful when you lock your elbow as you throw it." To demonstrate, he and Gene danced around sparring with each other, and though they both threw left jabs, they never landed with force. "Now it's your turn to try it, so I need a couple of volunteers."

Fr. Bonham's eyes went from boy to boy. No one moved. "Ok, why don't you, Freddy, and you, Darrell, square off and show them how it's done," he said at last. "At my command, come out and spar a bit."

Bonnie smiled with delight when Freddy looked at her and grinned. Then he puffed out his chest toward Darrell and jabbed the air in mock battle with his reddish brown gloves. This first time in boxing gloves did impress Freddy—about himself. With loud slaps, he pounded one glove against the other, and then poked the air again... this time with fierce energy. He felt very confident. He was ready.

"Try the various punches, but make an effort not to hurt each other too much," Fr. Bonham said. "And, remember, this isn't a real boxing match."

Freddy and Darrell faced each other and Fr. Bonham dinged a tiny bell. The two would-be boxers circled with little style, trying to mimic Fr. Bonham's bobbing and weaving. Jab, jab, went Freddy, brushing his new friend on the left cheek.

Darrell reacted with a swift uppercut that missed. Freddy countered with a left hook. This time Darrell responded with a left jab, remembering to lock his elbow.

Thunk!

The blow landed square on Freddy's nose and blood gushed out. It flowed down his face to drip crimson on his tee shirt.

"Time out!"

"That was a good blow, Darrell, but, maybe a bit harder than needed for this first lesson. Now, I guess we need to practice a little first aid. Bloody noses are easy to stop when you know what you're doing," Fr. Bonham said, opening a medical kit. "Here, Freddy, let me look at you."

Meanwhile, Darrell grinned and tapped his chest while Freddy turned toward Bonnie for sympathy. Her eyes weren't providing him comfort, instead they were smiling—and at Darrell. Thus, quicker than a three-minute round, Bonnie shifted her attention, appearing now to think Darrell was more fascinating.

Freddy stayed with the boxing lessons, hoping to win Bonnie back or impress some other girl. But nothing came of it, and he took a few more hits before the camp—and his boxing career ended for good.

While Freddy was trying to learn the art of boxing and impressing girls, George busied himself with the more everyday challenge of making a hand-tooled wallet.

THE LAND OF ARTS AND CRAFTS

Question: Does a hand-tooled wallet qualify as art? After all, what is art anyway? The skinny, longhaired lady named Miss Annie, who taught George's leather-working class, assured the kids that everyone should know art. But, just what did she mean?

George knew his dad did business with a guy named Art who had a gas and oil station in Belvue. Miss Annie, in her mid 30s, dressed in a paint-smudged smock, kept saying art used oil all right, not for cars and tractors, but for painting. It was confusing. How could you paint a tractor with oil? Did you use 30-weight?, he thought with a grin.

Miss Annie waved her long, red-painted fingernails and explained how everyone would learn to do a craft as an art project during camp.

At that point, Miss Annie swished back her long, gauzy, red-topped dress and answered all his questions at once. “Arts and crafts mean building something with your hands, and making it pretty. You boys will make fine tooled wallets, and the girls will make tooled purses.”

Relieved, George remembered making his dad a Christmas wallet out of cardboard at Prairie View School. He could do that. “Each of you take some of the leather,” Annie said, “and cut it from left to right, to make small pieces for wallets and larger sections for the purses.”

“That’s right, from your left, and now fold it like this. When you have your piece ready, you’ll have to share the hammers and awls.”

“Awls,” Darrell Horton’s younger brother, Dickie, whispered, “ain’t they them big night birds with googley eyes?” Dickie and George laughed.

“Use this awl,” Miss Annie said, “to punch holes in the edge of the leather. Then you can stitch the pieces together with these binding strips. Later in the week, you can tool in a name on the leather by pounding out the letters to spell *Dad* or *Mom*.”

Each day, George worked at cutting leather to fit the pattern…though he spent much time daydreaming. He awled, stitched, and worked his project and by the last day felt ready to tool the wallet. He hammered and hammered on the letters, all the while dreaming about lunch.

D. A. D. D. Oops! Now what was he going to do?

“That’s interesting,” Miss Annie said. “That’s a shame. What can we do about it? I have it, why don’t you just make it DADDY?”

So careless and embarrassed, George hammered away some more and added a Y, which made the whole word off-center. Too bad. I hope ‘Daddy’ likes it.

And so the week came to a close. George had a prized wallet to give his dad, and since Freddy had gotten a good education about boxing and girls, he’d have lots of stories to tell his friends back home.

After cleaning up the sleeping area and saying goodbye to everyone, the boys climbed in their dad’s car and headed home with wonderful memories. It had been a great camp…except for the Bonnie Wigglesworth affair.

The boys couldn't wait to get home and then go to church the next day. They had so much to tell. Freddy talked about the campfire music, the friends he'd made, and how he'd been trained as a boxer—omitting the bloody nose event and not a word about Bonnie. As for George, he talked of the huge gymnasium, the gobs of food he ate, and having dinner at night. And of course, his hand-tooled leather wallet story did not mention the off-centered word D.A.D.D.Y.

Both boys experienced new thoughts and feelings at Church Camp. Maybe these influenced their futures. And, what about those futures? What was in store for the two kids from a Kansas farm? Would they have more adventures like undercover undressing and learning the manly art of self-defense? Time would tell.

COMING SOON ~ FALL 2006

The Creep of Her Outfit

By

John and George Burgess

Freddy and George continue their antics in their next book, *The Creep of Her Outfit,* to be released in the fall of 2006. In this sequel, they experience the firecracker battle for independence, a tomcat from the sky, Lee Sure and Hi Gene, stink-bug-bait, 4-H entertainment, skinny-dipping, run-away show calves, and cornfield basketball.

Laugh as they encounter a triple threat cow, have fun dehorning, meet fair maidens, dodge the stripes, create implement art, hear of left-hand threaded pigs, torture the Hudson, forget some red football pants, and live through chiropractic dancing!

The Creep of Her Outfit promises more fun and self-inflected Shorty Brockman episodes, too. Poor Shorty, he just doesn't always get it right.